*With thanks to all of the chefs for giving
their time and creativity to this book, to
Harrison Vintners for their selection of wines,
to Shirley Marshall for all of her hard work, and to
Myburgh for his great photography.
Also to Malcolm Lewis and Michel Roux for
supporting the project from the beginning*

RELAIS & CHATEAUX®

ALL AROUND THE WORLD, UNIQUE IN THE WORLD

A TASTE
of RELAIS & CHÂTEAUX

97 RECIPES FROM SOME OF THE FINEST CHEFS IN THE UK AND IRELAND

sponsored by

www.yeschefmagazine.com

NETWORK
PUBLISHING LTD

First published in 2009 by Network Publishing Ltd.

Network House, 28 Ballmoor, Celtic Court, Buckingham MK18 1RQ

www.networkpublishingltd.com

Sponsored by Yes Chef! Magazine

www.yeschefmagazine.com

Printed on Consort Silk by Broglia Press (Dorset)

ISBN No: 978-0-9562661- 1-8

Printed in England

Publisher: Peter Marshall
Editor and Art Director: Shirley Marshall
Assistant Editor: Samantha Jones
Design Director: Philip Donnelly
Photographer: Myburgh du Plessis
Contributors: John Radford, Emma Sturgess

THE RELAIS & CHÂTEAUX NAME HAS LONG BEEN ASSOCIATED WITH EXCELLENCE. Each property is unique and works hard to retain its singular character. To be a member of the Relais & Châteaux collection is far more than the sum of its individual parts. Personality, talent and commitment start from the greeting guests receive on arrival to the goodbye they are offered on departure. Each member has a personal promise to ensure that guests are privy to moments of exceptional harmony, giving them a unique experience that leaves a lasting impression on the mind.

The restaurants within Relais & Châteaux UK & Ireland have chefs at their helms who are dedicated to sourcing the freshest and highest quality ingredients to create consistently exceptional dishes. Sourcing locally where possible, these chefs are passionate about the area in which their particular restaurant is situated and, as you will see from the pages of this book, they like to boast about it!

We have all enjoyed a warm camaraderie in the compilation of this book. I am proud to be associated with this family and especially the chefs within it. I hope you will enjoy reading about all of those behind these restaurants and that the recipes we have put together for you will bring delicious, memorable dishes into your home.

Michel

Michel Roux

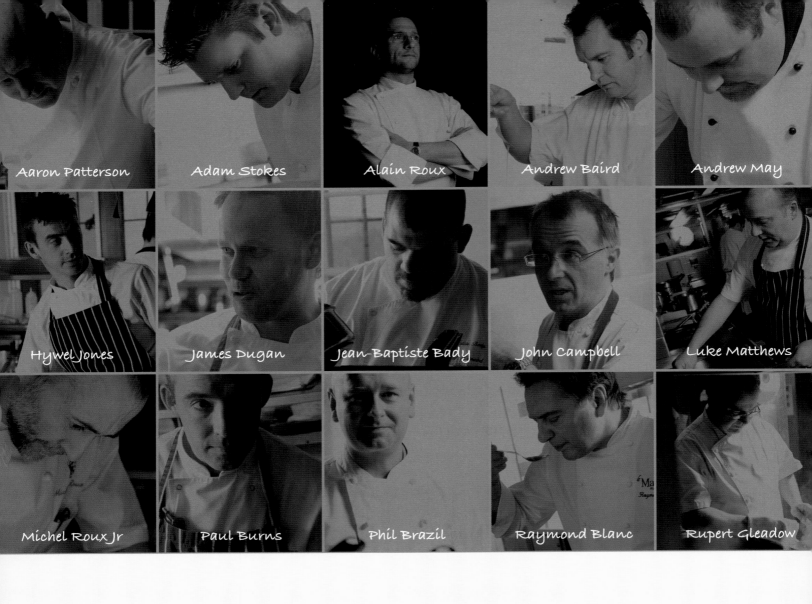

Aaron Patterson   Adam Stokes   Alain Roux   Andrew Baird   Andrew May

Hywel Jones   James Dugan   Jean-Baptiste Bady   John Campbell   Luke Matthews

Michel Roux Jr   Paul Burns   Phil Brazil   Raymond Blanc   Rupert Gleadow

Aaron Patterson Adam Stokes Alain Roux Andrew Baird Andrew May

Hywel Jones James Dugan Jean-Baptiste Bady John Campbell Luke Matth

Caines Michel Roux Jr Paul Burns Phil Brazil Raymond Blanc Rupert

Patterson Adam Stokes Alain Roux Andrew Baird Andrew May Bar

Hywel Jones James Dugan Jean-Baptiste Bady John Campbell Luke Matth

Caines Michel Roux Jr Paul Burns Phil Brazil Raymond Blanc R

Barry Quinion Colin Akrigg David Kelman Gordon Jones Heston Blumenthal

Mark Teasdale Martin Burge Matthew Gray Matthew Hodgkins Michael Caines

Russell Plowman Simon Haigh Shane Hughes Steven Titman

YES
CHEF!
MAGAZINE

contents

A Taste of Harrison Vintners

It has been an honour and pleasure, to select the appropriate wines to accompany this wonderful collection of recipes. At Relais & Châteaux, one does not pay a visit, one receives an experience! This has been the guiding principle for our selection of wines, all from independent growers and small estates, details of which are on pages 312 and 313.

Such wines are made for "Le Gastronomie" but, through the Relais & Chateaux association, can now be purchased, by guests, directly from us. Just go to our web site and click on "Relais & Châteaux"

To all who undertake a journey through this wonderful book, we wish "Bonne Route" and "Bon Appetit"!

www.harrisonvintners.co.uk

SOURCING LOCALLY

Fresh, local ingredients are all important
to the Relais & Châteaux chefs

Great chefs nurture all kinds of precious relationships: with the customer, the maître d'hôtel, even the favourite tasting spoon. But there's one essential dynamic which, in the past decade, has moved out of the culinary shadows. It's gone to cliché and back, but it's still true that even a Relais & Châteaux chef can't magic something special out of something substandard. The ingredients come first.

For many of the chefs, this is not only a truism but a muddy daily reality. Alain Roux's sorrel comes from the garden at The Waterside Inn; John Campbell shoots wild venison for The Vineyard's table; Le Manoir Aux Quat'Saisons is famous for its kitchen garden, which sends 90 types of vegetables towards the stoves. These projects represent the ultimate in using fresh, local produce, and there are plenty more reasons for doing so than to give the brigade a bit of fresh air in the garden.

Given the bewitching settings of their hotels and restaurants, it's not surprising that even chefs who are from somewhere else entirely can find themselves going native. They begin to insist on using that great local goats' cheese, lamb from the next field over, or wild mushrooms from nearby woods. For one, local means fresh: delicate vegetables and soft fruit won't need to see the inside of a refrigerated van, or lose flavour and sweetness on a long journey. 'There's no other journey that is so pure,' says John Campbell. 'For example, the mushrooms we pick, and red fruit from the local farm, don't go in the fridge, so you don't lose the flavour. There's no comparison.'

Using local suppliers also helps chefs to write menus that show off their location. In Cumbria, Sharrow Bay glories in a "local lunch" featuring a terrine of pheasant, partridge and grouse, noisette of local venison with red cabbage, and a marmalade bread and butter pudding. At Lower Slaughter Manor, the after-dinner savoury is revived with a Cotswold rarebit, and even at Le Manoir, where the French way rules, rhubarb and Gariguette strawberries sit happily together under a blanket of very English crumble topping.

At Gidleigh Park, on the edge of Dartmoor, Michael Caines has signature flavours that move from scented Thai purées to classic herbed butter sauces, but the restaurant's location is clear from the menu. 'For me, local, regional food is really important for our identity as a food destination,' he says. 'It shows how seriously we take produce, and it helps people get a sense of the region. The south west has one of the best larders in Europe, and Brixham crab and Dartmoor lamb, for example, really give people a flavour of the area.'

Seasonality goes hand-in-hand with local food, of course, and it's something that Michael expects from Relais & Châteaux properties. 'The chefs in the group are very conscientious when it comes to regional, seasonal produce,' he says. 'They're generally out in the countryside, so the local farmer might turn up with a few pheasant. Then, when you look at a menu in September and October, you see wonderful game.'

A countryside location isn't absolutely essential, however. Michel Roux Jr, of Mayfair's Le Gavroche, says, 'It's a bit difficult for me because the restaurant is in the middle of central London. Other than Hyde Park, I haven't got much greenery around me! But I use a small farm in Surrey. One of the owners will phone, sometimes from the field, and tell me that the baby leeks will be ready next week, or the pears are finishing, and that affects the menu. That's the kind of communication that top restaurateurs always aim for. If you're on first-name terms with your supplier, the produce will be better.'

Relationships with specialist suppliers can be nurtured over many years. They might grow specific varieties of vegetables to order, or know exactly which cheese will be in perfect condition for the weekend. Michael Caines admits to hoping his lamb man, Stuart Baker, doesn't fancy retiring just yet, while Michel Roux Jr trusts his west coast fishmonger to advise him on what's best. 'I speak to my fishmonger on the west coast every day,' says Michel. 'If it's not good enough he doesn't bother telling me! There are lots of unusual things that are great if they're treated properly and super-fresh, and that's where you need the communication.' And, as a Frenchman cooking in the heart of London, he's as committed to British produce as the chefs who have the natural larder on their doorsteps. 'It's phenomenal what these shores produce,' he says. 'Why would I want to serve Charolais when we've got absolutely stunning Angus?'

THE WATERSIDE

'A true
haven on the
River Thames'

INN

ALAIN ROUX

Alain Roux started in the pastry industry as an apprentice in 1984. He spent two years honing his pastry skills at Pâtisserie Millet in Paris, following the Roux family tradition. His first steps towards entering the family business were taken by working over the next six years at five different Relais & Châteaux restaurants in France. In 1992 he made the best move of his career, to The Waterside Inn at Bray to be under the guidance of the best teacher, his father, Michel.

Promoted to Sous Chef in 1995, Alain then became Joint Chef Patron at The Waterside Inn in 2001 and now runs the kitchen full time, bringing his own style to the menus and retaining the coveted 3 Michelin stars.

Serves 4

Preparation time: 50 minutes
Cooking time: 1 hour, 5 minutes

SOUPE DE POISSONS DE ROCHE SAFRANÉE AUX PÉTALES DE CABILLAUD ET SA TRANCHE DE PAIN AUX ALGUES MARINES

Rock fish soup lightly scented with saffron, garnished with flaked cod and a slice of seaweed flavoured bread

BY ALAIN ROUX

This dish reminds me of long summer days by the sea with the sun beating down on my back. It is the essence of the Mediterranean; simply fabulous.

INGREDIENTS

soup base:

1kg	assorted small rock fish (wrasse, rainbow wrasse, comber, perch, scorpion fish, blenny, sea bream, weever fish, tail of conger eel), cut into chunks
3 tbsp	olive oil
2	leeks, white parts, thinly sliced
100g	onions, thinly sliced
3	garlic cloves, crushed
500g	very ripe tomatoes, roughly chopped
1	bouquet garni, with a little dried orange peel and a branch of fennel
60cl	white wine
15cl	brandy
6cl	ricard

salt and freshly ground pepper

garnish:

300g	potatoes
250g	cod fillet
1 tbsp	chopped parsley
4	slices of seaweed bread
2	pinches of saffron threads

METHOD

soup:

Scale, gut, trim off the fins, wash in very cold water, drain and pat dry the assorted fish. Gently heat the olive oil in a saucepan, add the leeks, onions, garlic, tomatoes, bouquet garni and the fish for the soup and sweat over low heat for about 15 minutes, stirring with a spatula as often as possible. Deglaze with the alcohol.

Pour in 3.5 litres of boiling water and bring to the boil. Leave to bubble gently for 40 minutes, then pass the soup first through a vegetable mill, then through a conical sieve. Season to taste.

garnish:

Peel the potatoes and cut into 1cm cubes. Cook in lightly salted water, refresh, drain and put aside.

Poach the cod very gently in fish stock. Remove from the heat and leave aside to finish cooking off the heat.

to serve:

In a warm soup plate, place some flakes of poached cod and a few threads of saffron. Reheat in hot water or a steamer the potato cubes and place a few around the cod. Sprinkle a little chopped parsley on top. Pour the very hot fish soup and serve with a toasted slice of seaweed bread.

 RECOMMENDED WINE

Beaujolais Blanc – Domaine Pardon

Serves 4

Preparation time:	1 hour
Cooking time:	1 hour, 20 minutes

INGREDIENTS

risotto:

80g	butter
1 tbsp	onions, chopped
150g	carnaroli rice
6cl	dry white wine
60cl	vegetable stock
30g	grated parmesan
3 tbsp	cooked crab meat
1 tsp	flat leaf parsley, chopped

crab coral purée:

60g	crab coral
60g	mascarpone

squid:

8	small squid cleaned
60ml	olive oil
a few drops of lemon juice	
1	bay leaf
1	sprig thyme
salt and pepper	

vénéré rice:

4cl	olive oil
1 tbsp	onions, chopped
120g	Vénéré rice
5cl	dry white wine
45cl	fish stock
1	small courgette, finely diced

carpet shell clams:

1	shallot, chopped
20cl	dry white wine
1 tbsp	white wine vinegar
1	bay leaf
1	sprig thyme
32	carpet shell clams
1 tbsp	brioche crumbs

garnish:

4	crab claws, cooked and steamed to warm through
2	bulbs fennel cooked in saffron-flavoured vegetable stock, cut into quarters and warmed through
4 tbsp	parsley coulis

RISOTTO CRÉMEUX AU TOURTEAU DE CORNOUAILLES ACCOMPAGNÉ DE SES ENCORNETS AU RIZ VÉNÉRÉ ET CHAIRS DE CLOVISSES

Smooth risotto of Cornish hen crab, squid filled with "vénéré" rice and clams

BY ALAIN ROUX

This dish delivers both the crunch of the carnaroli rice with the softer texture of the venere rice and singing over the top of this is the creamy texture of the crab.

METHOD

risotto:

Sweat the onions with 40g of butter in a pan. Add the rice and cook until opaque. Add the white wine and reduce by one third. Add two thirds of the boiling vegetable stock, season with salt and stir once. Cook for 12 minutes. Add the remaining stock and cook for 3 minutes; the rice should still have a slight bite to it. Remove from the heat, add the parmesan and the rest of the butter and mix with a spoon. Add the crab meat and parsley. Mix gently and season. Cover the pan and set aside for 2 minutes before serving.

crab coral purée:

Pass the coral through a fine sieve. Add the mascarpone, whisk together, season and warm through just before serving.

squid (can also be cooked in a saucepan, if no vacuum machine):

Place all the ingredients in a vacuum-sealed bag. Cook in a bain-marie at 60°C for 15 minutes. Chill in iced water. Remove the squid from the bag and cut them open ready to be stuffed with venere rice. Place in a steamer to reheat just before serving.

vénéré rice:

Cook the vénéré rice like a pilau rice. Once the rice is cooked, add the diced courgettes, season and use to stuff the squid.

carpet-shell clams:

Cook the clams "marinière" style. Remove them from their shells and serve warm, arranging them on the risotto. Reserve 4 of the most attractive shells with the clam still inside, sprinkle with brioche crumbs and brown. Place one browned clam on one of the stuffed squid just before serving.

to serve:

Spoon the coral purée onto a warmed plate, place the risotto on top and dot with a few clams. Add a crab claw and the fennel quarters. Arrange the stuffed squid around them. Finish with a few dashes of warm parsley coulis.

 RECOMMENDED WINE

Pouilly Fuissé – Domaine de Bel Air - Macon

DOS DE SAUMON CUIT EN PAPILLOTE AUX AIGUILLES DE PIN MARIN, PETITES POUSSES DE PAK-CHOÏ EN FRITURE, NAGE À L'ANIS ÉTOILÉ

Fillet of salmon cooked "en papillote" with pine needles, served with deep fried leaves of pak-choï and a star aniseed sauce

BY ALAIN ROUX

I love to prepare this dish in late spring or early summer when wild salmon is at its best.
The marine pine needles add a wonderful smokiness to the dish.

Serves 4

Preparation time:	20 minutes
Cooking time:	35 minutes

INGREDIENTS

4	pieces of unskinned salmon fillet cut from the back, each about 70g
1 tsp	white peppercorns, crushed
½ tsp	coriander seeds, crushed
1 tbsp	Maldon salt flakes
80ml	olive oil
80g	long, marine pine needles, lightly rinsed in water if necessary and dried
100g	sea lettuce
12	leaves pak-choï

tempura batter:

45g	cornflour
185g	plain flour
½ tsp	bicarbonate of soda
½ tsp	Maldon salt flakes
475ml	ice-cold, lightly carbonated mineral water (e.g. Badoit or San Pellegrino)

star aniseed sauce:

1	shallot, sliced
2	button mushrooms, sliced
3	star anise
200g	vegetable nage or bouillon
50g	cream
50g	butter

METHOD

Preheat the oven to 180°C. Make two light incisions in the skin of each salmon fillet with a knife.

Mix together the crushed pepper, coriander and salt flakes. Smear both sides of the fillets with olive oil and sprinkle the flesh side with the seasoning mixture. Roll the pine needles in the remaining olive oil.

Cut a double thickness of foil into four 25cm squares. Divide the pine needles into 4 portions. Put two-thirds of each portion in the centre of each foil square. Place a salmon fillet on top, skin-side down, and sprinkle with the remaining pine needles.

Loosely fold up the ends of the foil to meet in the middle, fold them over and pinch the edges together to seal, without wrapping the fish too tightly.

Place the papillotes on a baking tray. Put this on a heat diffuser or direct heat for 3 minutes, then transfer to the oven and cook for 3 minutes if you like your salmon pink in the middle. Give it another 3 minutes in the oven if you prefer it well done.

batter:

To make the batter, put the dry ingredients into a bowl. Mix in the carbonated water a little at a time, stirring with long chopsticks; do not over-mix. Don't worry if the batter looks slightly grainy; this is quite normal. Use the batter straightaway. Heat the oil in a wok or deep-fat fryer to 160-180°C. Cook the tempura a few at a time, coating each pak-choï leaf separately. Pick up the leaves with the long chopsticks, briefly dip into the tempura batter so that it is barely coated, then drop into the hot oil. Repeat with a few more leaves turning them until golden all over. The tempura are cooked as soon as they rise to the surface; each piece will only take about 1 minute to cook. Remove immediately and drain on kitchen paper. Season with a little salt.

sauce:

In a saucepan, sweat with a little fresh butter the shallots and mushrooms with the star anise. Add the nage or bouillon and reduce by half. Add the cream and bring to the boil. "Monter" with the 50g of butter and season with salt and pepper. Pass through a fine chinois.

to serve:

When the salmon is cooked, remove it from the papillote, remove the pine needles and place on a plate. Heat some "sea lettuce" in the steamer then lay around and over the salmon. Garnish with the leaves of pak-choï cooked in tempura batter.

Drizzle a little sauce on the plate and serve.

 RECOMMENDED WINE
Saumur Blanc Multa Paucis – Domaine de la Paleine

PANACHÉ D'AGNEAU – SUFFOLK TEXEL – ET SA PASTILLA AUX CITRONS CONFITS MÉLI-MÉLO DE LÉGUMES SECS MITONNÉS ET JUS RELEVÉ AU RAS-EL-HANOUT

Selection of "Suffolk Texel" lamb and pastilla with confit lemon, served with a medley of simmered pulses and jus enhanced with ras-el-hanout

BY ALAIN ROUX

I first discovered this lamb whilst on a trip to "Gainsborough Country" and it is now a firm favourite of mine, which I like to combine here with flavours inspired by a recent trip to Marrakesh.

Serves 4

Preparation time: 40 minutes
Cooking time: 3 hours (maximum)

INGREDIENTS

lamb:

4	cutlets (chops) of lamb "Suffolk Texel" pan fried
1	Leg or loin of lamb "Suffolk Texel" oven roasted

pastilla:

100ml	lamb stock
150g	braised shoulder of lamb
½	sweet confit lemon, finely chopped
	filo pastry (4 pieces 10cm x 15cm)
	a little melted clarified butter

confit aubergine:

1	small aubergine cut in ½ cm dice
1 tbsp	olive oil
½	garlic clove, crushed
1	sprig of fresh thyme
2	confit tomatoes, in olive oil

pulses:

200g	medley of pulses (pearl barley, lentils, beans and peas), braised
8	caramelised button onions

sauce:

400g	lamb bones, chopped and roasted
½	onion, sliced
½	carrot, sliced
1	garlic clove
150ml	dry white wine
1.5 ltr	water
1	sprig of fresh thyme
1 tsp	spices "Ras-el-hanout"
	a little lemon juice

garnish:

½	sweet confit lemon, cut into thin wedges
4	sprigs of rosemary

METHOD

pastilla:

In a bowl, mix the stock, the lamb shoulder, the lemon and season with salt and pepper. Brush both sides of each piece of filo pastry and place some filling in the centre. Roll tight into a sausage shape. Pan fry with hot clarified butter until golden brown. Trim the edges at an angle and keep warm.

confit aubergine:

Pan-fry the aubergine with the olive oil and thyme. Season with salt and pepper. Finish with the garlic and the tomatoes. Drain and set aside.

sauce:

Brown the onion and carrot in a large saucepan. Add the lamb bones and the wine. Reduce by half. Add the water, the garlic and the thyme. Bring to the boil and simmer for 30 minutes, skimming occasionally, then strain into a clean saucepan. Add the spices and reduce to required consistency. Pass the sauce through a fine sieve and adjust the seasoning before serving, "monter" the sauce with a small knob of fresh butter and add a few drops of lemon juice.

to serve:

Spoon a bed of braised pulses on the left side of the plate and place two slices of roasted leg or loin of lamb on top and finish with the cutlet.
On the opposite side, spoon some aubergine and place the pastilla on it. Garnish with a sprig of rosemary and a piece of confit lemon wedge. Drizzle the sauce on the lamb and serve.

 RECOMMENDED WINE
Saumur Rouge Moulin des Quints – Domaine de la Paleine

Serves 4

Preparation time: 25 minutes
Cooking time: 25-30 minutes

Special equipment:
4 individual silver soufflé dishes (or oven proof china dishes) 8cm diameter, 3.5cm deep.

INGREDIENTS

3	egg yolks
35g	caster sugar, plus a pinch for the egg whites
10g	flour
150ml	milk
10g	butter
250g	mirabelles in syrup, drained and syrup reserved (can be made in season with fresh mirabelles, into a "classic" home made preserve)
45ml	mirabelle "Eau de Vie"
4	egg whites

for the soufflé dishes:

20g	softened butter
40g	caster sugar
4	sprigs of mint and icing sugar to serve

SOUFFLÉS CHAUDS AUX MIRABELLES
Warm golden plum soufflés
BY ALAIN ROUX

This warm, sweet dessert soufflé is one of the Roux favourites. The golden plums that I use here have a very delicate flavour. I invite you to try this dish and help to spread the word about this underused fruit.

METHOD

pastry cream:

Put the egg yolks and half of the sugar in a bowl and whisk until a pale light ribbon consistency. Sift in the flour and mix in thoroughly. In a saucepan bring the milk and the remaining sugar to the boil and pour onto the egg mixture and mix well. Return to the pan and bring to the boil over a gentle heat stirring continuously. Bubble for one minute and transfer into a bowl. Dust lightly with flakes of butter to prevent a skin from forming. Leave at room temperature.

the mirabelles:

In a saucepan reduce by half the reserved syrup. Add 150g mirabelles and cook for 5 minutes, then rub through a sieve. Set aside this purée at room temperature. Place the remaining mirabelles in a small bowl, pour over half the "Eau de Vie" and leave to macerate.

the soufflé dishes:

Using a pastry brush, coat the insides of the moulds with the soft butter. Pour the sugar into one dish and rotate so that the whole surface is coated with sugar. Pour the excess into the next dish and repeat with all the dishes.
Preheat the oven to 180°C.

the soufflé mixture:

Whisk the mirabelle purée into the pastry cream and the remaining "Eau de Vie". Beat the egg whites with a pinch of sugar until semi firm peaks. Using the whisk fold one third of the egg whites into the mixture, then with a spatula, gently fold in the rest of the egg whites. Spoon the mixture into the soufflé dishes so that they are half full. Divide between the dishes some alcohol-soaked mirabelles and keep a few to garnish the top of each soufflé after cooking. Fill to the top with the remaining mixture and smooth over the surface with a palette knife. Using the tip of a knife, run it around the edge of the moulds to take the mixture away from the dish, this will help the soufflés to rise.
Arrange the soufflés on a baking tray and cook for 6 to 8 minutes.

to serve:

Serve immediately; dusted with icing sugar, a few alcohol-soaked mirabelles (if any left!) and a sprig of mint.

 RECOMMENDED WINE
Coteaux de Saumur – Domaine de la Paleine

THE FAT DUCK

'Cooking principles: excellence, openness and integrity'

HESTON BLUMENTHAL

Heston Blumenthal has been described as a culinary alchemist for his innovative style of cuisine. His research pushes the boundaries of British gastronomy and enables a greater understanding of the way we register taste and flavour and the effects that nostalgia has on the palate. — a flair, which is prominent in the dishes at his restaurant, The Fat Duck. Heston opened The Fat Duck in Bray in August 1995, which has since gained three Michelin stars and worldwide acclaim for his multi-sensory approach to gastronomy. Heston is entirely self-taught. His formative years were spent travelling to various restaurants, vineyards, cheese makers and butchers throughout France carrying out extensive, thorough and determined research — a characteristic which soon became the trademark of his success.

THE SOUND
OF THE SEA

BY HESTON BLUMENTHAL

I chose these three dishes for very different reasons.

The Sound of the Sea shows just how important all of the senses are to our enjoyment of food. For me, emotion is a key ingredient. Listening to the sound of the sea through an iPod acts as a trigger for the diner to conjure up their own seaside memories. This dish crosses all cultural boundaries and, far from acting as a barrier between diners, it does just the opposite; bringing them together in a wonderful way.

Saddle of Venison, Celeriac and Sauce Poivrade, Civet of Venison with Pearl Barley, Venison and Frankincense Tea
This is a modern twist on a classical dish, venison with sauce poivrade. The addition of the frankincense tea accentuates the delicate gamey flavour of the venison but at the same time, provides a satisfying cleanser at the end of this main course.

The BFG
I am a 70's kid at heart and this is a 70's classic. Its name also ties in the slightly Willy Wonka feel to this dessert which includes a layer of chocolate aerated with a vacuum pump and a kirsch atomiser. When I visited the Black Forest researching this dessert, I realised that kirsch is the smell of the Black Forest and the essential ingredient in Black Forest Gateau.

THE SOUND OF THE SEA BY HESTON BLUMENTHAL

INGREDIENTS

for the ponzu:

65g	sake
2	whole fresh yuzu
1	whole fresh sudachi
700g	mirin
525g	rice wine vinegar
550g	tamari soy sauce
110g	"thin mouth" soy sauce (usu kuchi shoyu)
10g	katsuo bushi (dried bonito flakes)
15g	rishiri-kombu (dried kelp), browned on both sides over an open flame

for the miso oil:

250g	red miso paste
100g	white miso paste
5g	cod liver oil
250g	grapeseed oil

for the braised shiraita konbu:

1250g	mineral water
200g	glucose
25	sheets shiraita konbu
150g	mirin
425g	rice wine vinegar
65g	"thin mouth" soy sauce (Usu Kuchi)
8g	sea salt

for the cured halibut:

2	long sheets of dried konbu, soaked in cold water
350g	table salt
100g	caster sugar
55g	rooibos konbu tea
1	fillet fresh halibut

for the cured yellowtail:

350g	table salt
100g	caster sugar
2	yuzu, zest
1	fillet of young yellowtail (hamachi)

for the cured mackerel:

50g	unrefined caster sugar
50g	salt
20g	lemon zest
10g	lime zest
5g	coriander seed
one whole mackerel of around 350g weight	
olive oil as needed	
transglutaminase	

for the "sand":

10g	grapeseed or groundnut oil
20g	shirasu (baby eels or anchovies)
10g	kombu
80g	N-Zorbit M tapioca maltodextrin*
25g	ice-cream cone (dark, type), ground
30g	panko breadcrumbs, fried in grapeseed oil until golden brown, then lightly ground
2g	blue shimmer powder
3.5g	brown carbonised powder
140g	reserved miso oil
sea salt*	

This is essential to achieve the sand-like texture. National Starch developed it specifically to increase the volume of dry mixes and to absorb fats and oils to form a light, dry powder. Other types of tapioca maltodextrin do not absorb fat in the same way.

for the hijiki seaweed:

150g	dried hijiki seaweed
25g	"thin mouth" soy sauce (usu kuchi shoyu)
20g	mirin

for the "seashells":

1	Japanese lily bulb

for the "sea":

125g	carrots, peeled and finely sliced
125g	onions, finely sliced
75g	fennel, finely sliced
50g	leek, white and pale green parts only, finely sliced
50g	shallots, sliced
5g	garlic, finely sliced
25g	vermouth
100g	white wine (Chardonnay)
250g	razor clams, purged in several changes of fresh water
300g	mussels, purged in several changes of fresh water and beards removed
225g	cockles, purged in several changes of fresh water
1.75kg	water
35g	dried wakame seaweed
20g	kombu
15g	flat leaf parsley leaves and stems

for the final sauce:

800g	reserved ëseaí
200g	oyster juice
30g	white soy sauce (shiro shoyu)
table salt	
freshly ground black pepper	

to serve: (per portion)

10g	reserved "sand"
1 level tsp	reserved fried shirasu
1	reserved "seashell"
reserved ponzu	
2g	fresh codium spp. seaweed, washed in several changes of cold water and separated into pluches
2g	reserved hijiki seaweed
1	sheet of shiraita konbu cut into quarters reserved final sauce (at room temperature)
10g	soya lecithin
10g	sodium caseinate
micro ice plant for garnish	

METHOD

ponzu:

Pour the sake into a pan, bring to the boil over a high heat and flame off the alcohol. When the flames have died down remove the pan from the heat and set aside to cool. Wash the yuzu and sudachi, cut them in half and juice them, straining out any seeds. Discard any seeds from the fruit-skin halves, then cut the skins into quarters. Place in a large container along with the juice and the rest of the ingredients, and seal with an airtight cover. Refrigerate for 1 month, then strain the liquid through damp muslin and adjust the seasoning by adding tamari, thin mouth soy sauce or vinegar if necessary. Store in the fridge.

miso oil:

Fold all the ingredients together very carefully, then cover and refrigerate for 48 hours. Gently strain through damp muslin to separate the top layer of oil from the heavier miso below, and reserve the oil.

shiraita konbu:

Combine the water and the glucose in a pot wide enough for the sheets of shiraita konbu to lie out flat but not to wide for them to have room to float around during cooking (32cm is ideal). Remove the shiraita konbu from the package and place the sheets one at a time into a separate container of cold water, lying flat, so that each sheet is facing the same direction. Note: the sheets will be stuck together slightly and it is important for even cooking and marination that they be peeled off one at a time. Remove each sheet, one at a time, and wipe the viscous fluid off of it. Place each sheet facing the same direction into the pot with the water and glucose.

Bring the pot to a low simmer and cover the surface of the konbu with a sheet of muslin to keep it submerged in the liquid ensuring even cooking. Bring the water just to a simmer and set a timer for 20 minutes. Simmer the konbu gently for the 20 minutes and check the doneness (the konbu should be cooked through while retaining texture). Gently transfer the konbu into a 1/3 gastronorm pan so that the sheets are all facing the same direction, covering with the reserved muslin from the cooking process. Drain any liquid that has collected in the pan back into the pot and reserve the konbu at room temperature. Strain the liquid through a chinois into a container, rinse out the pot, and return the liquid to the pot.

Bring the remaining liquid in the pot up to a boil, first skimming any impurities that have risen to the surface, and begin to reduce the liquid down. Meanwhile heat the mirin in a saucepot and flame off the alcohol. Reduce the mirin by half and add to the reducing water mixture. Add the rice vinegar and reduce the mixture to a syrup. Remove from the heat and add the soy sauce and salt. Pour the hot liquid over the konbu. Wrap the container in clingfilm and refrigerate for 24 hours. Check the consistency of the liquid as well as the acidity and seasoning, if further adjustments are required drain the liquid into a saucepot and return to a simmer. Pour the liquid back over the konbu and refrigerate for a further 24 hours before using.

cured halibut:

Place 1 sheet of the softened konbu on top of a sheet of clingfilm. Combine the salt, sugar, and konbu rooibos tea. Coat the halibut piece with a generous amount of the cure and place onto the konbu. Lay the other piece of konbu over the fish and roll up in the clingfilm. Place the roll onto a drip rack and into a shallow container. Allow to cure in fridge for 10 hours depending on size. Rinse under cold running water for 5 minutes and dry with a towel. Wrap the fish in parchment and clingfilm.

cured yellowtail:

Lay down a strip of clingfilm. Combine the salt, sugar, and yuzu zest, coat the yellow tail with a generous amount of the cure and place onto the clingfilm. Roll the yellowtail in the clingfilm. Place the roll onto a drip rack and into a shallow bank box. Allow to cure in fridge for 12-14 hours depending on size. Rinse under running water and dry with C-folds. Wrap the fish in parchment and clingfilm.

cured mackerel:

Combine the salt, sugar, lemon zest, lime zest and coriander seed in a ingredients in a food processor and blend to a fine powder. Gut and fillet the mackerel. Run the tip of a sharp filleting knife down either side of the pin bones and bloodline in the centre of each fillet and remove this piece by gently pulling away using a pair of fish tweezers. Trim both fillets so that each is exactly the same length as the other and so that, when placed together, the two halves form a seamless ballotine. Remove a small amount of flesh from one of the fillets where the blue portion of the skin joins the fillet (but do not cut away the skin) to create a small flap that will overlap with the other fillet when the two pieces are joined together.

Place a layer of the ground sugar and salt cure onto a tray and place the mackerel fillets flesh-side down onto the cure. Cover with plastic wrap and refrigerate for one hour. Rinse the fillets under cold running water to remove the cure. Blot the fish dry. Lay down a piece of plastic wrap onto a work surface. Use a fine sifter to sprinkle Transglutaminase over the flesh of both fillets and then use a clean and dry pastry brush to dust off as much excess as possible. Lay one fillet skin-side down onto the plastic wrap and then lay the other fillet onto this (flesh-to-flesh) so that the pieces line up and the flap of trimmed skin overlaps slightly. The pieces should look like a trimmed, boneless fish. Carefully roll the plastic wrap around the fish and roll the ends to tighten the fish together (be careful not to distort the shape of the ballotine). Once the plastic wrap is tight around the fish tie the ends of the plastic wrap and refrigerate for at least four hours to bind the fillets together.

Finally, bring a pot of water to a boil and blanch the wrapped fish water for one minute and immediately plunge into ice cold water to prevent it from cooking. This process is to break the skin down without cooking any of the flesh. Slice the ballotine into 1cm thick slices and cover with clingfilm; refrigerate until needed.

"sand":

Place the grapeseed or groundnut oil in a small sauté pan over a medium heat until hot. Add the shirasu and sauté, stirring constantly, until they are golden brown. (If they are too dark, they will be bitter; too light and they won't be crisp enough. They will continue to brown after being removed from the pan.) Strain off the oil and drain the shirasu on kitchen paper. Grind the kombu to a fine powder, sift it, then weigh out 4g. Put 5g of the fried shirasu in a mixing bowl. Add all the other ingredients except the miso oil and salt, and combine. Add the miso oil, drizzling it in a light stream, and stir to obtain a wet sand consistency. Season with the sea salt and store covered until needed.

hijiki seaweed:

Soak the hijiki in warm water until softened (about 5 minutes), then drain off the water. Rinse with fresh water and drain again. Season with the soy sauce and mirin. Cover and refrigerate until needed.

"seashells":

Rinse off the sawdust that the lily bulb is stored in, then pat dry and cut out the core. Separate the individual layers of the bulb. Using a small knife, trim each layer to look like a seashell and store covered in fresh water. Blanch the "seashells" in salted simmering

water. As soon as they float to the surface, refresh in iced water, then drain and set aside. (They can become overcooked in a matter of seconds, so act quickly to retain the lightly crunchy texture).

"sea":

Put the vegetables, vermouth and white wine in a saucepan and simmer until translucent. Add water if necessary to prevent the vegetables from catching.
Add the shellfish and cover with the water. Bring the liquid up to 85°C/185°F, then cover and infuse for 25 minutes at this temperature. Remove the pan from the heat and add the wakame, kombu and parsley. Re-cover and allow to cool to room temperature. Skim off any impurities that have risen to the top. Pass the stock through a chinois and then through a sieve lined with damp muslin.
Cool over an ice bath.

final sauce:

Place the "sea", oyster juice and white soy sauce in a container and adjust the seasoning as necessary. Cover and refrigerate until needed.

to serve:

Place the "sand" on a plate and use a rigid card or spatula to shape it into a vertical strip about 2cm wide. Sprinkle the shirasu on top. Toss the "seashell" in the ponzu and place on the "sand". Toss the Codium seaweed in the ponzu and drain on kitchen paper. Place in a pile by the edge of the "sand". Place separate piles of the hijiki and shiraita konbu on the sand in the same manner. Drizzle the ponzu over the fish, then place them on top of each pile of seaweed. Place the final sauce in a container, add the soya lecithin and sodium caseinate, and foam the mixture using a hand-held blender. Spoon around the seafood to resemble the ocean crashing on to the beach. Garnish the dish with 3 pieces of ice plant and drizzle a bit more ponzu over the top. Serve with the iPod playing *The Sound of the Sea*.

♟ RECOMMENDED WINE
Buxus Villette Sauvignon Blanc – Domaine Louis Bovard – Vaud – Switzerland

SADDLE OF VENISON, CELERIAC AND SAUCE POIVRADE, CIVET OF VENISON WITH PEARL BARLEY, VENISON AND FRANKINCENSE TEA

BY HESTON BLUMENTHAL

Serves 4

INGREDIENTS

for the venison consommé:

2kg	venison bones
900g	Syrah wine
100g	olive oil
180g	carrots, peeled and finely sliced
120g	shallots, finely sliced
80g	celery, finely sliced
90g	leeks, finely sliced
140g	tomatoes, cored and chopped
35g	garlic, sliced
2	bay leaves
3g	sprig of thyme
	parsley leaves
	black peppercorns
2g	juniper berries
2.4kg	water
	tarragon leaves
	table salt

for the frankincense hydrosol:

50g	golden frankincense tears
100g	water

for the frankincense dilution:

100g	vodka
0.4g	reserved frankincense essential oil

for the confit of vegetables:

100g	extra virgin olive oil
140g	carrots, peeled and finely sliced
130g	onions, finely sliced
80g	leek, white and pale green parts only, finely sliced
30g	celery, finely sliced
5g	garlic, thinly sliced

for the tomato fondue:

500g	ripe vine tomatoes
	table salt
2	sprigs of parsley
2	sprigs of thyme
4	black peppercorns
½	star anise
1	clove
25g	extra virgin olive oil
80g	onions, chopped
10g	garlic, minced
8g	sherry vinegar
2g	tomato ketchup
	few drops of Worcestershire sauce
	few drops of tabasco sauce
	zest of ¼ lemon
	small pinch of saffron

for the sauce poivrade:

2.5kg	venison bones
900g	red wine (preferably Syrah)
50g	reserved confit of vegetables
50g	reserved tomato fondue

preheat the oven to 180°C/350°F/Gas 4.

for the gastrique:

15g	honey
2g	red wine vinegar
	reserved venison consommé
0.2g	bay leaf
0.4g	sprig of thyme
1g	juniper berries
0.5g	pink peppercorns
0.3g	black peppercorns

for the blood cream:

500g	venison bones (with some meat still attached)
500g	whipping cream

for the celeriac purée:

1kg	celeriac, peeled
200g	unsalted butter
400g	whole milk
	table salt
	black pepper

for the celeriac fondants:

2kg	celeriac, peeled
375g	unsalted butter
10g	table salt

for the civet base:

500g	chicken bouillon
10g	groundnut oil
300g	pearl barley
40g	shallots, chopped
1g	garlic, minced
150g	Madeira

for the red wine jelly discs:

100g	Shiraz wine
50g	Maury wine
0.8g	gellan F
0.08g	gellan LT100

for the venison medallions:

1	saddle of red deer, 10-18 months old (approximately 6.5kg)
	extra virgin olive oil
10g	sprigs of thyme

for the red wine foam:

This should not be prepared more than 12 hours before use.

200g	Shiraz wine
100g	Maury wine
8g	soy lecithin

for the grelot onions:
(per portion)

1	grelot onion

for the butter emulsion:

250g   unsalted butter
150g   water
5g   table salt

to serve:

(per portion)
reserved venison medallions
fine sea salt
fleur de sel
black pepper
reserved celeriac purée

clarified butter
reserved celeriac fondants
10g   chicken bouillon
2   reserved grelot onion halves
reserved butter emulsion
reserved sauce poivrade
2g   freshly sliced white truffle
reserved blood cream
20g   white chicken stock
reserved civet base
5g   cryogenically frozen foie gras,

cut into 1cm dice
5g   venison marrow, removed from the
          bone, soaked in lightly salted
          water to remove traces of blood
          and cut into 10mm cubes
15g   foie gras parfait, cubed
1g   sherry vinegar
reserved red wine jelly discs
reserved red wine foam
reserved venison consommé
8 drops   reserved frankincense dilution

METHOD

venison consommé:

Preheat the oven to 180°C/350°F/Gas 4. Place the venison bones in a pan and roast for 30 minutes or so, until lightly coloured. Pour the wine into a large pan, bring to the boil, then flame off the alcohol. Set aside until needed. Heat a large pressure cooker and add the olive oil. Add the vegetables and sweat until they are just starting to colour. Add the roasted bones, the flamed wine, bay leaves, thyme, 10g parsley, the juniper berries and 2g black peppercorns and cover with the water. Put on the lid, bring to full pressure and cook for 2 hours. Leave to cool before opening, then skim the fat from the surface. Pass the stock through a fine sieve lined with damp muslin into a large, rectangular container. Cover and freeze until solid. Line a perforated tray with a double layer of muslin large enough to hold the frozen stock in a single flat layer. Turn the stock on to the muslin-lined tray and place this over another tray to catch the stock as it defrosts.
Transfer to the fridge and allow to thaw slowly over 36-48 hours. Discard the gelled mass left in the top tray. Pour the filtered consommé into a large pan and reduce by half. Remove from the heat and allow to cool. Weigh the consommé, and for every 500g, add 7g tarragon, 5g parsley, 0.5g peppercorns and salt to taste. Cover and leave to infuse in the fridge for 12 hours. Strain the finished consommé through a fine sieve and divide into 65g portions. Refrigerate until needed.

frankincense hydrosol:

Set the bath of a rotary evaporator to 50°C/120°F. Combine the frankincense and water in the evaporating flask, attach and submerge in the bath. Using a pump, run iced water through the condensing coils. Begin rotating the flask and pull the vacuum to below 50mbars. Run the rotary evaporator for 3 hours. Collect the liquid in the receiving flask, remove the essential oil from the surface with a spoon or pipette and reserve.

frankincense dilution:

Combine the vodka and essential oil and mix thoroughly with a hand-held blender. Refrigerate in an airtight container until needed.

confit of vegetables:

Heat the olive oil in a saucepan over a medium heat, add the carrots and onions and cook until pale golden in colour. Add the leek, celery and garlic and cook until a rich caramel colour has developed. Set aside until needed.

the tomato fondue:

Bring a pan of water to the boil. Make a small incision in the tomatoes and blanch in the water for 10-15 seconds. Plunge into iced water to cool. Drain, remove the skin and cut the tomatoes in half. Scoop out and discard the cores. Place the flesh and seeds in a sieve set over a bowl. Sprinkle with ½ teaspoon salt, toss to combine and leave for 1 hour. Reserve the juice in the bowl, then chop the flesh into small dice and set aside. Make a bouquet garni by placing the parsley, thyme, peppercorns, star anise and clove in a muslin bag and tying securely. Set aside. Heat the olive oil in a pan, add the onions and sweat for 10 minutes. Add the garlic and bouquet garni and sweat for 5 minutes. Add the tomatoes and their juice, the vinegar, ketchup, Worcestershire sauce, Tabasco and lemon zest. Cook over a low heat for 2-3 hours, stirring regularly. After about 1-1½ hours of cooking, add the saffron. The fondue should have a nice dark colour and a jammy consistency. Keep refrigerated until needed.

sauce poivrade:

Place the venison bones in a pan and roast for 1 hour, or until lightly coloured. Place in a storage container. Pour the wine into a large pan, bring to the boil, then flame off the alcohol. Pour over the bones, adding enough water so that they are just covered. Add the confit of vegetables and tomato fondue, then cover and refrigerate for 48 hours. Transfer the bone mixture to a pressure cooker and top up with water to cover if necessary. Put on the lid, bring to full pressure and cook for 2 hours, skimming regularly. Take off the heat and leave to cool completely before removing the lid. Strain the liquid through a fine sieve into another pan. Bring to the boil and reduce to 10 per cent of the original amount. Pass through a fine sieve and set aside until needed.

gastrique:

Place the honey in a pan and warm over a medium-high heat until it begins to caramelise. Add the vinegar, reserved consommé, bay leaf, thyme, juniper berries and pink peppercorns. Return the pan to the heat and simmer for 5 minutes. Add the black peppercorns, freshly cracked, and infuse for a few minutes, until the aroma is sufficiently strong. Strain the sauce through a fine sieve lined with a double layer of damp muslin and refrigerate until needed.

blood cream:

Place the bones and cream in a saucepan and bring to 50°C/120°F. Cover and hold at this temperature for 30 minutes. Strain through a chinois and refrigerate the cream until needed.

celeriac purée:

Using a mandolin, slice the celeriac as thinly as possible. Melt the butter in a large saucepan over a medium heat and add the celeriac. Cook until completely soft, stirring to avoid it catching. When soft, add the milk and simmer for 5 minutes. Transfer to a blender and blitz to a purée. Pass the purée through a fine sieve using the back of a ladle and pour into a PacoJet beaker. Freeze completely, then pass through a PacoJet machine. Repeat this process 3 times, freezing between each processing. Transfer the purée to a pan and heat gently while stirring. Season to taste with salt and freshly ground pepper, then set aside to cool. Cover and refrigerate until needed.

celeriac fondants:

Preheat a water bath to 83°C/181°F.
Cut the celeriac into slices 15mm thick, then cut each slice into rectangles measuring 3 x 4cm. Place in a sous-vide bag in a single layer with the butter and the salt and seal under full pressure. Place the bag in the water bath and cook for 4½ hours (until cooked through but not

mushy). Remove and cool at room temperature for 15 minutes. Transfer to room-temperature water for 15 minutes, then place in iced water until thoroughly chilled. Keep refrigerated until needed.

civet base:

Line a tray with baking parchment and refrigerate until cold. Heat the chicken bouillon to just below simmering and keep hot. Place the oil in a pan over a medium heat and, when hot, roast the pearl barley until golden and nutty. Add the shallots and sweat until softened. Add the garlic and cook for 2 minutes. Pour in the Madeira, bring to the boil, then flame off the alcohol and reduce to a syrup.

Pour 200g of the hot chicken bouillon on to the barley and cook over a medium heat until the barley is just soft. Add more bouillon if required to achieve this.

Remove from the heat and spread the barley on to the chilled tray. When cool, divide into 22g portions and refrigerate until needed.

red wine jelly discs:

Cover a large, flat board with clingfilm, stretching it to ensure that there are no creases or air bubbles. Pour the wines into a pan, bring to the boil, then flame off the alcohol. Using a hand-held blender, add both gellans. Return to the heat and bring to the boil, stirring. As soon as the gellan has dissolved, pour on to the prepared board, tilting to spread the gel in a thin, even layer. Leave to set. Using a cutter 6cm in diameter, cut circles out of the jelly. Stack them between squares of baking parchment, place in a covered container and refrigerate until needed.

venison medallions:

Remove the individual loins from the saddle, keeping the rib bones attached. Then trim away the small fillets and reserve for another use, and French the individual bones. Place the loins in a sous-vide bag with the olive oil and thyme and seal under full pressure. Refrigerate for 48 hours. Remove the marinated loins from the sous-vide bag and wipe off any excess oil. Place several layers of clingfilm on a work surface and wrap it firmly around the loins, twisting the ends to tighten the package into a cylindrical shape. Refrigerate for at least 4 hours. Transfer the venison to a board, remove the clingfilm and cut the meat into 150g portions. Wrap each medallion in clingfilm, place in individual sous-vide bags and seal under full pressure. Refrigerate until needed.

red wine foam:

Pour the wines into a pan, bring to the boil, then flame off the alcohol. Remove from the heat and add the lecithin, stirring to dissolve. Cover until needed.

grelot onions:

Trim away any stalk on the onion and remove all but 0.5cm of the green top. Peel away the first 2 layers of the onion to expose the tender core. Remove as much root as possible, but keep the onion intact. Seal in a sous-vide bag at 15mbar, then cook in a microwave on full power for about 1 minute – long enough for the onion to be cooked through but still firm. Plunge the bag into iced water to prevent the grelot from overcooking. Once cool, remove from the bag and slice in half. Refrigerate until needed.

butter emulsion:

Combine the ingredients in a small pan and place over a medium heat. Emulsify with a hand-held blender and keep warm.

to serve:

Preheat a water bath to 60°C/140°F and another to 50°C/120°F. Place the venison medallions in the hotter water bath and cook until the internal temperature of the meat reaches 54°C/129°F. Transfer to the cooler water bath for 10 minutes.

Gently reheat the celeriac purée, adjust the seasoning, then cover and keep warm.

Place a small sauté pan on a high heat and add the clarified butter. Remove a fondant from the sous-vide bag and colour one side in the butter. Remove from the heat and pour off the butter. Add the chicken bouillon to the pan, gently shaking to coat the fondant. Keep warm.

Preheat a small sauté pan until very hot. Sear the cut side of a grelot half until golden and slightly charred. Keep warm. Cut the root end off the other half of grelot and separate the layers. Place in a small saucepan with enough butter emulsion to warm through. When hot, drain on kitchen paper and season. Keep warm.

Heat 30g of the sauce poivrade in a small saucepan and swirl in 1 teaspoon of the blood cream, heating gently to lightly thicken the sauce. Place the white chicken stock in a small pan, bring to a simmer and add 22g of the civet base. Stir and cook until the bouillon has been absorbed. Add 15g of both the sauce poivrade and the celeriac purée to bind the civet base. Stir and allow to reduce slightly. Add the diced foie gras and venison marrow, then remove from the heat. Add the foie gras parfait and sherry vinegar and adjust the seasoning.

Remove a venison medallion from the bag and drain on kitchen paper, leaving the clingfilm wrapping on the meat. Leave to rest in a warm place. Place the civet mixture in a small, warm bowl and position a jelly disc on top of it. Using a hand-held blender, froth the red wine foam and spoon over the jelly.

Cut the venison medallion across the grain into 5 slices, each 1cm thick. Remove the clingfilm and season the meat with fine sea salt, fleur de sel and sifted black pepper.

Place 60g of the celeriac purée on a warm plate. Place the grelots in butter emulsion on top of the celeriac purée. Trim the edges of the celeriac fondant, cut into 3 equal triangles and arrange on the plate. Place the slices of venison over the grelot. Place the seared grelot on the plate next to the venison. Spoon over 15g of the sauce poivrade, garnish with the white truffle, and serve.

Meanwhile, make the venison and frankincense tea. Heat 65g of the venison consommé to 65°C/149°F, add the frankincense drops and serve after the venison and civet as a kind of palate cleanser.

THE BFG!

(ALSO KNOWN AS THE BLACK FOREST GATEAU!)

BY HESTON BLUMENTHAL

Serves 4

INGREDIENTS

for the kirsch ice cream:

500g	whole milk
120g	egg yolks
200g	unrefined caster sugar
80g	kirsch
350g	sour cream

for the roast almond paste:

200g	whole blanched almonds
5g	egg white
5g	table salt

for the almond base:

40g	Amedei Toscano chocolate (32% cocoa solids), chopped
40g	amarena cherries
100g	reserved roast almond paste
15g	reserved chopped almonds
50g	feuilletine (caramelised puff pastry)

for the apricot pâté de fruit:

200g	unrefined caster sugar
3g	yellow pectin
250g	apricot purée
25g	glucose syrup
3g	malic acid
5g	amaretto liquor

for the kirsch ganache:

50g	unsalted butter
500g	Valrhona Guanaja chocolate (70% cocoa solids)
450g	UHT cream
70g	invert sugar syrup
110g	kirsch
3g	table salt

for the chocolate sponge:

225g	whole eggs
125g	unrefined caster sugar
50g	plain flour
30g	cornflour
30g	cocoa powder

for the soaking syrup:

100g	griottine cherries, in syrup
15g	kirsch

for the wood-effect base:

100g	unsalted butter
60g	plain flour
5g	baking powder
30g	sifted icing sugar
3g	table salt
60g	whole egg
30g	honey
15g	whole milk

for the wood grain:

100g	cocoa powder
20g	cornflour
180g	water
reserved wood-effect base	

for the dried vanilla cherry stems:

2	vanilla pods

for the chocolate shavings:

100g	Amedei Chuao chocolate (70% cocoa solids)

for the white chocolate mousse:

7.5g	leaf gelatine (170 bloom)
300g	white chocolate
500g	whipping cream
60g	kirsch
40g	egg yolks
10g	unrefined caster sugar
125g	whole milk
reserved chocolate sponge moulds	

for the dark chocolate mousse:

This should be made while the white chocolate mousse is setting.

5g	leaf gelatine (170 bloom)
150g	Amedei Chuao chocolate (70% cocoa solids)
200g	whipping cream
50g	egg yolks
50g	unrefined caster sugar
2g	table salt
150g	whole milk
reserved chocolate sponge moulds	

for the flocage:

This makes enough to cover 3 gateaux, but the surplus can be stored for later use.

500g	chocolate (70% cocoa solids)
200g	cocoa butter
reserved gateau	

METHOD

kirsch ice cream:

Pour the milk into a pan, bring to a simmer and remove from the heat. Place the egg yolks and sugar in the bowl of a food mixer and beat for 5 minutes. Pour in the warm milk, mixing gently to combine. Return the mixture to the pan and place over the heat, stirring, until it reaches 70°C/160°F. Hold at this temperature for 10 minutes to pasteurise. Cool over an ice bath. Cover and mature in the fridge for 8-24 hours. Stir in the kirsch and sour cream, then churn in an ice-cream machine to -5°C/23°F. Place a sheet of clingfilm on the surface of the ice cream, then cover and store in the freezer until needed.

roast almond paste:

Preheat the oven to 180°C/350°F/Gas 4 and line an oven tray with silicone paper. Combine all the ingredients in a bowl and spread over the prepared tray in a single layer. Bake for 10-15 minutes, or until golden brown. Remove and leave to cool. Roughly chop 15g of the almonds and set aside. Place the rest in a food processor and blitz until puréed. Set aside.

almond base:

Melt the chocolate in a bain-marie or microwave. Chop the cherries to roughly the same size as the almonds and stir into the chocolate along with the almond paste and chopped almonds. Fold in the feuilletine until the mixture comes together — it's important not to overmix. Line a baking tray with parchment and spread the mixture on it to a thickness of about 5mm. Score into strips measuring 12 x 7cm, then cover and refrigerate.

pâté de fruit:

Combine the sugar and pectin in a bowl. Place the apricot purée in a saucepan, bring to the boil and whisk in the pectin mixture. Whisk in the glucose syrup and continue to cook on a medium to high heat until it reaches 107°C/225°F. Set aside.
Dissolve the malic acid in the amaretto, then whisk into the apricot mixture, working quickly, as the syrup will now start to set. Pour into a bowl and leave to cool. When the gel has set, blitz with a hand-held blender until smooth and store in a piping bag until needed.

kirsch ganache:

Cut the butter into small pieces and set aside, covered, to reach room temperature. Finely chop the chocolate and melt gently in a bain-marie or microwave until it reaches about 50°C/120°F, but not more than 55°C/131°F. Set aside. Place the cream, invert sugar syrup, kirsch and salt in a saucepan and bring to the boil. Remove from the heat and very carefully add to the melted chocolate in three stages with the aid of a hand-held blender. (The aim is to emulsify, not to incorporate any air.) Line a 36 x 26 x 5cm tray with baking parchment. Blend the butter into the chocolate mixture, then pour into the prepared tray, cover and leave to set at room temperature for 48 hours. Cut the ganache into rectangles measuring 11 x 6cm, then cover and refrigerate.

chocolate sponge:

Preheat the oven to 180°C/350°F/Gas 4. Place the eggs and sugar in a bowl and whisk until thick and glossy. Add the remaining ingredients and fold together. Line a 29 x 19 x 3.5cm baking tray with parchment. Pour the cocoa mixture into the tray and bake for 15 minutes, or until firm to the touch. Cool on a wire rack, then cut into rectangles measuring 11 x 6 x 1.5cm. Using a round cutter 1cm in diameter, cut out 2 parallel rows of 4 holes in each rectangle and set aside.

soaking syrup:

Drain the cherries and set aside. Weigh out 40g of the syrup, add to the kirsch and mix thoroughly. Reserve until needed.

wood-effect base:

Preheat the oven to 180°C/350°F/Gas 4. Melt the butter in a small saucepan over a medium heat, stirring frequently, until it begins to brown and develops a nutty aroma. Strain the beurre noisette through a fine sieve and set aside.
Sift together the flour, baking powder, icing sugar and salt. Stir in 50g of the beurre noisette, then mix in the egg, honey and milk, incorporating them separately. Refrigerate until needed.

wood grain:

Preheat the oven to 180°C/350°F/Gas 4. Place the cocoa, cornflour and water in a bowl and whisk to a smooth paste. Using a home decorating tool designed for creating a wood-grain effect, dip the edge of it into the paste and using a rocking motion spread it over a silicone baking mat. Place in the freezer until set (about 1 hour). Allow the wood-effect base to come to room temperature, then spread it over the wood grain as thinly as possible. Place in the oven and bake for 8-10 minutes, or until golden brown. Transfer to a rack, leave to cool and store in an airtight container until needed.

dried vanilla cherry stems:

For the dried vanilla cherry stems
Top and tail the vanilla pods, split in half lengthways and scrape out the seeds (save for another use). Cut each pod in half widthways, and cut these into 3 lengthways strips. Tie a knot at the end of each strip to give the effect of a cherry stem. Set aside in a warm, dry place until needed.

chocolate shavings:

Run a small sharp knife along the block of chocolate to make shavings. Store in the freezer until needed.

white chocolate mousse:

Soak the gelatine in cold water and set aside. Chop the white chocolate and gently melt in a bain-marie or microwave. Set aside. Lightly whip the cream and kirsch to soft peaks and set aside. Whisk the yolks and sugar together for 5 minutes and set aside. Heat the milk in a saucepan to 60°C/140°F. Slowly pour it into the egg mixture while whisking constantly then return to the pan. Heat gently, stirring constantly, until it reaches 70°C/160°F, and hold at this temperature for 10 minutes. Squeeze the gelatine dry, then add to the saucepan and stir to dissolve. Pour the mixture into the melted chocolate and stir together. Fold in the cream, then pour immediately over the sponge in the moulds to a depth of 1cm. Refrigerate for about 1 hour to set.

dark chocolate mousse:

Soak the gelatine in cold water and set aside. Chop the chocolate and gently melt in a bain-marie or microwave. Set aside. Lightly whip the cream to soft peaks and set aside. Whisk the egg yolks, sugar and salt together until pale in colour (about 5 minutes). Heat the milk in a saucepan to 70°C/160°F, then slowly pour it into the egg yolks while whisking constantly and return the mixture to the pan. Heat gently, stirring constantly, until it reaches 70°C/160°F, and hold at this temperature for 10 minutes. Squeeze the gelatine dry, then add to the saucepan and stir to dissolve. Pour the mixture into the melted chocolate and stir together. Fold in the cream, then pour immediately over the white chocolate mousse to the top of the moulds. Level the surface with a palette knife, then freeze for 3-4 hours, until completely set.

assembly:

TO BUILD THE GATEAU, PART 1
(4-5 portions)
reserved almond base
reserved apricot pâté de fruit
reserved kirsch ganache
reserved chocolate sponge
8 reserved griottine cherries
reserved soaking syrup

Place a 12 x 7 x 6cm metal mould on a baking tray lined with parchment. Place an almond base strip in the bottom of each mould. Pipe a line of the pâté de fruit 1cm wide along the centre of it. Top that with a rectangle of ganache, followed by a rectangle of chocolate sponge. Place a cherry in each hole. Drizzle a little of the soaking syrup over the sponge and reserve.

TO BUILD THE GATEAU, PART 2
(4-5 portions)

reserved frozen gateau

Using a Parisian scoop 20mm wide, scoop out 2 parallel rows of 4 shallow indentations in the chocolate mousse layer of the gateau. Using a blowtorch, warm the outside of the mould and invert the contents on to a tray. Turn it over so that holes are on top. Using an offset palette knife, smooth the sides of the gateau.

the flocage

Chop the chocolate and cocoa butter and melt gently in a bain-marie or microwave. Pour into a paint spray gun and, working quickly, spray the gateau evenly on all sides. Refrigerate until the centre has defrosted (about 2-3 hours).

TO BUILD THE GATEAU, PART 3
(4-5 portions)
kirsch
reserved wood-effect base
reserved gateau
reserved chocolate shavings
reserved soaking syrup
8 amarena cherries, drained
reserved vanilla cherry stems
reserved kirsch ice cream

Pour the kirsch into an atomiser and secure the spraying nozzle. Place the wood-effect base on a serving tray and sit the gateau on top. Surround with the chocolate shavings, then push a skewer into each indentation to a depth of 2-3cm. Using a pipette, fill the skewer holes with the soaking syrup, making sure that it does not spill out. Place a cherry in each indentation, stalk end up. Stick a vanilla stem into each cherry and serve with the kirsch ice cream. Spray the kirsch atomiser into the air above the place settings.

 RECOMMENDED WINE
Quintessence du Clos –
Domaine Le Clos des Cazaux – Rhône

LE GAVROCHE

'Simply London's best. If the whole world is getting you down, grab your coat and make for Le Gavroche'

MICHEL ROUX JR

A graduate of Le Gavroche, Michel Roux Jr was born into fine cuisine. He received his schooling in its kitchens, and is imbued with its unique atmosphere and style. He spent time working at Charcutier Mothu and La Boucherie Lamartine in Paris as well as a spell in Hong Kong, although perhaps the most predominant influence on his work is the two years he spent under Alain Chapel, a man heralded as one of the most notable chefs of his generation. With two Michelin stars to his name, Michel has exceeded his impressive pedigree with his own inspiring, independent style.

Serves 4

Preparation time: 20 minutes
Cooking time: 10 minutes

SOUFFLÉ SUISSESSE

BY MICHEL ROUX JR

A timeless Gavroche classic: rich yet light, and definitely indulgent.

INGREDIENTS

45g   butter
45g   plain flour
500ml milk
5   egg yolks
salt and freshly ground white pepper
6   egg whites
600ml double cream
200g   Gruyère or Emmental cheese,
       grated

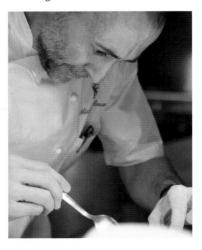

METHOD

Heat the oven to 200°C/400°F/gas 6.
Melt the butter in a thick-based saucepan, whisk in the flour and cook, stirring continuously, for about 1 minute. Whisk in the milk and boil for 3 minutes, whisking all the time to prevent any lumps from forming. Beat in the yolks and remove from the heat; season with salt and pepper. Cover with a piece of buttered greaseproof paper to prevent a skin from forming.
Whisk the egg whites with a pinch of salt until they form firm, not stiff, peaks. Add a third of the egg whites to the yolk mixture and beat with a whisk until evenly mixed, then gently fold in the remaining egg whites. Spoon the mixture into four well-buttered 8cm diameter tartlet moulds and place in the oven for 3 minutes, until the tops begin to turn golden.

to serve:

Season the cream with a little salt, warm it gently and pour into a gratin dish.
Turn the soufflés out into the cream, sprinkle the grated cheese over the soufflés, then return to the oven for 5 minutes. Serve immediately.

 RECOMMENDED WINE
Saint Saphorin Blanc – Louis Bovard – Vaud Switzerland

Serves 4

Preparation time: 10 minutes
Cooking time: N/A

LOBSTER MANGO SALAD

BY MICHEL ROUX JR

A light summer salad that's bursting with flavour and colour.

INGREDIENTS

2   cooked lobsters, 500-600g each
1   avocado, ripe but firm
1   mango, ripe but firm
2   spring onions, sliced
juice of 2 limes
peel of 1 lime, cut into thin strips
and cooked in a sugar syrup
12   basil leaves
4 tbsp   extra virgin olive oil
salt
green tabasco
endives leaves for serving (optional)

METHOD

Cut the lobster tail meat into medallions and all the rest into dice. Peel the avocado and mango and dice the flesh. Add the spring onions, lime juice and peel, torn basil leaves, olive oil and seasoning. Toss very gently.

to serve:
Serve the salad in glass bowls or spoon into little endive leaves.

 RECOMMENDED WINE
Fié Gris Blanc – Domaine de L'Aujardière, Loire

Serves 4

Preparation time: 45 minutes
Cooking time: 20 minutes

ROAST FILLET OF SEA BASS, PARSNIP PURÉE AND CARAMELISED GARLIC

BY MICHEL ROUX JR

INGREDIENTS

sea bass:

2 sea bass (600g each)
olive oil
3 shallots, sliced
80g button mushrooms, sliced
1 tbsp white wine vinegar
100ml dry white wine
400ml veal stock (see below)
salt and pepper
1 tbsp butter

veal stock:

(Makes about 3.5 litres)
1.5kg veal knuckle bones, chopped
1 calf's foot, split
1 large onion, roughly chopped
2 large carrots, roughly chopped
1 stick of celery, roughly chopped
5 ltr water
2 cloves of garlic
2 sprigs of thyme
½ tbsp tomato purée

caramelised garlic:

8 small shallots
20 cloves of garlic
olive oil

parsnip purée:

5 parsnips
120ml milk
1 tbsp butter
salt and pepper

parsnip crisps:

1 parsnip
oil for deep-frying

METHOD

veal stock:

Roast the bones and calf's foot in a hot oven (220°C/425°F/gas 7), turning occasionally until brown all over, then put them into a large saucepan.

Put the onion, carrots and celery into the roasting pan and roast until golden, turning frequently with a wooden spatula. Pour off any excess fat and put the roasted vegetable into the saucepan with the bones.

Put the roasting pan over high heat and add 500ml of the water to deglaze the pan; scrape the bottom with a wooden spatula to loosen all the caramelised sugars, then pour into the saucepan with the bones.

Add the remaining ingredients and bring to the boil. Skim off the scum and fat that come to the surface. Turn down the heat and simmer gently for 3 ½ hours, skimming occasionally. Pass through a fine sieve and leave to cool. This can be kept in the refrigerator for 8-10 days, or frozen.

sea bass:

Scale and fillet the sea bass, remove the pin bones using a pair of tweezers, rinse the fish and dry with kitchen towel. Score the skin of the fish several times with a sharp knife; this will help to prevent the fish from curling during cooking. Leave the bones (not the heads) to soak in cold water for the sauce.

Heat a little olive oil in a saucepan and cook the shallots for about 5 minutes, until golden and soft. Add the mushrooms and continue to cook for 10 minutes, stirring occasionally. Drain the fish bones, add to the pan and cook for 5-6 minutes. Add the vinegar and wine and let the wine come to the boil for 3 minutes, then add the stock, season lightly and simmer for 30 minutes, skimming at regular intervals. Pass through a fine sieve into a clean saucepan, bring back to the boil and whisk in the butter to thicken and gloss the sauce.

Heat a non-stick frying pan until smoking hot, add a few drops of olive oil, then add the fish, skin down, season with salt and pepper, and press the fish down with a palette knife if it begins to curl up. Once the skin is well browned, turn the fillets over and cook the other side; the whole process should not take more than 5-6 minutes, depending on the thickness of the fish.

caramelised garlic:

Peel the shallots and garlic. Blanch the shallots in boiling salted water for 10 minutes or until tender – cut them in half if large – then drain well. Put the garlic in a small saucepan of boiling salted water, bring to the boil for 2 minutes, then drain and change the water; repeat four times; drain well. Heat a little olive oil in a frying pan over medium heat, add the shallots and garlic and cook, shaking the pan so they don't stick, until caramelized.

parsnip purée:

Peel the parsnips and cut them into big chunks. Cook in boiling salted water until tender. Bring the milk to the boil and set aside. Drain the parsnips well, then put in a blender with the butter and some of the boiled milk and blend until totally smooth: the purée should be the consistency of double cream, so add more milk if necessary. Season and keep warm.

parsnip crisps:

Peel the parsnip and slice lengthways, using a mandolin to slice it as thinly as possible. Deep-fry in hot oil until crisp. Drain on kitchen towels to absorb any excess fat and set aside in a dry place.

to serve:

Spoon the parsnip purée on to warmed plates, make a hollow in the centre and fill with the caramelised garlic and shallots. Pour the sauce around the purée, place the fish on top and add a few parsnip crisps for decoration.

RECOMMENDED WINE

Les Terraces de Ch. Gris Blanc Nuits St Georges – Burgundy

Serves 2

Preparation time: 45 minutes

Cooking time: 30 minutes

WILD DUCK WITH GIROLLE MUSHROOMS

BY MICHEL ROUX JR

Game should always be cooked on the bone and served with seasonal accompaniments.

INGREDIENTS

1	wild mallard duck
80g	smoked duck breast
160g	girolle mushrooms, cleaned
2	shallots, peeled and chopped
1 tbsp	vegetable oil
1 tbsp	brandy
2 tbsp	Madeira
1 tbsp	chopped flat leaf parsley
2 dstsp	butter
salt, pepper	

METHOD

Trim and prepare the duck for roasting. Trim some of the fat off the smoked duck and cut into medium dice. Cut up the mushrooms if necessary. Take a cast-iron pan, small enough for the bird to fit in snugly, and heat up the oil until smoking. Place the seasoned duck in the pan and sear on all sides. Put in the oven at 200°C/Gas 6 for 10 minutes. Then add 1 spoonful of butter and continue to cook for a further 10 minutes, turning and basting twice. Remove the duck and leave in a warm place to rest. Discard most of the fat, leaving a little for cooking the shallots.

sauce:

In the same pan, cook the shallots over a moderate heat for a few seconds. Add the mushrooms and continue to cook until they are soft and render some of their water. Pour in the brandy and Madeira, bring to the boil and fold in the rest of the butter, the smoked duck and parsley.

to serve:

Serve the sauce hot with the roasted duck.

 RECOMMENDED WINE

Château de Pommard 1993 – Burgundy

SPICED CHERRIES IN KRIEK BEER
BY MICHEL ROUX JR

Delicious even for the non-beer lovers

INGREDIENTS

cherries:

1 ltr	Kriek beer (cherry-flavoured Belgian beer)
2	vanilla pods, split in half lengthways
1	stick of cinnamon
5	star anise
juice of 1 lemon and 1 orange	
½	zest of lemon, orange, and juice
½ tbsp	chopped ginger
300g	light brown sugar
1.5kg	cherries stoned
3 tbsp	kirsch liqueur

vanilla ice cream:

500ml	full fat milk
2	vanilla pods, split
6	egg yolks
125g	caster sugar
1 tsp	vanilla essence

METHOD

cherries:

Bring all the ingredients to the boil except for the cherries and Kirsch. Then add the cherries, cover and simmer for 2-3 minutes then leave to cool.

ice cream:

Bring the milk to the boil with the vanilla pods. Remove from the heat, cover and leave to infuse for 10 minutes.
Beat the egg yolks with the sugar until thick and creamy. Bring the milk back to the boil and pour on to the yolk mixture, whisking continuously. Pour the mixture back into the saucepan and cook over low heat, stirring continuously with a spatula, until the custard thickens slightly. Stir in the vanilla essence and pass through a fine sieve. Chill, then churn in an ice-cream machine until frozen.

to serve:

The cherries are delicious cold or warm but better if kept refrigerated for 24 hours. Add the Kirsch just before serving.

 RECOMMENDED WINE
Rasteau Rancio – Rhône

THE VINEYARD AT STOCKCROSS

'A distinct ambience
that you won't find
anywhere else.
A hidden gem waiting
to be discovered'

JOHN CAMPBELL

Since joining The Vineyard at Stockcross in January 2002,
Executive Chef John Campbell's food style has grown into some of the
best and most exciting food in Great Britain. Known as the cerebral chef,
John has a degree in International Culinary Arts, a host of accolades for his
food, as well as an enviable reputation within the industry. His genius lies
in combining complex elements into dishes that look and feel simple and
natural. He experiments with the effect that temperature has on flavour
— intensifying the taste and challenging the taste buds.

RISOTTO WILD MUSHROOMS, CEP ESPUMA, BALSAMIC

BY JOHN CAMPBELL

Serves 4

Preparation time: 35-45 minutes

Cooking time: 20 minutes

Special equipment:
iSi cream whipper

Planning ahead:
The mushroom nage and balsamic jelly can be made two days in advance, pickled trompettes can be made three days in advance and cep espuma can be made one day before.

 RECOMMENDED WINE

*Rosé de Kirwan –
Ch. Kirwan – Bordeaux*

INGREDIENTS

risotto base:

2kg	canaroli rice
10	shallots – finely chopped
1 ltr	white wine
2 ltr	chicken stock
10g	thyme
2	bay leaves
300g	olive oil

mushroom mix:

200g	chestnut mushrooms
200g	field mushrooms
200g	wild mushrooms (trompette, chanterelles, mousseron)

cep espuma:

200g	double cream
400g	milk
5g	salt
2g	truffle oil
1g	sherry vinegar
400g	cep purée

METHOD

cep purée:

200g	fine sliced onion
350g	fine sliced button mushrooms
250g	fine sliced field mushrooms
50g	unsalted butter
25g	dried cep
300g	Noilly Prat
750g	chicken stock
1	bay leaf
5g	thyme
1	clove of garlic
250g	cream
10g	salt

mushroom nage:

500g	sliced onions
100g	butter
25g	thyme
4	bay leaves
2kg	field mushrooms sliced
4kg	button mushrooms
16kg	water
100g	dried cep
50g	vegetable oil

pickled walnut jelly:

500g	pickled walnut juice
100g	balsamic vinegar
6g	agar

pickled trompette:

500g	trompette mushrooms
250g	olive oil
150g	vegetable oil
100g	white wine vinegar
100g	merlot vinegar
50g	sherry vinegar
juice of 1 lemon	
salt	

to finish:

5	pieces of celery cress
2g	finely chopped chives
10g	vegetable oil
3g	grated parmesan
20g	butter
200g	Cep purée
30g	mushroom mix
60g	risotto base
sherry vinegar, salt and truffle oil to season	
slice of black truffle	
150g	mushroom nage
3g	pickled trompette
cep espuma	
5	pieces of pickled walnut jelly
5	pieces of yellow chanterelles

risotto base:

Bring the chicken stock to the boil with the thyme and bay leaves and simmer for 10 minutes. Pour through a fine sieve and keep hot.

Gently fry the shallots with a good pinch of salt, taking care not to allow them to go brown in the olive oil until opaque.

Add rice and the wine and reduce until evaporated stirring continuously.

Add the stock to cover the rice continuing to stir, allow this to evaporate until the stock becomes thick and sticky then repeat the process, in all this should take about 8 minutes.

Once all the stock is used the rice should have a thick soup like appearance in the pan. Quickly remove the risotto onto trays and smooth flat. Cool quickly.

mushroom mix:

Trim the stalks from the mushrooms with a small knife.

Fill a bowl with cold water and place the mushrooms in the water. Gently run the mushrooms through your fingers whilst still in the water to clean them.

Carefully remove the mushrooms with your hands and place on a clean dry cloth.

Gently run the mushrooms through the cloth to dry them.

cep espuma:

Place all of the ingredients into a large pan and bring to the boil whisking from time to time.

Taste the mixture to check flavour and adjust as necessary with extra salt and sherry vinegar.

Pour into a cream whipper and "charge" with 2 N2O (nitrous oxide) gas canisters and shake vigorously. Dispense a little foam to check consistency then store the canister in a warm place around 50°C.

cep purée:

Colour the onions and garlic in a hot pan with the butter and a little vegetable oil.

Once golden brown add the Noilly Prat, thyme, bay leaf and dried cep and reduce until all of the liquid has evaporated.

Stir the mushrooms into the onions and continue to cook. Allow the liquids which have come out of the mushrooms to completely evaporate then add the chicken stock. Reduce by two thirds then add the cream.

Bring back to the boil then place the purée into a liquidiser and turn on full speed for 6 minutes.

Pour the purée through a fine sieve. Adjust the seasoning with salt and sherry vinegar then cover and cool.

mushroom nage:

Heat a large pan and add the vegetable oil. Add the onions, thyme, bay leaves and butter. Roast until golden brown.

Add the field mushrooms and continue to cook until dry.

Add the button mushrooms. Water will be released from the mushrooms, allow this to evaporate and the mushrooms to change to a dark brown roasted colour.

Add the water and bring to the boil. Add the dried cep, cover and leave to infuse for 12 hours.

Pour the nage through a colander and then through a cheese cloth.

pickled walnut jelly:

Place all of the ingredients into a pan and bring up to the boil whisking continuously.

Allow to boil for 1 minute then carefully pour onto a large square plate. Use a gas gun to disburse any bubbles which may have congregated on the surface of the jelly and allow to set.

Using a ruler and a pen mark 1cm indents around the 4 edges of the plate and cut the jelly into 1cm squares.

Store on the plate, clingfilmed in the refrigerator until required.

pickled trompette:

Using a small knife trim the root ends off the mushrooms.

Using just your fingers tear each mushroom into thin strands from top to bottom.

Fill a large bowl with cold water and add the mushrooms. Run the mushrooms through your fingers to remove any dirt. Carefully remove the mushrooms from the bowl with your hands and place on a clean dry cloth. Run the mushrooms through the cloth to dry them.

Mix the sherry and white wine vinegars with the olive oil.

Heat a large frying pan and add the vegetable oil. Add the mushrooms and the salt and fry for 1-2 minutes. Add the merlot vinegar. Once this has evaporated add the mixed vinegars and lemon juice and remove from the heat. Place into a container and allow to cool

to finish and serve:

Place 100g of cep purée in a pan and gently warm. Correct the seasoning with sherry vinegar and salt. Cover and keep in a warm place. Heat a round bottomed pan on the stove. Add the vegetable oil and the mushroom mix with a pinch of salt. Add half of the butter and roast the mushrooms until golden brown. Add the mushroom nage and then the risotto base. Using a plastic or wooden spoon carefully stir the risotto. When the nage has evaporated taste the rice to check it is tender, if not add a little more nage and continue to cook.

Once the rice grains are tender add the remaining cep purée and stir into the risotto.

Add the parmesan cheese and stir into the risotto. Remove from the heat and add the butter and a couple of drops of truffle oil. Season with salt and sherry vinegar then add the chopped chives.

Meanwhile, place a small frying pan on the stove and warm slightly. Add 10g of butter and melt. Add the chanterelles and gently fry for 1 minute. Season with salt and remove the pan from the stove. Remove the chanterelles with a spoon and place them on a clean cloth to drain.

Warm a round plate. Using a dessert spoon take half a spoon of cep purée.

Holding the spoon allow it to make contact with the plate at 12 o'clock. Without lifting the spoon let the purée run off onto the plate. Pause then slowly draw the spoon straight down the plate to 6 o'clock.

Place the very tip of the spoon in the purée at 12 o'clock and quickly pull the spoon to 10 o'clock.

Place the 5 pieces of walnut jelly equally spaced along the line of purée going to 10 o'clock.

Carefully spoon the risotto into the centre of the plate.

Arrange the pickled trompette around the edge of the risotto along with the chanterelles and the celery cress.

Direct the cream whipper into the middle of the risotto and carefully dispense the espuma onto the risotto to form a small mound of espuma.

Place a slice of truffle on top of the espuma and serve.

ORGANIC SALMON "MI-CUIT", SPICED LENTILS, FOIE GRAS
BY JOHN CAMPBELL

Serves 4

Preparation time:	45 minutes
Cooking time:	20 minutes

Planning ahead:

Pain d'epice can be made and raisins can be smoked three days in advance, vanilla salt and foie gras needs to made four days in advance and red cabbage purée needs to be made two days in advance.

INGREDIENTS

red cabbage purée:

1	red cabbage
5g	salt
150g	water
	cabernet sauvignon vinegar

smoked raisins:

200g	moelleux raisins
200g	wood chippings

vanilla salt:

500g	Maldon salt
5	vanilla pods

pain d'epice and seaweed mix:

1	loaf Pain D'epice
200g	latude du mere
4	egg whites
200g	icing sugar

soya dressing:

50g	white wine vinegar
150g	vegetable oil
100g	soya sauce

spiced lentils:

1kg	lentils du puys
500g	red onions, finely chopped
50g	vegetable oil
600g	soy sauce
600g	balsamic vinegar
460g	tomato ketchup
460g	sweet chilli sauce
125g	pickled ginger, finely chopped
15g	ground cumin
3 ltr	sparkling mineral water

apple and vanilla purée:

400g	Granny Smiths, peeled and finely sliced
40g	sugar
1	vanilla pod
100ml	water

foie gras:

1	lobe foie gras
5g	sugar
2g	salt
1g	pink salt
15g	Madeira

salmon:

	side salmon
300g	table salt
150g	sugar
2	vanilla pods
100g	whisky
500g	vegetable oil
5	coriander seeds
5	white peppercorns
2	star anise

to finish:

	freshly ground coffee powder
	Maldon salt
	coriander cress
1g	chopped coriander

METHOD

red cabbage purée:

Quarter the cabbage, remove the root and finely shred 380g.
Place in a pan with the salt and water and cover tightly with clingfilm.
Place on the stove and allow to steam until the cabbage is tender. (around 45 minutes)
Meanwhile, juice the remaining cabbage and measure 200g, set to one side.
Once the cabbage is cooked drain any excess water and place in a liquidiser along with the cabbage juice and turn on full power for 5 minutes. Pour into a large piece of cheese cloth, over a bowl and carefully bring the corners together and tie with string. Hang in a fridge over night with the bowl underneath to collect the liquids which will drain from the purée.
Open the cheese cloth and empty the contents into a mixing bowl.
Season with salt and cabernet sauvignon vinegar. Cover.

smoked raisins:

Place the raisins into a colander.
Place the wood chippings into a pan or bowl which the colander will fit into tightly without touching the wood chippings. Tightly cover with clingfilm.
Place the pan onto the stove and wait until you see smoke gather inside the pan. Remove from the heat and allow to cool without removing the clingfilm.
Take the raisins from the colander and cut into quarters.
Store in a container.

vanilla salt:

Heat an oven to 180°C then turn off.
Cut the vanilla pods in half lengthways with a small knife.
Scrape the seeds from the pods and place them in a mixing bowl. Add the Maldon salt and mix together. Place onto an oven proof tray and place in the oven for 2 hours to dry out. Using the end of a rolling pin, crush the salt mixture back down to resemble the original salt.
Store in a container in a cool dry area.

pain d'epice and seaweed mix:

Heat an oven to 220°C then turn off. Leave for 5 minutes.
Place the pain díepice onto a cooling wire. Place in the oven to dry out. This should take around 2-3 hours.
Place the latude du mere into a colander and wash for 20 minutes under cold running water to remove the salt.
Mix the egg whites and icing sugar together.
Tie string around an area which is cool. Individually dip each piece of the latude du mere into the egg mixture. Remove any excess mixture from the latude du mere and hang over the string. Allow to dry out for around 12 hours.
Place the pain díepice and the latude du mere into a food processor and pulse to form breadcrumbs.
Store in an air tight container in a cool dry place.

soya dressing:

Place the vinegar and oil into a liquidiser and turn onto full power for 2 minutes.
Gradually add the soya sauce and continue to liquidise for 1 minute.
Pour the dressing into a squirty bottle and store in the fridge until required.

spiced lentils:

Place the lentils in a pan along with the mineral water and place on the stove. Simmer gently until tender, around 40 minutes, then cool.
Heat a large pan and add the vegetable oil. Add the onions and the cumin and gently fry without colour until they become slightly opaque.
Add the vinegar and reduce to a syrup.
Add the remaining ingredients and simmer to a thick sauce consistency.
Remove from the stove and add the cooked lentils to this mixture and stir.
Place in a suitable container and cover and cool.
Store in the fridge until required.

apple and vanilla purée:

Scrape the seeds from the vanilla pod with a small knife.
Place the sliced apples, sugar and vanilla seeds and scraped pod into a small pan along with the water. Tightly clingfilm the pan and place it on the stove. Cook until the apples are soft, around 35 minutes.
Remove from the stove and empty the contents of the pan into a liquidiser. Turn onto full power for 5 minutes.
Pour the contents of the liquidiser through a fine sieve.
Place the purée in a container and store in the fridge until required.

foie gras:

Place the foie gras into a food bag and seal. Leave in a warm area to soften.
Place the sugar, salt and pink salt in a bowl and mix together. Set to one side for use later.
Once soft, lay on a clean cloth, smooth side down. Using the handle of a dessert spoon, make a sweeping incision through the middle of the lobe coming down and out to one side without splitting the lobe at the sides. Repeat for the other side of the lobe.
Using the spoon carefully remove the veins from the lobe paying attention not to pierce the lobe.
Once all of the veins have been removed, season the foie gras with the salt mixture and the Madeira.
Lay out clingfilm flat on the bench. Roll the foie gras into a sausage shape and place onto the clingfilm. Tightly roll the clingfilm around the foie gras 3 or 4 times. Using a cocktail stick pierce the clingfilm along the foie gras several times. Squeeze the ends of the clingfilm to disburse any extra liquids and air trapped.
Continue to roll in the clingfilm 4 or 5 more times then cut the clingfilm off.
Tie one end of the clingfilm. Holding the open end, roll the sausage away from you to tighten. Tie off the remaining end of clingfilm.
Place the foie gras in the freezer for 3 hours.
Take the foie gras out of the freezer and remove the clingfilm.
Heat a non stick frying pan on the stove until it starts to smoke,
Carefully place the foie gras into the pan turning every 10 seconds until you achieve a dark brown colour all around. Remove from the pan. Again, place a new piece of clingfilm on the bench and place the foie gras in the middle. Continue exactly as previously and place back into the freezer for a further 2 hours.
Heat a pan of water to 50°C. Place the foie gras into the pan and cook for 5 minutes.
Remove from the water and place back into the freezer for 30 minutes to chill quickly.
Once cool store in the fridge.

salmon:

Mix the salt, sugar and 1 split vanilla pod together.
Clean and trim the salmon sides removing the bones with tweezers.
Cut the side in half to make them more manageable.
Using a sharp knife carefully remove the fillet from the skin using a barrel motion running the knife between the fillet and blood line starting in the middle of the fillet and working towards the blood line then round and between the skin and the fillet.
Repeat this from the other side of the salmon. (For each side of salmon you should yield 4 barrels).
Check that all the blood and fat has been removed from each fillet.
Portion the salmon into 35g pieces.
Season a tray with 30g of the salt mix and pour on the whisky. Place the salmon on top of this mix and season a further 20g of the salt mix.
Turn the salmon over and leave to marinate for 20 minutes.
Wash the salmon in cold running water.
Fill a pan with the vegetable oil and remaining ingredients and bring up to 45°C. Place the salmon into the pan for 15 minutes taking care to regulate the temperature.
Remove and drain on a clean cloth.

to serve:

Warm 30g of the spiced lentils.
Fill a container with hot tap water and place a sharp knife into it.
Unwrap any clingfilm from the foie gras. Use the hot knife to take a slice from the foie gras around 5mm thick. Drizzle with the soya dressing and season with a little Maldon salt.
Using a teaspoon take a spoon of the apple purée. Place the spoon on the plate at the top. Allow the purée to fall onto the plate without the spoon leaving the plate. Slowly pull the spoon down and to the right to form a "swipe".
Place the tip of the spoon in the purée at the top of the plate and pull down and round to the left.
Place a small pile of red cabbage purée halfway down the swipe to the left.
Place 4 pieces of smoked raisin around the red cabbage purée.
Take a small pinch of the coffee powder and put a line through the swipe above the red cabbage purée with the powder.
Place the slice of foie gras on top of the red cabbage purée. Neatly arrange 2 springs of coriander cress around the foie gras.
Add the chopped coriander to the warmed spiced lentils and place through the middle of the swipe to the right.
Season the warm salmon with a little of the vanilla salt. Sprinkle with the pain d'epice crumbs to form a crust.
Place the salmon on top of the spiced lentils.
Drizzle the soya dressing around the dish taking care not to get any on the salmon or the foie gras.
Serve.

RECOMMENDED WINE
Buxus Villette Sauvignon Blanc –
Louis Bovard – Vaud

"ROAST CHICKEN" SMOKED GNOCCHI AND SWEETCORN

BY JOHN CAMPBELL

Serves 4

Preparation time: 60 minutes

Cooking time: 1 ½ hours

Planning ahead:
Chicken wings can be braised two days in advance, smoked gnocchi needs to be prepared one day in advance and the chicken jus can be made one day in advance, after you have prepped the chicken.

INGREDIENTS

chicken jus:

1kg	chicken wings (chopped small)
250g	sliced shallot
500g	chopped tomato
500g	veal jus
800g	chicken stock
150g	cabernet sauvignon vinegar (not home made)
100g	white wine vinegar
10g	tarragon
10g	chervil
100g	vegetable oil
200g	butter

sweetcorn purée:

500g	sweetcorn kernels
50g	sparkling water
7g	salt
	sherry vinegar

creamed leeks:

200g	leeks, washed and sliced thinly
25g	double cream
15g	chicken stock
5g	chopped black truffle
20g	butter
	salt
	sherry vinegar

smoked sweetcorn gnocchi:

250g	Desiree potato
150g	sweetcorn purée
1	egg yolk
65g	pasta flour
9g	salt
200g	wood chippings

chicken:

1	organic chicken
1	lemon
3g	thyme

braised chicken wing:

chicken wings from the whole chicken, tip removed and trimmed

50g	vegetable oil
½	carrot, peeled and chopped into 3cm pieces
½	stick of celery, chopped into 4 pieces
½	white of leek, washed and chopped into 3 pieces
1	peeled banana shallot chopped into 6 pieces
150ml	white wine
500ml	chicken stock
5g	thyme
2	bay leaves

chicken foam:

300g	braising liquor passed through cheese cloth
100g	milk
10g	butter
2g	soya lecithin
	sherry vinegar
	salt

to finish:

100g	butter
	sherry vinegar
	Maldon salt

INGREDIENTS

chicken jus:

Put the veal jus and chicken stock together in a saucepan and place on the stove. Reduce them to 700g and remove from the stove. Put to one side for use at a later stage.

Heat a large pan on the stove and add the oil. Place the chopped chicken wings into the pan and fry until they are golden brown.

Add the shallots and the butter and continue to fry stirring from time to time.

Once the shallots are golden brown remove the pan from the stove and empty the contents of the pan into a colander to drain the butter and oil.

Replace the pan onto the stove and replace the fried chicken wings and shallots, add the chopped tomatoes and vinegar and cook until all of the vinegar has evaporated.

Add the reduced stock and veal jus to the chicken wings and bring to the boil.

Using a ladle, remove any scum that has appeared on the surface of the sauce and reduce the heat so as the sauce is now simmering. Continue to simmer for 45 minutes.

Remove the pan from the stove and pour the contents through a colander, discard the contents of the colander.

Add the tarragon and the thyme to the sauce and leave in a warm area for 5 minutes.

Cut a large piece of cheese cloth and dampen with hot water.

Carefully pour the sauce through the cheese cloth.

Check the flavour of the sauce and season with salt and extra cabernet sauvignon vinegar if required.

Store in the refrigerator until required.

Before using the sauce, remove any fats which have solidified on the surface.

sweetcorn purée:

Fill a pan with hot water and place on the stove. Bring to the boil and add the sweetcorn kernels. Boil for 8 minutes.

Remove the pan from the heat and use a colander to drain the sweetcorn kernels from the water.

Place the kernels into a liquidiser and add the salt and sparkling water. Turn onto full power for 6 minutes.

Pour the contents of the liquidiser jug through a fine sieve.

Season with sherry vinegar and more salt if required.

Place into a container and cover. Store in the refrigerator until required.

creamed leeks:

Fill a pan with hot water and place on the stove. Bring the water to the boil.

Place the washed leeks into the boiling water and cook for 3 minutes. Meanwhile fill a container with iced water.

Remove the leeks from the boiling water with a slotted spoon and place into the container of iced water. Leave to cool for 3 minutes. Using a colander, drain the leeks from the iced water and place on a clean cloth. Draw the corners of the cloth together and squeeze out the excess water from the leeks.

Place a saucepan onto the stove to warm up. Add the butter and melt. Add the leeks and gently fry without colour for 2 to 3 minutes. Add the chicken stock and reduce until the liquid in the pan thickens slightly.

Add the cream and bring to the boil. Reduce the cream until it is thick. Remove the pan from the stove and add the chopped truffle. Season the leeks with salt and sherry vinegar. Remove from the pan and place in a container to cool. Cover and store in the refrigerator until required.

smoked sweetcorn gnocchi:

Prick the potatoes with a sharp knife and place in the microwave. Set on full power and cook until soft.

Remove from the microwave and cut in half. Place each half in turn on a fine sieve and, using a plastic scraper, push the potatoes through the sieve taking care not to allow any skin to go through the sieve.

Place the potato into a mixing bowl and add the sweetcorn purée along with the egg yolk and salt. Mix together then add the flour.

Knead the mixture to form a dough, cover with clingfilm, and set in a cool area to rest for 30 minutes.

Meanwhile fill a pan with hot water and place on the stove. Bring the water to the boil. Fill a container with iced water and set to one side for use at a later stage.

Place the now rested gnocchi dough onto a lightly dusted, clean work surface. Knead for a minute or two. Using a knife cut pieces off the dough and weigh to 10g each. Rub a little pasta flour on your hands and taking a 10g piece of dough roll to form a ball shape. Take a fork and dip it in the pasta flour. Whilst still holding the gnocchi dough in your hand use the fork starting at the base roll the gnocchi ball until you reach the tip of the fork using slight pressure. You should be left with an oval shape piece of dough with four grooves through one side of it. Place the piece of gnocchi onto a lightly floured tray. Repeat this process for each piece of dough.

Carefully place the gnocchi into the pan of boiling water. When they float to the surface of the pan remove, with a slotted spoon and place in the iced water. Allow to cool in the water for 5 minutes then drain, using a colander. Place onto a clean dry cloth and gently dry then put into a clean colander.

Place the wood chippings into a pan or bowl which the colander will fit into tightly without touching the wood chippings. Tightly cover with clingfilm.

Place the pan onto the stove and wait until you see smoke gather inside the pan.

Remove from the heat and allow to cool without removing the clingfilm.

Remove the clingfilm from the pan and carefully place the gnocchi into a clean container. Lightly drizzle with vegetable oil and store in the refrigerator until required.

chicken:

Preheat an oven to 300°C.

Using a boning knife make an incision in the chicken skin halfway up the thigh of the chicken. Pull the skin down to the carcass and pull the thigh down and away from the breasts to dislocate the joint. Use the boning knife to remove the leg from the chicken. Repeat this process for the other leg.

Holding the chicken wing away from the carcass use a boning knife to cut through the joint closest to the chicken breast. Repeat this process for the other chicken wing. Retain the wings for use at a later stage.

Using a boning knife cut through the chicken carcass following the line on each side where the breast meets the ribcage. Pull the carcass back and cut through to remove the back of the chicken.

Trim any excess skin at the neck of the chicken and place the now chicken crowns onto a wire oven rack.

Place the rack in the oven for 3 minutes. Remove and cool.

Put the lemon and the thyme inside the chicken crown and place in a food bag. Seal tightly.

Fill a pan with water and place on the stove. Bring the water up to a temperature of 68°C. Place the food bag containing the chicken into the pan of water and place a weight on top of it to ensure it remains submerged during the cooking process. Cook the chicken for 72 minutes taking care to regulate the heat so as to maintain the water at 68°C.

Meanwhile fill a large container or sink with plenty of iced water.

Remove the food bag from the pan and plunge into the iced water using the weight once again to keep the bag submerged at all times. Keep the bag in the iced water for 2 hours.

Remove the food bag from the iced water and open it. Remove the chicken and place it on a clean chopping board.

Using a sharp knife run the blade down the side of the chicken's breast bone from the tip to the base taking care to stay as close to the bone as possible, continue to follow the wishbone down with the knife blade. Carefully use the tip of the knife running the blade across the ribcage to remove the breast from the carcass.

Repeat this process for the remaining breast and discard the carcass.

Using a sharp knife neatly trim the chicken breast removing any excess skin and fat. Turn the breast over and using the knife remove the vein from the chicken fillet.

Place each breast into a clean food bag and seal. Store in a container of ice in the refrigerator until required.

To reheat fill a pan with water, place on the stove and heat it up to 50°C.

Place the food bag containing the chicken breast into the water for 15 minutes.

Heat up a frying pan on the stove and add a little vegetable oil.

Remove the food bag containing the chicken breast from the water and open it.

Dry the breast with a clean cloth and season with table salt.

Gently fry the breast, skin side down, in the oil to colour the skin.

Remove from the pan and place on a clean chopping board.

Using a sharp serrated knife trim the head and tip of the chicken breast on an angle. Carve the breast through the middle again on an angle. Season each piece with Maldon salt.

braised chicken wing:

Heat a saucepan on the stove and add the vegetable oil. Fry the chicken wing until golden brown.

Add the carrot, celery, leek, and shallot and continue to fry until the vegetables are golden brown.

Add the white wine and the chicken stock and bring to the boil. Reduce the heat so as the stock is simmering and add the thyme and bay leaves. Continue to simmer until the wings are tender, around 1½ hours.

Using a slotted spoon, remove the wings and place on a tray. Leave in a cool area until the wings are cool enough to handle but not cold.

Meanwhile pour the braising liquor through a fine sieve and return to a clean pan.

Place the pan on the stove and bring the liquor to the boil. Reduce the liquid by half.

Pour into a clean container, cover and cool. Store in the refrigerator for use later.

Take the cooled chicken wings and using your finger carefully remove the bones taking care not to break any of the skin on the wing.

Store on a clingfilmed tray in the refrigerator until required.

To reheat pour a little of the braising liquor into a saucepan and place on the stove. Bring the liquor to the boil and reduce the heat slightly so the liquor is simmering. Add the wings and reheat in the liquor for 5 minutes.

Remove with a slotted spoon, drain on a clean cloth and season with Maldon salt.

chicken foam:

Place all of the ingredients into a saucepan and put onto the stove. Bring the foam to the boil.

Season with salt and sherry vinegar.

Cool the foam to 50-60°C. Using a hand blender, pulse the foam until bubbles form on the surface of the liquid.

Use a spoon to scoop the foam from the liquid taking care not to take any of the liquid with it.

to serve:

Warm a little of the sweetcorn purée in a saucepan on the stove.

Remove from the stove and season with salt and sherry vinegar, place in a warm area.

Heat a frying pan on the stove and add the butter. Gently fry a gnocchi until it is golden brown. Season with salt and remove from the pan with a spoon. Drain on a clean cloth.

Place a little of the leeks in a saucepan and warm on the stove. Again, season with salt and sherry vinegar. Place in a warm area.

Place a little of the chicken jus in a saucepan and warm on the stove. Season with salt. Place in a warm area.

Using a dessert spoon place a small pool of sweetcorn purée in a bowl at 12 o'clock. Place the tip of the dessert spoon in the pool of purée and draw straight down the bowl to 6 o'clock.

Place a small pile of the leeks in the centre of the bowl with a dessert spoon.

Lay a piece of the roast chicken breast against the leeks. Put the gnocchi against the chicken touching the leeks.

Place the chicken wing on top of the leeks using the chicken breast to support it.

Carefully use a dessert spoon to pour sauce over the chicken and wing allowing a little to run down onto the bowl.

Place a little of the foam on top of the chicken wing and chicken breast. Serve.

RECOMMENDED WINE
Fleurie Domaine Pardon et Fils –
Cru de Beaujolais En Magnum

Serves 4

Preparation time:	45 minutes
Cooking time:	N/A

Planning ahead:
The mango sherbert needs to be prepared four days in advance, the cucumber sorbet needs to be prepared two days in advance (but turned on the day) and the vanilla yoghurt jelly can be made the day before.

INGREDIENTS

cucumber soup:

4	cucumbers, juiced
200g	stock syrup
70g	lime juice

cucumber and lime sorbet:

300g	water
340g	sugar
110g	glucose
6	cucumbers, juiced
300g	yoghurt
2	limes, juiced

lime jelly:

50g	sugar
50g	lime juice
100g	water
1.8g	agar

mango foam:

100g	passion fruit purée
200g	mango purée
200g	stock syrup
100g	water
3	leaves gelatine

vanilla yoghurt jelly:

330g	yoghurt
70g	stock syrup
2	vanilla pods with the seeds removed and retained
2	leaves gelatine

mango sherbet:

300g	mango purée
4g	tartaric acid
10g	sugar

to finish:

aphillia cress

🍷 **RECOMMENDED WINE**
Quintessence du Clos – Domaine Le Clos des Cazaux – Rhône

CUCUMBER, LIME, MANGO, YOGHURT

BY JOHN CAMPBELL

METHOD

cucumber soup:

Pour all of the ingredients into a bowl and whisk together.
Pour through a fine sieve and store in a jug in the refrigerator until required.

cucumber and lime sorbet:

Put the water, sugar and glucose into a saucepan and place on the stove. Bring to the boil.
Remove the pan from the stove and add the remaining ingredients.
Pour through a fine sieve and store in the refrigerator for 12 hours.
Churn in an ice cream machine until the mixture thickens but does not freeze. Remove and store in a covered container in the freezer until required.

lime jelly:

Place all of the ingredients into a pan and bring up to the boil whisking continuously.
Allow to boil for 1 minute then carefully pour onto a small square plate. Use a gas gun to disburse any bubbles which may have congregated on the surface of the jelly and allow to set.
Using a ruler and a pen mark 2cm indents around the 4 edges of the plate and cut the jelly into 2cm squares.
Store on the plate; clingfilmed in the refrigerator until required.

mango foam:

Fill a container with cold water and add the gelatine.
Place the stock syrup and water into a pan and warm on the stove.
Remove the pan from the stove. Remove the gelatine from the container of water and add to the pan containing the stock syrup, stir until the gelatine dissolves.
Add the passion fruit purée and mango purée.
Pour into a cream whipper and "charge" with 2 N2O (nitrous oxide) gas canisters and shake vigorously.
Place the cream whipper in the refrigerator for at least 4 hours before you require it.
To serve remove from the refrigerator and shake vigorously.

vanilla yoghurt jelly:

Fill a container with cold water and add the gelatine.
Pour the stock syrup into a saucepan and add the vanilla seeds. Place the pan on the stove and warm.
Remove the gelatine from the water and add to the stock syrup. Stir until the gelatine has dissolved.
Add the yoghurt and whisk until the liquids have emulsified.
Pour through a fine sieve. Place the jelly into a container and cover. Refrigerate for 5 hours before you require it.

mango sherbet:

Preheat an oven to 250°C then turn off.
Using a palette knife spread a thin layer of the mango purée onto a non stick baking mat.
Place the baking mat into the oven and allow to dry out for 6 hours.
Remove the mat from the oven. Peel the purée from the mat and place in a food processor.
Add the tartaric acid and sugar and turn onto full power for 5 minutes.
Remove the contents of the food processor bowl into a fine sieve. Shake the sieve so all the fine sherbet falls through the sieve onto a piece of baking parchment.
Place the sherbet from the baking parchment into an air tight container. Store in a cool dry area until required.

to serve:

Place a small jug in the freezer to chill.
Use a dessert spoon to scoop a piece of the yoghurt jelly and place it at 7 o'clock in a bowl.
Put a piece of lime jelly in the bowl at 5 o'clock. Carefully place a pinch of mango sherbet at 2 o'clock.
Place a sprig of aphillia cress in the yoghurt jelly.
Remove the jug from the freezer and pour a little of the cucumber soup into the bowl.
Using an ice cream scoop, ball the cucumber sorbet and place in the centre of the bowl.
Shake the mango espuma and direct the nozzle at the sorbet. Dispense a little of the espuma onto the sorbet.
Serve.

Serves 4

Preparation time: 1 hour, 20 minutes
Cooking time: N/A
Planning ahead:
The sorbet needs to be prepared two days in advance (but turned on the day) and the muscovado sponge can be made the day before.

INGREDIENTS

chocolate ganache:

125ml   milk
125ml   double cream
4   yolks
25g   sugar
350g   dark chocolate
100ml   cold milk

muscovado sponge:

1Kg   muscovado sugar
1Kg   butter
1Kg   egg
1Kg   soft flour
50g   baking powder

vanilla and white chocolate mousse:

200g   Philadelphia cream cheese
2   vanilla pods
325g   double cream
200g   white chocolate

yoghurt crème fraîche sorbet:

200g   crème fraîche
300g   yoghurt
500g   milk
4   yolks
270g   sugar
50g   glucose

soaking syrup:

400g   griottine syrup
50g   Kirsch

griottine syrup:

400g   soaking syrup

tempered chocolate:

100g   dark chocolate pistols

chocolate sauce:

250g   cocoa powder
570g   water
750g   sugar

to finish:

4   griottine cherries
100%   chocolate

BLACK FOREST GATEAU

BY JOHN CAMPBELL

METHOD

chocolate ganache:

Mix the cream and milk together in a saucepan and place on the stove. Bring to the boil.
Meanwhile mix the sugar and the yolks together in a bowl.
Pour the boiled milk and cream over the yolks and sugar whisking continuously.
Pour the mixture back into the pan and return to the stove.
Gently warm the mixture stirring continuously with a wooden spoon until it thickens and coats the back of the spoon.
Remove the pan from the stove and stir in the chocolate until the mixture emulsifies.
Stir in the cold milk to the mixture and refrigerate in a piping bag.
This needs to be out for ½ an hour before serving.

muscovado sponge:

Preheat an oven to 180°C.
Line a baking tray with silicone paper.
Place the sugar and butter together in a mixer and whisk until light and fluffy.
Gradually add the egg.
Meanwhile sift the flour and the baking powder together.
Slow the mixer and carefully fold in the flour and baking powder so as not to lose any of the air incorporated into the mixture.
Using a plastic scraper place the mixture into a lined baking tray and bake in the oven for 10-15 minutes.
Remove from the oven and check to see if the cake is cooked by placing a sharp knife into the centre of the sponge, leave for a few seconds and then remove the knife. If the blade comes out clean the sponge is ready, if not return to the oven for a few more minutes then repeat the process until the blade comes out clean. Cool quickly.
Remove from the tin. Using a sharp serrated knife slice the sponge into 1cm thick slices.
Trim away the crusts and trim into rectangles 2cm by 4cm.
Store in an air tight container.

vanilla and white chocolate mousse:

Place the cream cheese into a mixing bowl and whisk on an electric mixer until the cheese softens. Scrape down the sides of the bowl from time to time.

Fill a saucepan with hot water and place on the stove to boil.
Using a sharp knife split the vanilla pod lengthways. Use the knife to scrape the seeds from the pod.
Put the seeds in a mixing bowl along with the chocolate and place on top of the pan of water to melt.
Once melted add to the now softened cream cheese.
Meanwhile pour the cream into a mixing bowl and semi whip with a whisk. Put to one side for use at a later stage.
When the mixture is smooth fold in the cream. Store in the refrigerator in a piping bag until required.

yoghurt crème fraîche sorbet:

Pour the milk into a saucepan and add the glucose, place on the stove. Bring to the boil and remove from the stove.
Mix the yolks and sugar together in a mixing bowl. Pour over the milk whisking continuously and return to the saucepan. Place back on the stove and heat gently continuing to stir with a wooden spoon until the mixture coats the back of the spoon. Remove from the stove. Place the crème fraîche and yoghurt into a mixing bowl and whisk in the cooked mixture. Pour the sorbet base into a container and place in the refrigerator for 12 hours then churn in an ice cream machine and store in the freezer until required.

soaking syrup:

Place both ingredients in a mixing bowl and mix together.
Store in a squeezy bottle.

griottine syrup:

Pour the syrup into a saucepan and place on the stove.
Bring to the boil and reduce by half.
Cool and store in a squeezy bottle.

tempered chocolate:

Cut sheets of acetate into strips 1cm by 9cm.
Fill a saucepan with hot water. Put two thirds of the chocolate into a mixing bowl and place on the pan of water. Place on the stove and gently warm stirring with a plastic spoon. Use a thermometer to monitor the temperature of the chocolate constantly. Once the chocolate reaches 40°C remove the pan from the stove and continue to stir. As soon as the chocolate

reaches 51°C add the remaining chocolate and remove the bowl from the pan.

Continue to stir the chocolate until the temperature drops to 28°C. Using a hair dryer gently reheat the chocolate to 32°C.

Thinly spread the chocolate onto the sheets of acetate with a palette knife and allow to cool and set. If the chocolate cools below 30.5°C reheat it to 32°C with the hair dryer. Store the chocolate in a cool dry place until required.

chocolate sauce:

Put all of the ingredients into a pan and place on the stove. Bring to the boil whisking continuously.

Remove from the stove and place in a container to cool.

Store in the refrigerator until required.

to serve:

Remove the ganache from the refrigerator 30 minutes prior to serving the gateaux along with the griottine syrup.

Using a knife quarter the griottine cherries. Gently warm 50g of the chocolate sauce in a pan on the stove.

Use a pastry brush to place 4 strips 10cm long, two horizontal around 7cm apart and two vertical, 6cm long through the horizontal strips evenly spaced.

Take two pieces of the muscovado sponge and drizzle liberally with the soaking syrup. Place the muscovado sponge diagonally through the chocolate sauce adjacent to each other.

Pipe three nuggets of ganache in a triangle pattern inside the sponges then follow with the white chocolate mousse. Place the cherries on the mousse and around the sponge and randomly place droplets of griottine syrup around the plate.

Fill a container with cold water. Take the sorbet from the freezer. Using a dessert spoon dip it in the cold water, roll the spoon through the sorbet to create a roche. Place the roche on top of the sponge. Repeat the process and place the second roche, opposite the first, on the other piece of sponge.

Take two pieces of the tempered chocolate; place one of them horizontally using the sorbet to hold the chocolate in place and the other vertically.

Using a fine microplane, carefully grate the 100% chocolate over the whole plate.

🍷 RECOMMENDED WINE
Rasteau Rancio – Rhône

GIDLEIGH PARK

> 'Cooking is my passion. I love it and I can never see myself not being in the kitchens'

MICHAEL CAINES

Michael Caines is one of Britain's most acclaimed chefs. AA Chef's Chef of the Year in 2007 and awarded an MBE in 2006 for services to the hospitality industry. In 2000, Michael founded Michael Caines Restaurants and took over food and beverage operations at The Royal Clarence, Exeter, Britain's first hotel. A chance encounter with Andrew Brownsword led to the creation of the ABode Hotel group, of which Michael is an Operational Partner and Director, in overall charge of all food and beverage operations throughout the fast-growing group. Michael is also Executive Chef at Gidleigh Park, the acclaimed and prestigious country house hotel on the edge of Dartmoor at Chagford, Devon, where he has earned his reputation – as well as two Michelin stars, and also at its Michelin starred sister hotel, The Bath Priory Hotel, Restaurant and Spa in Bath. Both properties serve distinctive modern European cuisine utilising the finest local and regional produce and ingredients.

Serves 4

Preparation time: 2 hours
Cooking time: 45 minutes

Special equipment:
Blender
Non-stick pan

Planning ahead:
Make the celeriac purée, the soy truffle vinaigrette and the French vinaigrette in advance.

INGREDIENTS

12   scallops
celeriac purée
soy and truffle vinaigrette
mixed salad
chopped chives
olive oil
salt and pepper
French dressing

celeriac purée:

200g   celeriac, chopped
15g   celery, chopped
15g   onions, chopped
150ml   water
150ml   milk
25g   unsalted butter
pinch of salt and pepper to season

soy and truffle vinaigrette:

25g   shallots sliced
50g   button mushrooms
10g   soy sauce
25g   veal glace
30g   olive oil
20g   truffle juice
5ml   truffle oil
2   sprigs of thyme,
          fresh (80g/bunch)
100g   olive oil

french vinaigrette:

300ml   vegetable oil
100ml   white wine vinegar
salt and pepper
sprig of thyme
clove of garlic.

SCALLOPS WITH CELERIAC PUREE AND SOY AND TRUFFLE VINAIGRETTE

BY MICHAEL CAINES

This is a wonderful dish which incorporates the rich soy and truffle vinaigrette with the smooth, creamy flavour of the celeriac. This contrasts beautifully with the meaty scallops which are delicate in flavour against the intense flavour of the soy and truffle. This has become one of my signature dishes over the years.

METHOD

purée:

In a saucepan sweat the onion, celery and salt with the butter, add the milk and water then the celeriac and pepper. Bring to the boil and reduce to a simmer. Cook out for 30 minutes and then allow to cool. Pass off through a colander and then place into a robot coupe and blend until fine. Remove from the robot coupe and then pace into a blender and blend to a very fine purée.

soy vinaigrette:

Sweat the shallots in the 30ml of olive oil and a pinch of salt and lightly colour.
Add the mushrooms and thyme and sweat for a further 2 minutes. Add the soy sauce and reduce to nothing, now add the truffle juice and reduce by half.
Add the veal glace and bring to the boil, place into a blender and blend to a fine puée.
Warm 100g of olive oil and add to the pulp, then add the truffle oil. Correct the seasoning and then pass through a fine sieve. Place into a plastic bottle and use at room temperature.

french vinaigrette:

Mix all the ingredients together in a bottle and shake before using.

to serve:

Pan fry the scallops in a non-stick pan in olive oil.
Dress some celeriac onto the plate, and then some soy vinaigrette.
Now place 3 scallops onto the plate and top with the salad dressed in the French vinaigrette.

 RECOMMENDED WINE
Fié Gris Blanc – Domaine de L' Aujardière – Loire

Serves 4

Preparation time: 3 hours
Cooking time: 30 minutes

Special equipment:
Blender

Planning ahead:
Prepare the lentils and also the pumpkin and cumin purée in advance. Ask your butcher to prep your pheasant for oven ready.

INGREDIENTS

2   pheasants oven ready or dressed pumpkin and cumin purée (recipe as below)
thyme
garlic
salt/pepper
lentils (recipe as below)
non-scented oil
unsalted butter
sugar
toasted pumpkin seeds
200g   button onions

pumpkin and cumin purée:

250g   pumpkin (Crown Prince)
2g   cumin seeds
20g   butter
1 tsp   pumpkin oil
50ml   chicken stock

lentils:

250g   green lentils
1ltr   water
8   cloves of garlic, peeled
150g   shallots, peeled
400g   smoked bacon trimmings
1   onion, cut in half and spiked with cloves
150g   carrot cut into 4, lengthways
100g   thinly sliced lardons, blanched
1   small bouquet garni (thyme, bayleaf, parsley stalks and celery bound with leek and tied together with string)
1 (heaped) tsp chicken bouillon
chopped parsley
butter
salt/pepper

ROAST PHEASANT WITH LENTILS, AND PUMPKIN AND CUMIN PURÉE

BY MICHAEL CAINES

Love this dish for the autumn and winter, pheasant is surprisingly mild in flavour and not as strong as some might think. The sweetness of the pumpkin with the cumin spices adds another dimension to the mild game flavour that you get from the pheasant. The soft and smoky lentils hold up well against the other flavours, yet bring to the dish an earthy flavour and a soft texture.

METHOD

lentils:

Place the lentils into a saucepan and cover with water (not the litre), bring to the boil and pass through a colander then refresh with cold water. Place the lentils back in the saucepan and add the water, garlic, shallots, onion, carrots, bouquet garni, bouillon and bacon trimmings. Bring to the boil and reduce to a slow simmer, cook out for approximately 45 minutes. Once the lentils are cooked allow to cool and then remove the garnish (onion, bacon, bouquet garni etc.). Strain the lentils from their juices and place into a pan, heat and add a knob of butter. Now add the blanched lardons and season, finally add some chopped parsley. Keep back for later use.

pumpkin and cumin purée:

Toast the cumin seeds in a dry pan until light brown. Place the butter into a pan and cook the cumin seeds for a few seconds before adding the peeled and chopped pieces of pumpkin. Add a pinch of salt and cook for 10 minutes. Add chicken stock and bring to the boil. Place a lid onto and cook for 20 minutes.
Place into a blender and blend to a fine purée, now add the pumpkin oil and season with salt and pepper.

pheasant:

Stuff the birds with the thyme, 2 garlic cloves, salt and pepper; season the outside of the bird and then heat a roasting tray and add a drop of non-scented oil and unsalted butter. Place the birds into the tray on their sides and put into a preheated oven at 200°C for 5 minutes, turn onto the other side for a further 5 minutes then finally onto the back with the breast facing up for 5 minutes. Remove from the oven and leave to rest for 10 minutes.

to serve:

Place the button onions in a shallow saucepan and cover with water. Add a pinch of sugar, salt, pepper and a knob of butter. Bring to the boil and reduce the water, colour the onions and place onto a tray. Reheat the pheasant in the oven and then warm the lentils, be careful not to dry them out, then add the button onions and keep warm. Take the pheasant out of the oven and remove the legs and breast. Dress some pumpkin purée onto the plate, now place the lentils in the middle of the plate and put the portioned pheasant on top.

Serves 4

Preparation time: 2 hours
Cooking time: 15 minutes

Special equipment:
A thick bottomed pan

Planning ahead:
Braise off the chicory, soak the raisins and also caramelise the walnuts three days in advance.

INGREDIENTS

4   80g pieces of duck foie gras
braised chicory
raisins soaked in Jasmine tea
dried orange powder
caramelised walnuts
orange segments

braised chicory:

25g   butter
50g   onions chopped small
200ml   orange juice
50ml   chicken stock
8   baby chicory (or 2 large)
1   garlic clove, peeled and chopped
1   small bay leaf
1   sprig of thyme
salt and pepper
orange dust

raisins soaked in jasmine tea:

5g   tea
200ml   boiling hot water
100g   raisins

caramelised walnuts:

150g   walnuts
200ml   stock syrup

PAN-FRIED DUCK FOIE GRAS WITH BRAISED CHICORY WITH ORANGE AND RAISINS

BY MICHAEL CAINES

This is a gorgeous dish. The rich, fatty flavours of the foie gras are cut and contrasted by the citrus orange and sweet, plump raisin fruit. The braised chicory gives a wonderful contrast of texture and slight bitterness on the palette. This is a recent addition to my menus that has proved to be a very popular dish.

METHOD

braised chicory:

Sweat the onions and garlic in the butter with a pinch of salt no colour. Add the orange juice, chicken stock, thyme and bay leaf. Add the baby chicory and bring to the boil, season with salt and pepper. Cover with a parchment paper and braise in the oven until soft. Leave to cool.
Remove the garnish and pass off the liquid, store the braised chicory in the stock.
Take some of the stock and bring to the boil, add a pinch of orange dust and season with salt and pepper, now add a drop of orange juice. Reserve for later.

raisins soaked in jasmine tea:

Infuse the tea with the boiling hot water and leave to stand until the water is warm. Place the raisins into a jar or plastic container and then pass the tea through a fine sieve onto the raisins.
Leave to soak for 3 days before using to allow the raisins to plump up.

caramelised walnuts:

Place the walnuts into the stock syrup and cook until 110°C, remove using a draining spoon and place into a fryer at 190ºC until golden brown.
Remove and place onto parchment paper and lightly salt. Once cool, take a few and chop with a knife for the topping of the foie gras.

to serve:

In a hot pan, pan-fry the foie gras colouring both sides, remove from the pan and top with the chopped walnuts, a dusting of orange powder and some sea salt. Leave to rest in a warm place.
Now reheat the chicory in its stock, and warm the raisins in their juices. Cut chicory in half, dress in the middle of the plate, sprinkle the raisins around then place the foie gras on top. Add a few caramelised walnuts, orange segments and then sauce with the butter sauce.

Enjoy!

 RECOMMENDED WINE
Château La Truffière – Monbazillac

Serves 4

Preparation time: 2 hours

Cooking time: 20 minutes

Planning ahead:
Make the herb purée in advance and if possible poach off the quail in advance and refresh in iced water. The gnocchi can also be made in advance and is suitable for home freezing.

INGREDIENTS

2	oven ready quail
herb purée	
rosemary gnocchi	
poached quail eggs	
chopped parsley	
unsalted butter	
salt and pepper	

herb purée:

1	small shallot, sliced
10g	butter
100g	spinach raw
25g	parsley cooked and refreshed
50ml	cream
10g	chervil picked
6g	garlic purée

poached quail eggs:

12	quail eggs
500ml	water
10ml	white wine vinegar
5g	salt

potato and parmesan gnocchi:

250g	Binjte potato, cooked and puréed
50g	onions finely chopped
5g	rosemary chopped
25g	grated parmesan
50g	plain flour
25g	butter, unsalted
2	egg yolks
salt and pepper	

🍷 RECOMMENDED WINE
Château Beauportail Rouge – Pécharment

ROASTED QUAIL WITH HERB PURÉE AND ROSEMARY GNOCCHI

BY MICHAEL CAINES

A wonderful herbaceous dish. The herb purée is earthy and intense and contrasts beautifully with the meatiness of the quail, which is delicate in flavour and balanced beautifully by the purée of herb. The rosemary is just strong enough to add an extra element to the gnocchi.

METHOD

herb purée:

In a stainless steel saucepan sweat the shallots in the butter, no colour. Add the spinach and chervil and continue to sweat until the spinach is cooked.
Place into a blender with the blanched parsley and garlic purée, bring the cream to the boil and then add to the blender. Blend the mixture until smooth and correct the seasoning.
Remove from blender, place into a container and keep warm.

poached quail eggs:

Place the water, vinegar and salt into a saucepan and bring to the boil. Crack 6 eggs into a small bowl with water and 10ml of white wine vinegar, leave for 30 seconds and then add to the boiling stock.
Bring to the boil and then reduce to a simmer, once the eggs are well formed and ready remove and place on ice. Repeat until all are poached
Trim and tidy the eggs and place onto a tray with cloth. To reheat, simply drop them back into hot water.

potato and parmesan gnocchi:

Sweat off the onions in the butter until soft and transparent, no colour. Add to this the chopped rosemary and stir well. Leave to cool.
Cook off the potatoes and pass through a fine sieve, mix into this the onions and rosemary, egg yolks and parmesan and check the seasoning before adding the flour. Bring together and then place onto the table and shape, dusting with flour, then cut into a 5mm dice.
Cook the gnocchi in salted boiling water for 3-4 minutes or until doubled in size, drain. Toss the gnocchi in foaming butter and finish with chopped parsley, finish the sauce with chopped tarragon.

to serve:

Season the quail and in a roasting tray heat some unsalted butter, place the quails into the tray and into a preheated oven at 190°C for 6 minutes. Remove from the tray and take off the breasts and legs and trim.
Reheat the herb purée and the quail eggs.
Dress the plate with the herb purée, and the dressed 5 gnocchi onto the plate, then add the 3 quail eggs and finally dress the 1 breast and 1 leg onto the plate and serve.

Enjoy!

Serves 4

Preparation time: 6 hours

Cooking time: N/A

INGREDIENTS

chocolate sablé:

1kg	flour
800g	butter
8	egg yolks
10g	salt
400g	icing sugar
100g	dark chocolate
50g	cocoa powder

This sablé pastry must be refrigerated for about 2 hours before using.

dark chocolate mousse:

200g	dark chocolate
80g	milk
200g	cream
1	eggs

chantilly cream:

300g	double cream
25g	icing sugar

seeds of 1 vanilla pod

Whisk together. Reserve in the fridge.

white chocolate ice cream:

1 ltr	milk
100g	sugar
10	egg yolks
400g	white chocolate (melted on a bain-marie)
50g	milk powder
2 dl	whipping cream

hazelnut parfait:

chocolate tears:

200g	dark chocolate tempered

clear acetate paper

60mm	ring

pate a bombe:

12	egg yolks
150g	caster sugar
60g	water

Italian meringue:

300g	egg whites
150g	glucose
150g	sugar
60g	water
400g	hazelnut praline milk chocolate

(melted on a bain-marie)

300g	whipped cream
50g	Frangelico
200g	chopped milk chocolate pistols
250g	hazelnut nougatine

hazelnut nougatine:

1kg	caster sugar
500g	glucose
400g	toasted and peeled

TRIO OF CHOCOLATE: DARK CHOCOLATE MOUSSE ON A SABLE BISCUIT, MILK CHOCOLATE PARFAIT AND WHITE CHOCOLATE ICE CREAM

BY MICHAEL CAINES

This trio of chocolate has become a wonderful signature dish of mine. This is a great dish for all chocolate lovers! It is a fairly technically-tricky dish, but is worth the efforts involved. The highlight for me is the wonderful hazelnut and milk chocolate that work together beautifully. This contrasts well with the bitterness of the dark chocolate and the white chocolate ice cream is a perfect balance to both.

METHOD

chocolate sablé:

Sift the flour and cocoa powder into a mixing bowl and rub into the softened butter until the mixture resembles fine grains of sand.
Add the icing sugar, egg yolks and then pour in the melted chocolate. Bring together and remove from the bowl and refrigerate for 2 hours
Roll out at number 2, cut out some discs with a plain cutter, bake for 10 minutes at 160°C

dark chocolate mousse:

Place the chocolate in bowl and melt over a bain-marie.
Place the eggs into a jug and bring the milk and cream to the boil.
Using a Bamix, blend the boiling milk and cream into the eggs, then stir the mixture into the melted chocolate, using a whisk at first and then a maryse.
Pour into pre-clingfilmed number 5 rings.
This recipe makes 10 number 5 rings
Leave to set in the fridge for at least 2 hours.

white chocolate ice cream:

Cream together the egg yolks and the sugar until white and stiff.
In a saucepan combine the milk, milk powder and cream, and bring to the boil.
Pour some of the milk onto the creamed eggs and sugar, whisking continuously.
Return the mixture to the saucepan and over a medium heat cook out to 85°C.
Strain through a chinoise and then pour in the melted white chocolate.
Churn and keep at minus 18°C.

hazelnut parfait:

To make the chocolate tears ,cut the acetate paper into long strips 15mm by 100cm long.
Then coat them with the tempered chocolate thinly.
Pick up the end of the strip and join both ends

together and then shape into a tear shape into the circle. Leave to set and place into a fridge.
To make the pate a bombe, mix together the sugar and water and bring to the boil. Cook until 120°C and then pour into the whipping egg yolks and continue whisking until cool. Remove from the bowl and place into a large mixing bowl.
Now make the Italian meringue by cooking the sugar, glucose and water together until 120°C, then pour carefully onto the whipping egg whites.
Now add the melted hazelnut chocolate to the pate a bombe mix, with the Frangelico. Fold in the whipped cream and then the Italian meringue. Sprinkle in the chopped milk chocolate and the hazelnut nougatine and fold in.
Place into a piping bag and fill the chocolate tears with the mixture.
Freeze at -20°C until served

hazelnut nougatine:

Roast the hazelnuts on a roasting tray in the oven, place into a cloth and rub them to remove the skin, separate from the skin and keep warm.
Cook the sugar and the glucose to a blond caramel. Add the hazelnuts and mix in.
Cool down on non-stick tray until cold. Use immediately after it is cooked.
Place into a robot coupe and blend until coarse in texture, but not fine.

to serve:

(On a long plate, from right to left).
Place a chocolate mousse on a sablé biscuit, add a small quenelle of chantilly topped with a chocolate curl.
Cover the top of the milk chocolate and hazelnut parfait with crushed nougatine Finally sandwich a ball of white chocolate ice cream between 2 discs of tempered chocolate.

 RECOMMENDED WINE

Cristallo Vin de Fraise – Thurgau – Switzerland

LE MANOIR AUX QUAT' SAISONS

'Perfection in food, comfort, service and welcome'

RAYMOND BLANC

Raymond Blanc is acknowledged as one of the finest chefs in the world; his exquisite cooking has received tributes from every national and international guide to culinary excellence. At the age of 28, Raymond Blanc opened his first restaurant, "Les Quat' Saisons" in Summertown, Oxford. After just one year, the restaurant was named Egon Ronay Restaurant of the Year and a host of other accolades including Michelin stars followed. It was in 1984, however, that he fulfilled a personal vision, creating a hotel and restaurant in harmony when he opened Le Manoir aux Quat' Saisons in Great Milton, Oxford. Le Manoir is the only country house hotel in the UK which has achieved two Michelin stars for a total of 25 years.

Serves 4

Preparation time: 15 minutes

Cooking time: 2 minutes

Planning ahead:
The vinaigrette can be made several
days in advance.

INGREDIENTS

2	bunches baby leeks, trimmed and washed
15g	Dijon mustard
15g	white wine vinegar
30g	water
1g	sea salt
½ g	pepper, white, freshly ground
45ml	groundnut oil (or any unscented oil)
20g	sliced black truffle **(*1)**

LEEK AND TRUFFLES WITH MUSTARD VINAIGRETTE

BY RAYMOND BLANC

This is a perfect light starter with the minimum of ingredients.

METHOD

Slice only the green part of the leeks at an angle ½ cm thick and blanch in boiling water for 1-2 minutes and refresh in ice water.

In a large bowl mix the mustard, vinegar and water. Season with the salt, pepper and slowly add the oil, whisking all the time. Taste and correct the seasoning.

Drain the leeks thoroughly and put in a separate bowl, mix in 4 tablespoons of the mustard dressing. Taste and add more if you need to. **(*2)**

Arrange the leeks in the middle of four starter plates in a neat circle. Top with the slices of truffle and spoon around a little of the remaining dressing.

Chef's notes (*):

*1   Fresh truffles will always be better if you are lucky enough to get hold of some. But you can buy quality preserved truffles available in good delis and supermarkets.

*2   You need just enough to coat and lightly season the leeks.

Variation:

You could replace the truffle with sautéed langoustines, prawns, scallops, cooked and sliced Jerusalem artichokes.

 RECOMMENDED WINE
Beaujolais Blanc – Pardon et Fils

Serves 4

Preparation time:	20 minutes and
	1 hour marinade
Cooking time:	N/A

Special equipment:
Japanese mandolin

Planning ahead:
The tuna can be marinated a week in advance and frozen until needed.

INGREDIENTS

8	hand dived scallops medium, thinly sliced
100g	tuna, marinated (see below), cut into 1mm thin strips
4	pinches salt
4	pinches cayenne pepper
15ml	Seville orange, juice
20ml	olive oil, extra virgin
4g	banana shallot, finely diced, washed and drained
2g	chives, chopped
8g	caviar Ocietra
100g	fennel salad (see below)
2g	shiso cress, 6 leaves each
4g	micro herb

tuna marinade:

100g	tuna loin trimmed
4.5g	grey salt
3g	Seville orange zest, grated
2g	lemon zest, grated
2g	basil stalks, chopped
2g	black peppercorns, crushed

fennel salad:

100g	fennel, finely sliced
4	pinches sea salt
5ml	Seville orange juice
15ml	olive oil, extra virgin
2g	lime zest, blanched 3 times in boiling water and chopped fine
8g	ginger, sliced fine and blanched 3 times in boiling water
½ g	cayenne pepper
5g	fennel seeds, soaked over night and toasted in a dry pan
20g	rocket leaves

CEVICHE OF TUNA AND SEA SCALLOP WITH SHAVED FENNEL SALAD

BY RAYMOND BLANC

My cuisine is very much modern French but at all times seasonal, using tastes and textures from elsewhere to enrich my French traditions. This light summer dish is a perfect example – the tuna is from the Mediterranean.

METHOD

tuna marinade:

On a large piece of clingfilm (big enough to wrap around the tuna twice) place the piece of tuna, mix together the rest of the ingredients and evenly sprinkle on both sides of the fish. Tightly wrap in the clingfilm and leave to marinade in the fridge for 1 hour.
Wash off the marinade, pat dry and store in the freezer tightly clingfilmed.

fennel salad:

In a large bowl mix all the ingredients together except for the rocket. Taste, correct the seasoning and put to one side until needed. This should only be done up to 10 minutes before you are ready to serve, and mix in the rocket at the last minute to prevent it from wilting.

ceviche:

On a large square plate, arrange the sliced scallops into three lines running from the top to the bottom. In between the scallop rows place the sliced tuna.
Season the scallops only with the salt and pepper.
On top of each row of scallops place a thin line of shallot, chives and three small amounts of caviar evenly spaced.
Finish with a small amount of fennel salad in the middle and garnish with the Shiso and micro herbs.

 RECOMMENDED WINE
Calamin Grand Cru Blanc – Louis Bovard – Vaud – Switzerland

Serves 4

Preparation time: 20 minutes
Cooking time: 15 minutes

Special equipment:
Blender
Sieve

Planning ahead:
You can have all the ingredients sliced and your wine weighed out the day before.

INGREDIENTS

fish:

4 x 150g	turbot, filleted and portioned, brushed with butter, lemon, salt and pepper **(*1)**
20g	butter, unsalted
50g	½ shallot, small peeled and sliced
2g	sea salt (1 pinch)
0.5g	white pepper (1 pinch), freshly ground
120g	button mushrooms, washed and sliced
100ml	dry white wine (chardonnay)
80ml	water

vegetable garnish and oysters:

20g	butter, unsalted
30ml	water
200g	spinach, washed
85g	cucumber ribbons **(*2)**
60g	samphire grass
4	whole native Colchester oysters, size 2, opened and kept in their juices in a small saucepan.

sauce:

200ml	strained cooking liquor, see above
60g	cucumber skin
12g	wasabi paste
1g	lecithin – soya based **(*3)** (optional)
40g	butter
1g	lemon juice

BRAISED FILLET OF TURBOT, OYSTER, CUCUMBER AND WASABI JUS BY RAYMOND BLANC

This has been a classic dish at Le Manoir for many years. But as all Manoir dishes it is about details which are not always easy to duplicate in your own home. I have 40 chefs in my kitchen. Maybe the best way to enjoy it is at Le Manoir.

METHOD

sauce and fish:
Preheat the oven to 190°C – Gas Mark 5 – 170°C fan assisted
In a sauté pan on a medium heat, sweat the shallots in the butter for 2 minutes. **(*4)**
Add the sliced mushrooms and sweat for a further minute.
Add the wine and boil for approximately 5 seconds – taste **(*5)**
Place the fillets of fish on the mushrooms, bring the liquid to the boil and cover with a lid
Cook in the preheated oven for approximately 5 minutes. Remove from the oven, spoon out the fish on to a large buttered serving dish and keep warm. **(*6)**
Strain the juices into a large jug blender, pressing on the shallots and mushrooms to extract as much juice as possible. Reserve.

finishing the sauce:
In a large jug blender, blitz together the hot cooking juices, cucumber skin, wasabi paste, lecithin, butter and lemon juice. Strain and reserve.

vegetable garnish and oysters:
Divide the butter and water into two saucepans. Spinach in one and cucumber and samphire in the other. Add a tiny pinch of salt to the spinach. Cover with a lid.
On a high heat bring the pans of vegetables to a quick boil. The spinach will take one minute, the cucumber and samphire 30 seconds. Just barely warm the oysters in their own juices. Place the turbot back in the oven for one minute. And bring your sauce to the boil.

serving:
Place the spinach in the middle of each plate, with the cucumber and samphire around. Top with the fish and oyster, spooning the sauce over and around.

Chef's notes (*):

*1   Peel the cucumber, reserving the skin, then use a mandolin or a sharp knife to cut ribbons from the cucumber, turning as you go, until you are left with the seeds, which can be discarded.

*2   This can be done a few hours in advance. The melted butter mixed with the lemon juice and salt will season the fish first. Then the fish is refrigerated; the butter will solidify and prevent the salt from curing the fish.

*3   Lechithin is an emulsifier that you can find in many vegetables, seaweeds, eggs etc. Here we are using a natural extract of soya beans in a powdered form. Once emulsified with liquid it will produce a light airy sauce. It is optional.

*4   By sweetening the shallots you will convert the starches into sugars adding a sweetness to your sauce.

*5   The wine is boiled in order to remove some of the alcohol content and to reduce the acidity. The aim is to leave enough acidity to give depth of flavour; if reduced too much, the sauce is likely to be very flat.

*6   Once the fish has been taken out of the oven, it is rested for 3 minutes. This will allow the residual heat to finish cooking the fish perfectly, and also some of the juices to escape. This will be used to enrich the sauce.

Variation:
The fish could be portioned on the bone and cooked which would provide more flavour to the sauce. The bones of the fish could be chopped up and softened with the sliced mushrooms to provide more depth of flavour.
This dish offers many variations: tomatoes, mustard, basil and leek could also be used.
Fillets of brill, plaice, lemon sole, etc. can be used instead.

ROASTED WINTER VEGETABLES

BY RAYMOND BLANC

This is a lovely way to cook and present your seasonal vegetables, using what is available and as local as possible you can maximise the vitamins, minerals, flavour and textures.

Serves 4

Preparation time: 20 minutes

Cooking time: 2 hours

Planning ahead:
All elements of this dish can be cooked a day in advance and reheated to order.

INGREDIENTS

roasted beetroot, pumpkin and onions:

2	candy beetroot, washed and quartered
2	golden beetroot, washed and quartered
160g	pumpkin discs, cut 3cm round and high
	baby onions, peeled and trimmed
30g	olive oil
30g	water

sea salt and freshly ground black pepper

pumpkin purée:

200g	pumpkin, peeled and diced 2cm
10g	unsalted butter
2g	sea salt
1g	black pepper, freshly ground
5ml	hazelnut oil

mushroom fricassee:

5g	shallot, finely chopped
15g	butter unsalted
2g	garlic, finely chopped
100g	seasonal mushrooms (chanterelles, trompettes, girolles)
10g	flat leaf parsley, chopped
1	squeeze lemon juice

sea salt and freshly ground black pepper

garnish:

15g	butter
30ml	water
100g	spinach
8	parsnip ribbons, deep fried
12	sage leaves, deep fried
100ml	Port reduced by 2/3rds
100ml	red wine until it thickens **(*1)**

METHOD

roasted beetroot, pumpkin and onions:

Preheat your oven to 110°C.
In a small casserole with a lid, sweeten the vegetables on a medium heat in the olive oil with a little seasoning for 5 minutes. Add the water and cook in the preheated oven for 40 minutes to 1 hour until they are soft but still hold their shape. **(*2)**

pumpkin purée:

In a medium sized saucepan on a medium heat, gently cook the pumpkin in the butter, with a little seasoning and cover with a tight fitting lid. Stir regularly to ensure it does not stick to the bottom.
When the pumpkin begins to break down and release its moisture, turn up the heat to evaporate as much of the liquid as possible, stirring all the time.
Purée the pumpkin in a food processor until smooth, taste, correct the seasoning and add a little hazelnut oil to finish.

mushroom fricassee:

This should be cooked at the last moment when you are ready to plate up.
Sweat shallots in the butter on low heat for one minute. Add the garlic, turn up the heat and add all the wild mushrooms apart from the black trumpets, cook for 30 seconds, then add the trompettes. Add a pinch of salt and pepper and cook for one minute, stir in the parsley and add a squeeze of lemon juice.

to finish the dish and garnish:

Preheat your oven to 180°C.
Reheat your beetroot, pumpkin and onions in the oven for 8-10 minutes.
Warm your purée in a small pan and cook your mushrooms.
In a separate medium saucepan, bring the butter and water to the boil, creating an emulsion; add a pinch of salt and the spinach. Cook until it has just wilted, drain and keep warm.
To dress the plates, spoon the pumpkin purée in the middle of each plate and spread it lengthways, avoiding the edges. Arrange all the other ingredients on top of the purée and spoon the red wine and port reduction around.

Chef's notes (*):

*1 Reduce the wines until they coat the back of your spoon; taste and add a little caster sugar if the concentrated tannins of the wines becomes too overpowering.

*2 This slow method of cooking the vegetables ensures all the starches are converted into sugars giving maximum flavour and will leave them with a soft melting texture without becoming a purée or falling to pieces.

Variation:

This dish can be made all year round by using the best seasonal vegetables. Replace the beetroot, pumpkin and onions with carrots, celeriac, Jerusalem artichokes, new season garlic cloves, butternut squash, grelot onions, small red thai shallots. Use seasonal mushrooms, ceps, giroles, chanterelles, trompettes, morels, oyster, pied bleu.

 RECOMMENDED WINE
*Brouilly Domaine Tavian –
Cru de Beaujolais*

Serves 4

Preparation time: 40 minutes
Cooking time: 25 minutes

Special equipment:
Ice-cream machine, 7cm pastry rings,
piping bag, silicone tray, mandolin.

Planning ahead:
You can make the ginger sauce and dried
pear slices a day in advance.

INGREDIENTS

almond clafoutis:

100g	ground almonds
100g	icing sugar
6g	cornflour
100g	unsalted butter, softened
1	medium egg
3g	vanilla extract

caramel croustillant:

35g	milk, full cream
75g	unsalted butter
95g	caster sugar
2g	Pectin powder NH
30g	glucose powder
15g	plain flour

caramelised pear:

2	whole pears, comice, peeled, halved, cored and cut with 7cm pastry ring. (keep the trimmings for the sorbet)
32g	unsalted butter
150g	caster sugar
30ml	white wine, Chardonnay

ginger sauce:

60ml	whipping cream
60ml	milk, full cream
8g	fresh ginger, grated
20g	caster sugar
2	egg yolks, organic
¼ leaf	gelatine, softened in cold water

dried pear slices:

½	Comice pear (small and slightly under ripe)
15ml	stock syrup (100g caster sugar, 100ml water boiled)

pear sorbet:

400g	Comice pear purée (freshly made)
20ml	lemon juice
10ml	alcohol, eau de vie de Poire William
1g	vitamin C powder
50g	caster sugar (according to sweetness)

pear dice:

100g	Comice pear, peeled, cored and diced 5mm
20ml	alcohol, eau de vie de Poire William
3g	fructose
dash	lemon juice

CARAMELISED PEAR CROUSTILLANT AND ITS OWN SORBET

BY RAYMOND BLANC

One of the new Le Manoir dishes, simple and one
of the greatest experiences using Comice pears.

METHOD

almond clafoutis:

Preheat your oven to 160°C.
In a large bowl mix together the almond powder, icing sugar and cornflour. Gradually mix in the softened butter, then, in a separate bowl beat together the egg and vanilla extract and add this to the mixture. Reserve in the fridge for a minimum of one hour to let it set slightly.
Line a tray with greaseproof paper, lightly grease the pastry rings and using a piping bag evenly fill the rings by one third.
Cook for about 8-10 minutes until lightly golden.

caramel croustillant:

Preheat your oven to 180°C.
In a medium saucepan heat together the milk and butter to a gentle simmer.
In a bowl mix together the sugar, pectin, glucose. Mix this into the hot milk and bring to the boil. Remove from the heat and add the sieved flour.
Pour onto a tray between two sheets of greaseproof paper, roll thin and freeze for 30 minutes in order to remove the top layer of paper.
Bake in the preheated oven for 7-8 minutes.
Allow to cool slightly before you cut out your 7cm discs and reserve.

caramelised pear:

In a non stick pan, bring the butter and sugar to a light brown caramel. Add the pieces of pear and colour on both sides for two minutes each. Pour in the wine and simmer until just soft in the middle, take off the heat and leave to cool before draining off the cooking liquor. Reserve until needed.

ginger sauce:

In a medium pan, bring the milk and cream to a simmer and infuse with the freshly grated ginger for 30 minutes. In a bowl mix together the egg yolks and sugar. Strain off the milk and whisk into the egg mixture. Pour back into the saucepan and cook on a medium heat for two minutes until it coats the back of the spatula, stir in the drained gelatine and cool over an ice bain-marie. Reserve in the fridge until needed.

dried pear slices:

Preheat your oven to 110°C.
Using a mandolin, slice the pear lengthways as thin as possible, place directly onto a Teflon tray. Brush with the stock syrup and cook for about 30 minutes until dry and crisp with no colour.

pear sorbet:

In a blender blend all the ingredients together and churn in an ice-cream machine straight away. Reserve in the freezer until needed.

pear dice:

Mix all the ingredients together just before you are ready to serve.

to serve:

In each medium serving bowl pour a small amount of ginger sauce into the middle top with the warm clafoutis, the warm caramelised pear half and cover with the caramel croustillant. Garnish with the pear dice, pear sorbet and a dried pear slice.

 RECOMMENDED WINE
Cadillac – Château de L'Orangerie – Bordeaux

LONGUEVILLE MANOR

ANDREW BAIRD

Having worked in some of the best kitchens in the UK during his training and taking on the position of Head Chef at Longueville Manor at an early age, Andrew turned his back on books and the media and set out to be innovative and individual. He immersed himself in local ingredients, of which Jersey has some of the finest in Europe, together with regional methods of cookery. His involvement with the local farming and fishing communities ensures that he has a true understanding of where all of his ingredients have originated and this in turn translates to the finest quality contemporary dishes on the plate.

Mussels ~ Local
£1-80 lb

'A taste of Jersey'

98

Serves 4
Preparation time: 1 hour
(excluding stock and tomato confit)
Cooking time: 10 minutes

This dish is made with six components
1.   Lobster
2.   Lumo ham cannelloni
3.   Plum tomato infusion
4.   Preparation and cooking
      of vegetables
5.   Preparation and cooking of
      the couscous
6.   Preparation of the chicken stock

INGREDIENTS

4 x 300g Bobby lobsters (Bobby = lobster
          without claws)
160g   Lumo cured ham
1 x 20g   Perigord truffle
8   vine ripened plum tomatoes
olive oil

chicken stock:

1	carrot
1	onion
1	celery stick
1	leek
4	bay leaves
12	peppercorns
50g	parsley
2 ltr	water
600g	chicken bones

garden vegetables:

4	baby fennel
8	baby carrots
8	mange tout
8	fine French beans
4	garden asparagus
4	lemon grass
4	caper berries

cous cous:

1	red pepper
1	courgette
100g	couscous
100ml	chicken stock (see recipe)

to finish:

20g	blue maw seeds
20g	pine nuts
10g	red aramath
10g	baby sorrel
10g	chervil
10g	shizo cress
walnut oil	
balsamic	
salt and pepper	

POACHED TAIL OF JERSEY LOBSTER WITH LUMO CURED HAM CHOWDER, GARDEN VEGETABLES AND MICRO SALAD

BY ANDREW BAIRD

This dish is a tasty assembly of our prized local lobster, our home grown garden vegetables with a burst of flavour from the Lumo ham and plum tomatoes.

METHOD

lobster:

If available, buy baby lobster without claws. These are often far cheaper than "select".
Straighten the lobster tail and tie a knife or similar metal object to the tail to keep it straight during cooking.
Heat a large pan of salted water to boiling point.
Place the trussed lobster into the water for 7 minutes.
Remove from the heat and drain off the water.
Refresh until cool in cold water and drain well.
Remove the head and peel the tail.
Carefully remove the intestine and rinse.
Slice into five slices and put aside.

chicken stock:

Peel carrots and onion. Wash the leek and celery and keep whole. Place in a heavy pan with all the other ingredients, bring quickly to the boil and skim. Simmer on a gentle heat for 3 hours skimming all the time. Once cooked, pass through a chinoise quickly.

garden vegetables:

Peel the carrots.
Peel the asparagus.
Top and tail mange tout and French beans.
Trim the fennel.
Cook lightly in an emulsion of seasoned chicken stock and olive oil for a few minutes until tender.
Drain and leave to cool.

cooking the cous cous:

Peel and dice the red pepper. Heat in a little olive oil until tender. Add the Chicken stock, salt, pepper and diced courgette.
Bring to simmer.
Remove from heat and place in a bowl and cover until cool.
Once cool stir through with a fork.

lumo ham cannelloni:

Lay two layers of clingfilm on a flat surface.
Making an oblong, place the Lumo Ham on the film.
Place the dressed couscous down the centre.
Slowly draw the far side of the clingfilm towards you, wrapping the cous cous to form a cylinder.
Unwrap and leave aside.

plum tomato confit:

Bring to the boil a large pan of boiling water.
Remove vine and stalks from the tomatoes.

Place tomatoes in water for 10 seconds.

Immediately place in cold water – the skin should be easy to remove.

Drain and cut into quarters.

Place on a tray and rub with olive oil.

Load tray into a preheated oven at 150°C for 4 hours to achieve an intense tomato flavour.

Cut into oblongs and leave aside.

to assemble:

Place the tomato confit and cannelloni parallel to each other on an oblong plate.

As shown run a line of blue maw seeds down the long edge of each plate.

Place the sliced lobster tail on top of the tomato confit and dress with sliced perigord truffle, baby fennel, shizo cress and chervil.

Place the remainder of the baby vegetables and salad on top of the Lumo ham cannelloni.

Use your flare to dress the plate with balsamic, herbs and oil.

 RECOMMENDED WINE
Dezaley Red
Rouvinez Vins – Valais – Switzerland

ROAST FILLET OF ANGUS BEEF WITH OXTAIL RAVIOLI, GRILLED FOIE GRAS AND WOODLAND MUSHROOMS

BY ANDREW BAIRD

This is a dish created with the finest ingredients available. Angus beef is some of the best beef in the world and with the foie gras and ceps, the combination is just divine.

Serves 4

Preparation time:
5 hours (including cooking of oxtail and chicken stock)

Cooking time:
20 minutes

Special equipment:
Pasta machine

Planning ahead:
Not all butchers will stock the finest beef and oxtail, so order ahead.

 RECOMMENDED WINE
Buxus Villette Sauvignon White
Louis Bovard – Vaud – Switzerland

INGREDIENTS

400g	Angus Beef fillet
1kg	oxtail on the bone cut into 10cm sections
60g	foie gras
200g	ceps
20g	morels
2	bok choy
100g	haricot beans
*6ltr	chicken stock (recipe x3)
*250g	pasta dough (recipe x1)
*250ml	red wine/oxtail sauce (recipe x1)
*250ml	cep purée (recipe x1)
*100ml	cep cream (recipe x1)
100g	carrot
100g	leek
100g	celery
20g	onion
4	bay leaf
12	peppercorns
1	bottle red wine
50g	tomato purée
1	egg yolk
	olive oil
200g	smoked bacon
30ml	cream (single)
5g	chives

chicken stock (x3):

1	carrot
1	onion
1	celery stick
1	leek
4	bay leaves
12	peppercorns
50g	parsley
2 ltr	water
600g	chicken bones

pasta dough:

250g	pasta flour
2	whole free range organic eggs
3	egg yolks from organic free range eggs
1g	saffron stems
10ml	water
5g	salt

cep purée:

250g	ceps
30g	shallot
1	garlic clove
200ml	chicken stock
50ml	double cream
50ml	Madeira wine
15g	unsalted butter
	salt and pepper to taste

cep cream:

40ml	cep purée
60ml	chicken stock

METHOD

chicken stock:

Peel carrots and onion. Wash with the leek and celery, keep whole. Place in a heavy pan with all the other ingredients, bring quickly to the boil and skim. Simmer on a gentle heat for 3 hours skimming all the time. Once cooked, pass through a chinoise quickly.

cooking oxtail and making sauce:

The sauce for this dish comes from a reduction made from the liquor that the oxtail is cooked in. Trim the oxtail of any excess fat. Ideally the oxtail should be cut into 10cm sections. Your butcher will be happy to do this.

Peel carrot and onion. Wash leek and celery and roughly chop.

Roast oxtail in a preheated oven at 200°C for 15 minutes. Remove from the roasting tray and place in a deep saucepan.

Drain any excess fat from the roasting tray and add the roughly cut vegetables. Turn the oven down to 180°C and cook for 10 minutes

Add 50 g of tomato purée and stir in.

Add mixture to the saucepan with the oxtail

Deglaze the roasting tray with the red wine. This simply means removing all the meaty bits. Bring the wine to simmering point and then pour this into the oxtail mix. Bring everything to the boil and reduce volume by half.

Cover the oxtail with chicken stock (see recipe) and simmer for approximately 4 hours, making sure you don't reduce. Top up if necessary with water.

Once cooked, remove oxtail from the liquor and cool before removing the meat from the bones. Take care to discard any gristle and fat.

Pass the liquid through a chinoise and reduce to approximately 1 litre. This should give you a nice balance of oxtail and red wine flavours.

Once the oxtail has cooled – flake it with the back of a fork and roll into small balls. You will need approximately 1 teaspoon of sauce per oxtail ravioli. Cover and place in fridge until you have made the ravioli.

pasta dough:

Sieve the pasta flour and place in a bowl or food processor.

Beat the whole egg and egg yolks and pass through a chinoise.

Infuse the saffron stems in 100ml of hot water. Leave to cool. Add 3 tablespoons of the saffron infusion to the pasta flour together with the eggs and salt.

Process in food processor or knead by hand until the mix comes together. Don't worry if at this stage it is still slightly dry.

Place in a plastic bag – a freezer bag is ideal and rest for two hours.

Remove from the bag and knead again. It should come together to form a smooth pasta dough.

cep purée:

Peel and slice the shallots.

Crush the garlic.

Place butter in a heavy bottomed pan and melt over a medium heat.

Add shallots and garlic.

Wash and roughly cut the ceps.

After 4-5 minutes the shallots and garlic should be sweated down without any colour.

Add ceps and continue cooking. You will see the ceps soften.

At this point add the Madeira wine. The alcohol will evaporate and reduce only slightly.

Add the chicken stock. Bring back to the boil and reduce until the mixture becomes sloppy.

At this stage add the cream. Bring back to the boil and liquidise.

Pass through a muslin or chinoise.

Season to taste and it is ready to use.

cep cream:

Simply mix the ingredients together and blend with a hand blender.

Heat and hand blend just before serving ravioli. Bring the pasta dough to room temperature. This will take a good hour.

Using a pasta machine, roll out the dough on its finest setting. Dust the work surface with flour to stop it sticking. Using a set of round cutters, select one approximately 70mm and cut forming 8 circles.

Place the ball of oxtail in the centre and using a little egg yolk around the edge place the second circle on top. Take care to expel all air.

Cook and serve by adding a few drops of olive oil and a good pinch of salt to a pan of simmering water. Cook for approximately 3 minutes. Drain and serve immediately.

haricot beans:

If using dried haricot beans soak overnight.

Cover with chicken stock (see recipe), add a bay leaf and the smoked bacon.

Simmer for approximately 1 hour until tender.

At this stage remove bacon and bay leaf and reduce the chicken stock until it has almost disappeared. Add cream and simmer until the sauce coats the beans. Serve with a few snipped chives.

the assembly:

Cut the beef fillet into 4 equal 100g pieces

Season with salt and pepper and using a heavy duty frying pan seal and colour the beef all over.

Place in the oven for 4 minutes at 180°C.

Leave to rest.

Cut the bok choy in half and blanch in salted water for 2 minutes. Drain and coat in warm butter and season.

Using a large round main course plate, warm the cep purée and using a dessert spoon place an elongated tear drop around the plate as shown in the picture. Season the foie gras and pan fry until golden on both sides

Using the foie gras oil in the pan, gently sauté the morels and ceps and place on plate as shown.

Add the bok choy – opening up the leaves to form a half moon shape.

Heat and add a dessert spoon of the creamed haricot beans together with the pâté of foie gras and woodland mushrooms.

Heat the red wine/oxtail sauce, cep cream and ravioli.

Cut the beef fillet into two and place on top of the bok choy and finish with the ravioli, red wine sauce and cep cream.

HAZELNUT SABLÈ WITH "JIVARA" CHOCOLATE, SESAME ICE CREAM AND A BALSAMIC REDUCTION

BY ANDREW BAIRD

"Jivara" chocolate is one of the finest available. Delicately combined with a hazelnut sablé and sesame ice cream, with the contrasting flavour of reduced balsamic, an outstanding dessert.

Serves 4

Preparation time: 3 hours

Cooking time: 40 minutes

Special equipment:
Ice cream maker

Planning ahead:
Depending on your ice cream maker, you may need to make it 24 hours ahead.

INGREDIENTS

hazelnut sablè:

400g	peeled roast hazelnuts
570g	unsalted Jersey butter
225g	sugar
700g	flour
7g	salt
2	vanilla pods
200g	egg yolks

jivara chocolate cream:

250g	milk
250g	whipped cream
100g	egg yolks
50g	sugar
250g	chocolate "Valrhona Jivara"

sesame ice cream:

1ltr	milk
200g	cream
50g	milk powder
6g	salt
2g	agar agar
150g	egg yolk
120g	sugar
40g	trimoline

balsamic reduction:

20ml	balsamic vinegar

METHOD

hazelnut sablè:

Chop hazelnuts and mix with butter, sugar and salt. Place in a mixer and beat until the mix becomes pale.
Fold in flour and egg yolks and sugar mix together with the seeds from the vanilla pods.
Place between two sheets of silicone paper and roll out to approximately 3mm.
Place in a refrigerator and chill for 20 minutes
Cut into oblong shapes and bake in the oven at 180°C for approximately 8-10 minutes.
Leave to cool.

jivara chocolate cream:

Whisk egg yolks and sugar in a mixing bowl until they become pale.
Heat milk and cream to 85°C then put onto egg yolks with sugar mix and slowly mix until luke warm.
Warm the chocolate until it just melts and add to the mixture. Leave to cool
Once cool place in the refrigerator in a piping bag ready to use.

sesame ice cream:

Mix egg yolks, milk powder, agar agar and sugar until pale.
Heat milk and cream to 85°C.
Pour over sugar and egg mixture.
Return to a heavy based saucepan and heat until it coats the back of a spatula.
Add pectin, trimoline and salt then pass through a conical strainer.
Add sesame seed and leave to cool
Then ideally freeze and Pacojet or churn in a traditional ice cream maker.

balsamic reduction:

Simply reduce the balsamic vinegar over heat until a syrupy consistency is obtained.

 RECOMMENDED WINE

Quintessence du Clos –
Domaine Le Clos des Cazaux – Rhône

SUMMER LODGE COUNTRY HOUSE & SPA

'Dorset is a gourmet's paradise, fuelled by an abundance of superb local ingredients and wonderful home-cooked food'

STEVEN TITMAN

Steven Titman has developed a cuisine of international fame since joining Summer Lodge Country House & Hotel as Head Chef in 2004. He prefers to use a wide variety of locally sourced, fresh produce to create dishes which allow the flavours to speak for themselves. Steven began his career at Longueville Manor in 1994 as Chef de Partie before moving abroad to Germany in 1998 to work at the Restaurant a la Table in Dortmund. He returned to working at a Relais & Châteaux property in the form of The White Barn Inn in Maine, USA in the autumn of 2000 where he continued to work as Chef de Partie and later progressed to become the junior Sous Chef.

Serves 4

Preparation time: 1 hour

Cooking time: 10-15 minutes

Planning ahead:
The purée and confit potatoes can be prepared a day in advance.

PAN SEARED LYME BAY SCALLOPS WITH SWEET SHALLOT PURÉE, CONFIT MARIS PIPER POTATOES, PARSLEY AND CAPER DRESSING

BY STEVEN TITMAN

This dish really showcases the quality of the local scallops. The sweetness of the scallops with the shallots and the acidity from the capers is a perfect combination.

INGREDIENTS

12	Lyme Bay scallops (ask your fishmonger to remove them from the shell for you)
8	large shallots (peeled and thinly sliced)
50g	sugar
30g	sherry vinegar
200ml	cream
50g	butter
1 tbsp	baby capers
1	bunch flat leaf parsley (finely sliced)
1 tsp	Dijon mustard
2	Maris Piper potatoes
1	clove garlic
1	sprig thyme
150ml	olive oil
1	lemon (zested)
sea salt	
4	small portions of mixed salad

METHOD

Place the shallots in a saucepan and cook slowly in the butter over a moderate heat until soft and translucent. Add the sugar and cook until this turns to a light caramel, then add the sherry Vinegar. Cook for 2 minutes, then add the cream and bring to the boil.
Place the mixture in a blender and blend until smooth.
Peel the potatoes and cut into discs approximately the diameter of a 10 pence coin (or the same diameter as your scallops). Place in a shallow pan with the garlic, thyme, olive oil and a pinch of salt and cook slowly over a low heat for approximately 1 hour. Remove from the heat, and strain, saving some of the oil for use in the dressing.
For the dressing mix the mustard, capers, parsley and 4 tablespoons of olive oil (saved from cooking the potatoes) together.

to serve:

Place the potatoes on a tray, sprinkle with sea salt and lemon zest and place in a medium oven to warm.
Reheat the shallot purée over a gentle heat (being careful not to boil). Heat a frying pan on the stove, then sear the scallops over a high heat for 2-3 minutes on each side. Finish with a little butter and squeeze of lemon juice.
Place 3 teaspoons of the shallot purée across the middle of the plate, then place the three potato discs on top of each. Place the scallops on top of each potato and a little of the dressing over each scallop. Finish the plate with a small salad garnish.

 RECOMMENDED WINE
Saumur Blanc Multa Paucis –
Domaine de la Paleine – Saumur

Serves 4

Preparation time: 45 minutes

Cooking time: 5-6 hours (including braising time)

Special equipment:
1 x Isi cream whipper (with 2 x gas cartridges)
Metal rings
Butcher's string
Mandolin

Planning ahead:
The shoulder can be cooked and finished a day or two in advance, therefore much reducing the cooking time on the day.

INGREDIENTS

braised shoulder of lamb:

1	lamb shoulder (de-boned and trimmed)
2	onions, 1 chopped and 1 finely diced
2	carrots, 1 chopped and 1 finely diced
3	garlic cloves
1 tbsp	tomato purée
100ml	tomato juice
200ml	red wine
500ml	lamb or chicken stock
1	celeriac, finely diced
1	swede, finely diced

potato ring:

2	large Maris Piper potatoes

potato foam:

300g	potato purée
75g	milk
100g	cream
50g	butter
salt and freshly milled black pepper	

roast loin of lamb:

2 x 200g lamb loins

rosemary jus:

2	sprigs rosemary finely chopped

savoy cabbage:

6	rashers streaky bacon, cut into lardons
1	onion, finely chopped
1	Savoy cabbage, shredded

ROAST LOIN OF DORSET LAMB AND BRAISED SHOULDER "SHEPHERD'S PIE" WITH SAVOY CABBAGE AND ROSEMARY JUS

BY STEVEN TITMAN

The signature dish of Summer Lodge for nearly five years now, this dish combines two cuts from the Dorset lamb. The shoulder is braised and then made into a rich Shepherd's pie and the loin is simply roasted. The flavours are kept quite simple so the true flavour of the lamb preparations shine through.

METHOD

braised shoulder shepherd's pie:

Season the lamb shoulder and sear in a hot frying pan. Place the lamb in a deep casserole dish. In the same frying pan add the chopped onions, carrots and garlic and cook for 3 minutes.
Add the tomato purée and cook for a further 2 minutes then adding the tomato juice, red wine and stock. Bring to the boil and pour over the shoulder.
Cover the dish and place in a slow oven (140°C) and braise for 5 to 6 hours until the shoulder is falling apart. Remove the shoulder, allow to cool a little and flake the meat or roughly chop.
Meanwhile, strain the cooking juice and reduce in a saucepan until well flavoured and sauce consistency.
In a clean saucepan cook the diced carrot, onion, celeriac and swede until soft (but not puréed). Add the diced shoulder and continue to cook on a low heat. Add a little of the sauce to bind the lamb and vegetables together. Save the rest of the sauce to one side.

potato ring:

Thinly slice the potato lengthways with a mandolin.
Wrap a length of greaseproof paper around a metal ring and then carefully arrange the potato slices onto it, securing with a piece of string.
Deep fry until golden brown. As the potato cooks the ring and paper should fall away allowing the potato to cook evenly on both sides whilst maintaining its shape
Drain on a piece of kitchen towel.

potato foam:

Gently heat up the potato purée with the milk, cream and butter. Season to taste. When the potato has the consistency of whipping cream place in a cream whipper and charge with the gas.

to serve:

Season and sear the loins in a hot pan and roast for approximately 7 minutes, turning half way through the cooking. Remove from the oven and allow to rest.
In a hot pan add the bacon and chopped onion and cook until the onions are soft. Add the shredded cabbage and cook for a further 2 minutes.
Place the potato ring onto the plate and half fill with the shepherd's pie (a ramekin can be used if the potato rings are not made).
Arrange the cabbage in front of the shepherd's pie and place 3 slices of lamb on top. Finally place the potato foam on top of the shoulder mix. Add the chopped rosemary to the sauce and spoon a little of the jus around the lamb.

 RECOMMENDED WINE
LOIN – Moulin des Quints Rouge –
PIE – Cuvée la Paleine Red
Domaine de la Paleine – Saumur

Serves 4

Preparation time: 1 hour (including freezing the sherbert and granité)

Cooking time: N/A

Special equipment:
Ice cream machine (if possible)

Planning ahead:
The sherbert and granité can be prepared the day before, also the jelly can be made in advance.

INGREDIENTS

lemon curd:

2	eggs
125ml	lemon juice
80g	sugar
60g	butter

lemon sherbet:

475ml	milk
170g	sugar
2.5	lemons, zest and juice

lemon thyme granité:

500ml	water
100g	sugar
50g	lemon thyme
50g	lime Juice

lemon thyme jelly:

375g	water
60g	sugar
75g	lemon thyme
2	gelatine

SUMMER LODGE TRIO OF LEMON, LEMON CURD, LEMON SHERBET AND LEMON THYME JELLY

BY STEVEN TITMAN

A nice light dessert, ideal to finish dinner. The different flavours and textures all combine to produce a well balanced dessert.

METHOD

lemon curd:

Stir beaten eggs, sugar and juice over a pan of hot water until thick.
Remove from heat and whisk in diced butter.

lemon sherbet:

Bring all except the juice to the boil. When cold (it must be completely cold to prevent the mix from curdling) strain and add lemon juice. Either churn in an ice cream machine or place in a round bottom bowl in the freezer, stirring every 20 minutes until set.

lemon thyme granité:

Heat the water and sugar to make a syrup. Add the lemon thyme and lime juice whilst hot and leave to infuse (at least one hour).
Strain into a flat tray and place in the freezer.

lemon thyme jelly:

Boil the water and sugar to make a syrup and leave to cool until completely cold.
Blanch the lemon thyme in boiling water for 2 minutes and then plunge into iced water (this will help preserve the colour).
Blend the lemon thyme and syrup together, strain and add gelatine to a small amount then mix with rest (this will also help to preserve the colour). Pour into 4 martini glasses approximately 3cm high and place in the fridge to set.

to serve:

Remove the martini glasses from the fridge and pour the lemon curd on top of the jelly. Next, scrape the granité with a fork and place a layer of this on top of the lemon curd. Finally finish with a scoop of the lemon sherbet.

Chef's tip:

Try a layer of crumbled meringue in between the layers to add another texture. Dried lemon thyme and confit lemon slices will enhance the decoration.

RECOMMENDED WINE
Coteaux de Saumur –
Domaine de la Paleine – Saumur

CHEWTON GLEN

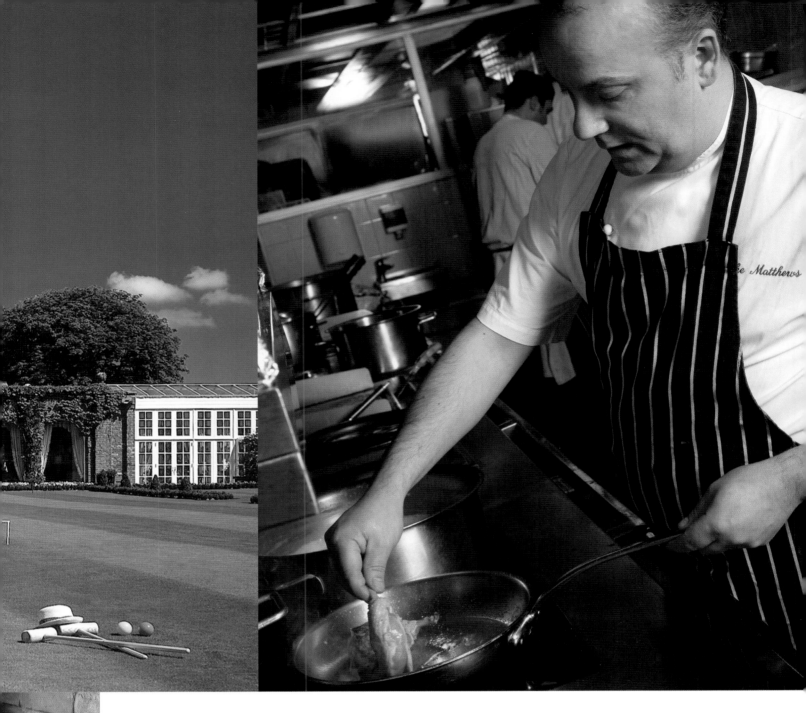

'I am driven by satisfying my guests. Many of them enjoy simple food made with top quality ingredients and cooked with the same care as the more complex dishes'

LUKE MATTHEWS

Luke has been at Chewton Glen since 1993; he spent ten years as Senior Sous Chef and then in November 2003 was appointed Executive Chef. Luke is a local man, having attended school, and subsequently college, in Bournemouth. After finishing his apprenticeship, aged 20, Luke had a brief sojourn at Chewton Glen with Chef Pierre Chevillard which was an inspiring catalyst in his early career path. He then worked in the Channel Islands before moving to one of the first gastro-pubs in Oxfordshire then heading to the South of France as Sous Chef at Hotel Les Bories, Gordes. Following on from another 18 months at Bishopstrow House in Warminster he finally came home to Chewton Glen, again in the capacity of Senior Sous Chef before taking over as Executive Chef.

Serves 4

Preparation time: 1 hour
Cooking time: 10 minutes

Special equipment:
Deep fat fryer
Whisk

INGREDIENTS

scallops:

12	large hand-dived scallops removed from the shell and cleaned (ask your fishmonger to do this for you)
2 tsp	salt
2 tsp	madras curry powder

cauliflower beignets:

12	small cauliflower florets
500g	self raising flour
1 tbsp	white wine vinegar
2 tbsp	madras curry powder
1 tsp	salt
1 pint	sparkling water

cauliflower purée:

1	head of cauliflower with the stalk and outer leaves removed
50g	unsalted butter
50g	double cream
1 tbsp	lemon juice
salt	

parmesan velouté:

2	shallots chopped
1	bunch of thyme
1	bay leaf
250ml	Noilly Prat
500ml	chicken stock
250ml	double cream
60g	grated parmesan
3	large pieces of parmesan rind
salt	

truffle vinaigrette:

100ml	chardonnay vinegar
100ml	truffle oil
200ml	olive oil
sugar	
salt	
chopped truffle (optional)	

pea shoots:

1	bunch of pea shoots

HAND-DIVED SCALLOPS CAULIFLOWER AND CURRY, PARMESAN AND TRUFFLE

BY LUKE MATTHEWS

Chosen scallops are my favourite shellfish and a very popular dish at the hotel.

METHOD

Start by preparing the parmesan velouté. Sweat the shallots in a pan with a little oil. Add the thyme, bay leaf and the alcohol then reduce until almost dry. Next, add the chicken stock and the parmesan rind to the pan and reduce by half. Finally add the cream and bring to the simmer. Simmer for 5 minutes then whisk in the grated parmesan, simmer for a further 2 minutes then pass through a fine sieve and season with salt. Keep warm.

To prepare the cauliflower purée start by finely chopping the cauliflower, reserving 12 small florets for the beignets, then sweat it down in a pan with the butter and lemon juice. Cover the pan with a lid and do not allow the cauliflower to colour. Once the cauliflower is soft and cooked add the cream and bring to the simmer. Transfer the mixture to a blender and purée until silky smooth then season with salt and pass through a fine sieve into a pan to keep warm.

Now, prepare the batter for the cauliflower beignets, whisk together the dry ingredients then whisk in the sparkling water bit by bit until a double cream consistency is reached. Set aside until needed.

To prepare the truffle vinaigrette whisk together all the ingredients until emulsified.

to assemble:

Set up four plates. Dress each plate with a few drags of cauliflower purée using your spoon to pull the purée across the plate. Dust the cauliflower florets in flour then dip into the batter and deep fry in a pan with some oil or a deep fat fryer until golden coloured and crispy. Drain onto a clean paper towel and season with salt. Warm the velouté through in a pan. Place a large non-stick pan on the stove to warm up for cooking the scallops. Season the scallops with curry powder and salt and pan fry for 45 seconds on each side until a nice golden colour is achieved. Remove them from the pan and place onto a tray with the cauliflower beignets. To dress the plate, place three scallops onto each plate along with three cauliflower beignets, dress the pea shoots with some truffle vinaigrette and place on top of the scallops, finish the plate with a nice drizzle of velouté.

Chef's tip:

Make sure the pan for cooking the scallops is very hot for searing otherwise the scallops will "stew" in the pan and become rubbery. Also, keep the beignet batter in a bowl over ice water as this will help to achieve an extra crispy batter.

Serves 4

Preparation time: 2 hours
Cooking time: 25 minutes

Special equipment:
Fine sieve
Sharp carving knife

INGREDIENTS

2	racks of lamb, French trimmed
8	lamb sweetbreads, soaked in water overnight and blanched in chicken stock

crust:

100g	Dijon mustard
100g	dark brown sugar
200g	pistachio nuts crushed

spinach:

500g	spinach
100g	finely chopped shallot
100g	watercress
2	eggs
2	egg yolks
250g	butter

polenta:

250g	polenta
1 ltr	milk
2 tbsp	chopped rosemary
100g	finely chopped shallot
110g	parmesan cheese grated
salt and pepper	

sauce:

100g	finely chopped carrot
100g	finely chopped shallot
100ml	white wine
1 ltr	lamb stock
200ml	veal stock
16	black olives stoned and cut in half

RACK OF LAVERSTOKE PARK LAMB PISTACHIO CRUST, SWEETBREADS AND BLACK OLIVE JUS

BY LUKE MATTHEWS

Laverstoke park lamb is probably the best quality lamb I have ever tasted and works very well with the pistachio crust.

METHOD

spinach:

Start by blanching off 250g of the spinach and refreshing in ice water. Arrange onto a work surface in one even layer to form a square shape. Sauté off the remaining spinach in butter, with 100g of shallots and the watercress,s then allow to cool. Once the mixture is cool add the eggs then spread it onto the spinach square, roll the square in to a sausage shape. Steam for 5 minutes.

polenta:

Bring the milk up to a simmer with the rosemary and 100g of shallot to infuse. Whisk in the polenta and cook out until soft. Finish the polenta with parmesan cheese and some olive oil. Season the polenta well with salt and pepper then spread onto a tray lined with clingfilm and allow to set.
Once the polenta has set cut out 4 nice pieces and sauté in olive oil until golden and crispy on either side.

lamb:

Season all over with salt and pepper and seal on all sides in olive oil and butter. Place the racks on to a roasting tray and allow them to cool. Mix the Dijon mustard together with the sugar and then paint it on to the racks, use the glaze as a glue to stick on the pistachio crumbs thickly and evenly. Roast the racks in the oven at 170°C for 15 minutes, this will be pink, then leave them to rest.

sauce:

Sweat down the carrot and the remaining 100g of shallot until a golden colour is achieved. Then add the white wine and reduce by half. Then add the lamb stock and reduce until a glace consistency is achieved. Finally, add the veal stock and reduce down until the sauce will coat the back of a spoon. Season the sauce then strain it. Finish the sauce with the olives.

lamb sweetbreads:

Cook in a hot pan with some oil until golden and crispy. Then finish them with a few knobs of butter and some salt and pepper.

to serve:

To finish the dish place the polenta and spinach on the plate, along with the sweetbreads. Carve the lamb and place two pieces of meat on each plate, then sauce the plate.

Chef's tip:

Prepare the polenta and spinach elements of the dish the day before, leaving you just to finish and assemble the dish the next day.

 RECOMMENDED WINE
*Clos Louie Rouge –
Côtes de Castillon – Bordeaux*

Serves 4

Preparation time: 3 hours, 15 minutes

Finishing time: 10 minutes

Special equipment:
Acetate
Sugar thermometer
Greaseproof paper

INGREDIENTS

parfait:
50g   water
125g   caster sugar
2 x   egg whites
250g   coconut purée
150ml   whipped cream

coconut sorbet:
200ml   water
200gs   caster sugar
500g   frozen coconut puree
25ml   lemon juice

chocolate:
250g   dark chocolate

bananas:
2 x   bananas
butter and sugar

ICED COCONUT PARFAIT
BY LUKE MATTHEWS

Coconut reminds me of holidays and I love anything chocolate.

METHOD

coconut sorbet:

First make a stock syrup by bringing the water and sugar to the boil. Allow to cool then add the frozen coconut puree and lemon juice. Mix together then churn in an ice cream machine.

parfait:

Make Italian meringue by boiling the water and sugar to 116°C, whisk egg whites to soft peak then pour onto sugar syrup.
Mix the purée and lightly whipped cream together. Fold into the rest of the ingredients. Line a baking tray with greaseproof paper pour in the mousse making it approx 2cm deep then freeze. Cut frozen parfait to 2cm x 8cm rectangles.

chocolate:

Temper the chocolate by warming 200g over a bain marie to 45°C then remove from heat and stir in remaining chocolate to bring down temperature to 27°C. When this is achieved, heat chocolate back to 32°C. Spread the tempered chocolate between two sheets of acetate and smooth out, when almost set, using a ruler cut chocolate to 2cm x 8cm rectangles.

banana:

Caramelise the banana in a little butter and sugar in a hot frying pan.

to serve:

Melt a little chocolate and paint this in a neat stripe down the centre of the plate. Sandwich the coconut parfait with the chocolate rectangles and place on the plate, top with a spoon of the chocolate sorbet and caramelised bananas.

Chef's tip:
Prepare the sorbet and parfait at least one day in advance. Chocolate can be made a few days before and kept in an air tight container.

RECOMMENDED WINE
Quintessence du Clos –
Domaine Le Clos des Cazaux – Rhône

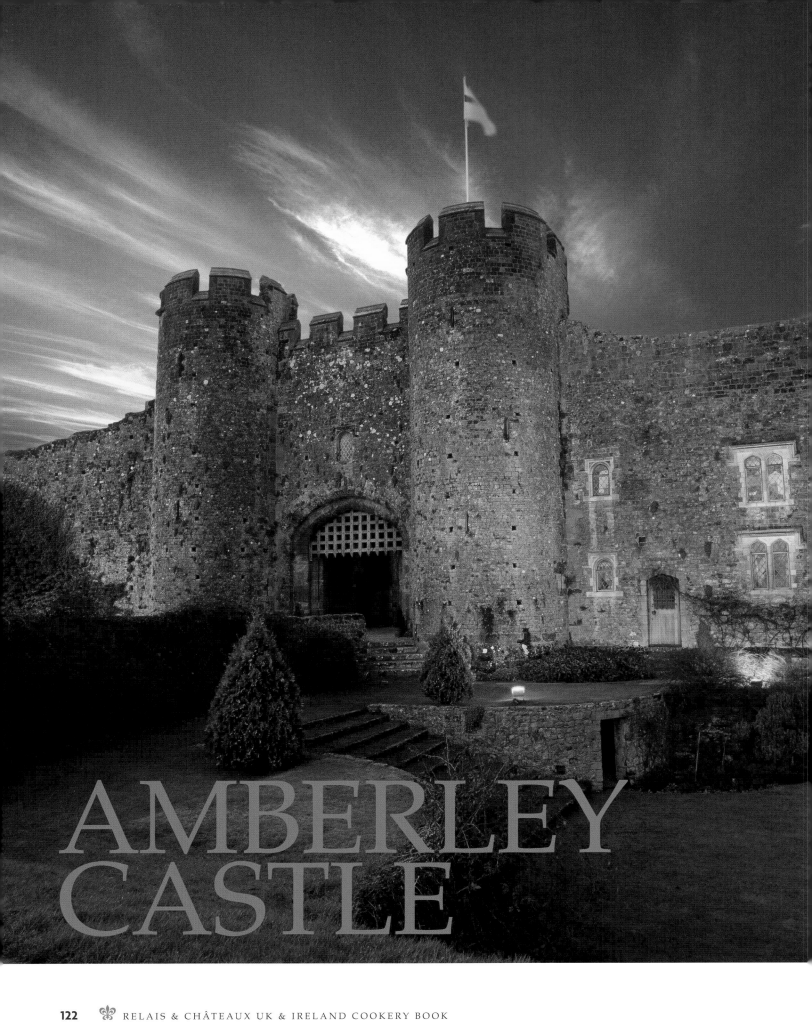

AMBERLEY CASTLE

'The eclectic style in the restaurant reflects both the Castle's exciting history and contemporary influences, with the best locally produced seasonal ingredients used to complement imaginative dishes and gastronomic delights'

JAMES DUGAN

In 2006 James joined Amberley Castle as Head Chef, and felt that Amberley's breathtaking location, nestled at the foot of the South Downs, was the perfect location for him to strive to achieve his first Michelin star, having worked in Michelin-starred restaurants for his entire career. James has a modern European take on food, utilising local produce within a 30 mile radius of the Castle, and works with a young, enthusiastic team that brings new ideas and possibilities with endless combinations of flavours and styles to his kitchen.

Serves 4

Preparation time: 2 hours

Cooking time: 5 minutes

Special equipment:
Pasta machine

Planning ahead:
The soup can be made the day before with the macaroni.

INGREDIENTS

minestrone soup:

2	onions
	fennel bulb
2	garlic cloves
1	carrot
2	rashers smoked streaky bacon
500g	plum tomato
2 tbsp	tomato purée
900ml	chicken stock
1	bay leaf

salmon:

4 (80g)	organic salmon portions

pasta:

140g	egg yolk
250g	of pasta flour
2 tbsp	olive oil
2 tbsp	water

garnish:

2	plum tomato
1	carrot
4	asparagus
2	Parma ham

poaching liquor:

100ml	white wine
200ml	fish stock

ORGANIC SALMON MINESTRONE WITH MACARONI

BY JAMES DUGAN

I have chosen this and the following two dishes due to the fact that they have aesthetic value and show good use of British and European produce.

METHOD

minestrone:

Cut all the vegetables small to minimise the time of cooking, sweat the onions down in olive oil for a few minutes until soft add the fennel, garlic and carrot for approximately 5 minutes then the chopped bacon, bay leaf and tomato purée.

Finally, add the chopped tomatoes then the stock and bring to the boil, simmer for 30 minutes lightly purée in a blender and pass through a sieve, season lightly with salt and pepper to your taste.

pasta:

Place the pasta flour, yolks, olive oil and water in a bowl mix until mixture comes together, knead until you achieve a smooth texture to the dough then rest for 30 min in the fridge.

Using a pasta machine roll the dough down to a number 2, lightly flour the surface of the pasta, taking a long skewer roll the pasta over to form a roll, cut the pasta slide the skewer out and allow to dry, once dry cut to 2 to 3 inches in length, repeat the process several times until you have sufficient macaroni to do the job, approximately 4 per portion.

Blanch the pasta in boiling water until cooked then refresh in cold water.

garnish:

Peel and cut the carrot into a small neat dice 5mm/5mm blanch in boiling water until cooked then refresh in cold water.

Cut the base off the asparagus and lightly blanch in boiling water, refresh and cut to cylinders of similar sizes to the carrots.

Blanch the tomatoes in boiling water for 10 seconds then refresh in ice water, remove skin and seeds and discard, then dice the flesh to the same size as the carrots.

Cut the Parma ham into a dice of similar size to other garnishes.

assembly:

Bring the fish stock and wine to the simmer, lightly season, place the salmon into the stock and allow to poach for 2-3 minutes.

Bring the soup to the boil and check seasoning, meanwhile arrange the garnish in the bottom of your serving bowls.

Warm through your pasta, season and arrange on top of the garnish, lay the salmon over the pasta and finally pour the soup around the salmon.

Finish with some leaves and croutons.

 RECOMMENDED WINE
Chablis 1er Cru Vaillons –
Domaine Long-Depaquit – Burgundy

WEST COUNTRY RED MULLET, SWEET AND SOUR CARROTS, TOMATO FONDUE AND SCOTTISH LANGOUSTINES

BY JAMES DUGAN

Serves 4

Preparation time: 3 hours

Cooking time: 10 minutes

Planning ahead: The purée, polenta, fondue and sauce can be

made the day before.

INGREDIENTS

red mullet:

4	120-140g red mullet fillets
8	medium langoustines

sweet and sour carrots:

20	baby carrots
100ml	rice wine vinegar
150g	Brown sugar
5g	ginger
1	lime juice and zest
4	cardamom pods, split

tomato fondue:

250g	plum tomato "concasse"
1	shallot
1	garlic clove
1 tsp	tomato purée
50ml	white wine
½ tsp	thyme

spiced carrot purée:

3	carrots
50g	butter
1	pinch cumin
1	pinch caraway seeds
2	pinches curry powder
300ml	water

sauce:

shells from langoustines	
1	shallot
1	garlic clove
1	carrot
1	bay leaf
1	star anise
1 tsp	tomato purée
30ml	brandy
200ml	water
50ml	whipping cream

polenta:

125g	polenta
10g	cream cheese
70g	parmesan
370ml	chicken stock

METHOD

sweet and sour carrots:

Peel and blanch the carrots in boiling water, refresh and set aside.
Boil the vinegar, sugar, ginger, limes and cardamoms together and reduce by two thirds, allow to cool then place the carrots into infuse until needed.

fondue:

Sweat the finely chopped shallots and garlic in olive oil until soft, add the thyme tomato purée and then deglaze with white wine, reduce by ½, add the skinned and deseeded tomatoes to the pan and cook out over a gentle heat until fondue is reduce to a purée form with little moisture. Pass through a coarse sieve and season with salt pepper and a little of the reduced vinegar mix from the carrots.

carrot purée:

Melt the butter then add the spices, then peel and grate carrots and add to the spices, allow to gently cook down for 5-10 minutes or so.
Cover with the water simmer for approx 30 minutes, strain through a sieve reserving the liquor.
Blend the carrot mix adding the stock until the mix freely blends, season and pass through a fine sieve.

sauce:

Roast the shells in olive oil until golden, remove from the pan and set aside, add the vegetables to the pan, sweat until golden then add the star anise, bay leaf and purée, deglaze with brandy then return shells to the pan and top with water, simmer for 30 minutes pass off and reduce liquor to a glace.
Add cream bring to the boil season and set aside for use.

polenta:

Bring the stock to the boil add the polenta and stir continuously over a medium heat until polenta grain softens.
Remove from the heat, add the cream cheese, parmesan and season, shape into quenelles using two teaspoons, chill and deep fry until golden. When needed, season.

assembly:

Gently sauté the mullet until golden, approximately 3-4 minutes, sauté the langoustine in the same pan during the last 20 seconds of cooking, remove and set aside.
Warm the carrots in the vinegar mix, warm the fondue, carrot purée and fry the polenta until golden.
Lay down the carrots, place the mullet on top, then place the langoustines on top of the mullet, spread the purée, fondue and polenta next to the fish, top with leaves, warm the sauce and serve.

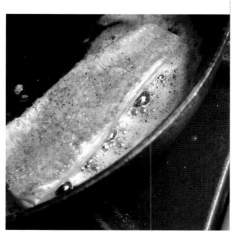

 RECOMMENDED WINE
Les Terrasses du Château Gris Blanc –
Nuits-St-Georges – Burgundy

SPICED FIG CAKE, LEMON JELLY AND TOASTED ALMOND FOAM

BY JAMES DUGAN

Serves 4

Preparation time: 6 hours plus

Cooking time: 13 minutes

Special equipment:

Hand blender to lift the almond foam

Planning ahead:

All can be done the day before with the exception of the foam, which needs to be made prior to serving.

INGREDIENTS

spiced fig cake:

150g	butter
60g	plain flour
45g	ground almonds
½ tsp	ground cinnamon
½ tsp	ground ginger
½ tsp	ground mixed spice
180g	caster sugar
2 tbsp	honey
4	egg whites
½ tsp	baking powder
1	fig

lemon jelly:

100ml	lemon juice
100ml	water
1½	gelatine leaves
60g	caster sugar

fig ice cream:

200ml	milk
50ml	whipping cream
2	yolks
40g	caster sugar
160g	figs, puréed

fig cream:

80g	figs, puréed
50g	whipping cream
45g	caster sugar
100g	eggs
100g	unsalted butter
1	gelatine leaf

chocolate case:

100g	dark chocolate

almond foam:

50ml	whipping cream
200ml	semi skimmed milk
40g	caster sugar
100g	flaked almonds

🍷 **RECOMMENDED WINE**
Rasteau Rancio –
Rhône

METHOD

spiced fig cake:

Whisk the egg white with the sugar until stiff, place the butter into a pan and lightly cook to a nut brown colour add the honey and allow to cool. Take the flour, spices, almonds, sugar and baking powder and sieve it into the whites, fold in gently, once incorporated fold in the butter.

Place into a mould measuring 3 inches wide x 2 inches high and cut a fig into ¼ then set each piece into one of the sponge mixtures, set aside until ready for use.

lemon jelly:

Soak the gelatine in cold water until soft, warm the lemon, sugar, and water until sugar is dissolved add the gelatine and pass through a sieve into a container.

Pour the solution into a martini glass and place into the fridge to set up.

fig ice cream:

Bring to the boil your cream, fig purée and milk.

Mix together your eggs, sugar and pour over the hot milk solution, return to a gentle heat and stir to a light coating consistency, remove from the heat, strain through a sieve and allow to cool, once cool churn through your ice cream machine.

fig cream:

Warm your fig purée and cream together, mix the eggs and sugar together and pour over the hot cream solution, return to a gentle heat and stir continuously until it thickens to a good coating consistency. Remove from the heat, add the softend gelatine and butter until fully dissolved strain through a fine sieve and cool, refrigerate for 8 hours before use.

chocolate case:

Melt your chocolate and spread it onto 2 acetate sheet measuring 5 inches x 10 inches, then roll them into a cylinder trying to leave a circumference of 0.5-1 inch, wrap this in clingfilm to hold the shape whilst the chocolate is setting. Give them 10 hours to set at room temperature. When ready to cut use a warm thin knife and cut to size required.

almond foam:

Toast your flaked almonds in the oven until golden then place cream, milk and sugar into a pan with the almonds, place on a low heat and infuse for 1 hour.

Pass through a sieve and keep warm, blend with a hand blender when needed to lift the foam.

assembly:

Bake the fig cake at 180°C for 13 minutes, turn out onto the slates garnished with a little purée, place the glass down and top with the ice cream then the foam, last of all fill the chocolate tubes with the fig cream and serve.

GRAVETYE MANOR

MARK RAFFAN

Mark was born and bred just a few miles down the road from Gravetye Manor where he has spent most of his professional career starting as a Commis Chef in 1981 and culminating in becoming co-owner with Andrew Russell in 2004. Mark's professional career spans some four years as apprentice at the Eaton Restaurant in Hove, Sussex, followed by three years as a Commis Chef at Gravetye, one year at the Walper Terrace Hotel in Kitchener, Ontario, Canada, followed by one year at Le Gavroche under Albert Roux, two years as Sous Chef at Gravetye and then three years as Head Chef and a penultimate three and a half years as Executive Chef to King Hussein of Jordan. Mark then returned to Gravetye where he now lives with his wife Paula and four children Georgia, Charlie, Harry and Archie.

Serves 4

Preparation time:	30 minutes
Cooking time:	10 minutes

SEARED HEBREDIAN SCALLOPS WITH A FRICASSEE OF COCKLES MUSSELS AND LANGOUSTINE

BY MARK RAFFAN

This is one of my favourite fish starters it is light with great subtle flavours of the sea, the sweetness of the caramelised scallops and langoustine is balanced with the natural saltiness of the cockles and mussels. A great dish for summer.

INGREDIENTS

12	large diver caught scallops (cut out of the shell and roe discarded)
500g	fresh live mussels (cleaned and washed)
500g	fresh live cockles (cleaned and washed)
12	large fresh langoustine (peeled, keep the shells for the sauce)
2	peeled shallots (roughly chopped)
½	head of garlic (roughly chopped)
1	bottle of white wine
500ml	double cream
2	tomatoes (peeled, deseeded and chopped)
1	small leek (cleaned and sliced into roundels)
1	small bunch of chives (chopped)
1	small bunch of parsley
1	small selection of micro herbs for garnish
150g	butter
salt and pepper for seasoning	

METHOD

Place a heavy bottomed saucepan onto the stove and let it get very hot, pour the white wine into another pan and bring to the boil. Place the mussels into the hot pan and add half the boiling wine, cover with a lid and let steam for two minutes until all the mussels have opened pour out of the pan into a colander keeping the cooking juices. Repeat the same process for the cockles. Set aside 12 of the mussels and 12 of the cockles in their shells for the garnish, pick the rest out of the shells and keep to one side.

Pour both of the cooking liquors into a pan add the garlic shallots parsley and langoustine shells. Reduce by half. Add the cream and reduce again by one third whisk in the butter and then pass into a clean pan season and keep warm.

Place a small pan onto the stove add a small knob of butter and then the leeks. Gently sweat until soft. Season with salt and pepper and keep warm.

Place a heavy bottomed frying pan onto the stove add a little oil and get nice and hot. Season the scallops with sea salt and black pepper. Place the scallops into the pan and fry for aproximately one and a half minutes turn over and cook for a further one and a half minutes. Take out of the pan and drain onto kitchen paper, season with a little lemon juice.

Place the sauce back onto the stove and bring up to the boil take off of the heat and add your cockles, mussels (both in and out of the shell), langoustine tomato and chives. Let warm through, do not reboil as this will make your shellfish tough.

to serve:

To plate the dish take 4 warm big bowls, place a little of the leek into the bowl, arrange three scallops on top of the leek, arrange three of each of the cockles, mussels (in the shell) and langoustine tail around the scallops. Spoon around the remaining cockles, mussels, tomato and chives. Garnish with a little micro herbs and serve immediately.

RECOMMENDED WINE

*Vacqueyras Vieilles Vignes Blanc –
Domaine Le Clos des Cazaux – Rhône*

Serves 4

Preparation time:	30 minutes
Cooking time:	20 minutes

CANNON OF SPRING LAMB WITH GRATIN POTATOES, ASPARAGUS AND MINTED HOLLANDAISE

BY MARK RAFFAN

Spring is one of the most exciting times of the year for me the first arrival of locally bred spring lamb cutting the first heads of asparagus from our walled kitchen garden and grabbing a bunch of our mint on the way back to the kitchen. This is what cooking is all about.

INGREDIENTS

1	loin of spring lamb
4	Desiree potatoes
12	asparagus tips
4	portions of fresh Spinach picked and washed
4	portions lamb sauce (see recipe below)
4	portions mint hollandaise (see recipe below)
250ml	cream
2	cloves garlic
salt and pepper	

for the sauce:
This can be made well before cooking the dish

1 kg	roasted lamb bones
1	carrot peeled and diced
1	onion peeled and diced
1	stock of celery peeled and diced
1	leek peeled and diced
1	head garlic
3	sprigs of rosemary
3	sprigs of thyme
1	glass of white wine
1 ltr	stock, preferably veal

for the hollandaise:

1	whole egg
1	egg yolk
2 tbsp	reduction
250g	butter
2 tbsp	fresh chopped mint

for the reduction:

1	shallot, chopped
6	black peppercorns
1	sprig tarragon
50ml	white wine
5ml	white wine vinegar

RECOMMENDED WINE
Vacqueyras Grenat Noble Rouge –
Domaine Le Clos des Cazaux – Rhône

METHOD

potatoes:

Peel the potatoes and slice each potato into 3 even slices.
Cut out with 1 inch diameter pastry cutter.
Bring the cream and crushed garlic to the boil.
Season with salt and pepper.
Place all the potato discs into cream and gently cook until potatoes are soft.
Take out of the cream and place on a baking tray, spoon a little of the sauce over each potato disc.
Place to one side ready for finishing.

asparagus:

Peel the asparagus and cut off the tips about 3cm long.
Slice the rest into roundels on the angle.

spinach:

Place a large pan onto a hob stove, heat until almost smoking then add a little olive oil and butter. Plunge in the washed spinach and vigorously stir until totally wilted. Season with salt and pepper and turn into a colander to drain. Lightly press the excess juice from the spinach and keep warm ready for serving.

lamb:

Seal the lamb in a hot pan and place in a hot oven for approximately 6 minutes. Take out and leave in a warm place to rest for a further 6 minutes.

the sauce:

Sauté all the chopped vegetables, garlic, thyme and rosemary in a heavy bottomed pan until lightly browned. Deglaze with the white wine then add the roasted bones and the veal stock and reduce on a high heat by two thirds.
Strain through a fine sieve.
Season with salt and pepper and keep ready for use.

hollandaise:

Melt the butter and keep warm.
Place the egg yolks and reduction into a round bottomed bowl, whisk over a pan of boiling water until egg mix becomes like a smooth thick double cream.
Take off the heat and gently whisk in the warm melted butter and add the freshly chopped mint.
Season and keep in a warm place ready for use.

the reduction:

Place in a saucepan and reduce by three quarters and strain.

to assemble:

To plate the lamb take a warm oval plate and place three small piles of spinach horizontally along it.

Place a gratin potato on top of each pile of spinach and slice the lamb into three even medallions. Season with a little salt and then place these on top of the potato.

Place one asparagus tip onto each piece of lamb and then nape with a little of the minted hollandaise and sprinkle the asparagus roundels around.

Carefully sauce the dish and serve immediately.

Chef's tip:

I have been buying my English Lamb from L.A. Miller and Son for the past ten years. I find using a local village butcher works extremely well as they know the quality I require and are always in close contact concerning the quantities and cuts I require. Peter Miller sources all his lamb personally so I always know that I will get the best quality available.

Serves 4

Preparation time: 15 minutes

Cooking time: 20 minutes

INGREDIENTS

125g	butter
250g	caster sugar
125g	soft flour
4 medium	eggs – separated
550ml	milk
2½	lemons, juice and grated zest

double cream, to serve

LEMON PUDDING

BY MARK RAFFAN

This was my grandmother's recipe and has always been a real favourite.

METHOD

Place the softened butter in to a food mixer, add the sugar and beat until white and fluffy. Slowly add the egg yolks, followed by the lemon zest and juice. Turn speed of mixer down to as slow as it will all go and add the flour and mix slowly until well incorporated, then slowly add all the milk. The mixture will go very runny and will look split but don't worry, this is correct!

Whisk up the egg whites to peak in another bowl, then fold them into the lemon mixture. Fill 4 x 4 inch diameter ramekins right to the top and bake in a bain-marie at 160°C for 20 minutes.

to serve:

Serve with thick double cream.

 RECOMMENDED WINE

Coteaux de Saumur –
Domaine de la Paleine – Saumur

LOWER SLAUGHTER MANOR

'Queen of the Cotswolds'

DAVID KELMAN

David started his career at Bodysgallen Hall hotel as a Commis in pastry. After three and a half years and at the position of Chef de Partie he left to go to a larger hotel. Three years later he returned to Bodysgallen as a Junior Sous Chef and after a short time was promoted to Senior Sous Chef and then helped the Head Chef gain three rosettes and the hotel gain four red stars. Four years later David had the opportunity to move to the Cotswolds and Lower Slaughter Manor, and the chance to make a reputation for himself and the hotel. So far he has had four great years at Lower Slaughter, and the hotel has gained three AA rosettes and Relais & Châteaux property status since he has become Head Chef.

Serves 4

Preparation time: 1-2 hours
Cooking time: N/A

Planning ahead:
The trout needs to be prepared 48 hours in advance.

INGREDIENTS

1	fillet of trout from a 1-2kg trout (remove all pin bones)

salt mix:

200g	sea salt
200g	granulated sugar
1	lemon (chopped small)
30g	coriander
1	sprig of thyme
100ml	white wine
1	chilli (chopped)
20g	ginger (peeled and chopped)
2	cloves of garlic (crushed)
2	shallots (sliced)

marinated cucumber:

1	peeled cucumber
30g	ginger (finely grated)
¼	red chilli (finely chopped)
15g	toasted sesame seeds
2 tbsp	sesame seed oil
100ml	extra virgin oil
2 tbsp	fish sauce
3 tbsp	soy sauce
20g	chopped coriander

wasabi mayonnaise:

100g	mayonnaise
1 tsp	lemon Juice
	wasabi paste

for garnish:

mixed salad or micro cress
sliced radish
herb oil (optional)

HOME CURED DONNINGTON TROUT, WHITE RADISH, SESAME MARINATED CUCUMBER, WASABI MAYONNAISE AND MICRO CRESS

BY DAVID KELMAN

Using local freshwater trout and combining it with the marinated cucumber and wasabi mayo brings out the clean wonderful flavours from the trout.

METHOD

trout:

Mix all the ingredients in a bowl, except for the trout.
Place ½ the salt mix into a deep container (which is long and deep enough for the trout).
Lay the trout on top of the salt, skin side down and then pour the rest of the salt over the top.
Leave in the fridge for 36 hours.
Remove from the fridge and wash off any salt mix.
Pat dry and put in the fridge wrapped in clingfilm.

marinated cucumber:

Using a peeler, make ribbons of cucumber but don't peel the seeds.
Mix the rest of the ingredients and place the cucumber into the mix, season with salt and pepper.
Place into the fridge for 1-2 hours.

wasabi mayonaise:

Mix the wasabi paste, mayonnaise and lemon juice. Use as much wasabi as you like, it all depends on how hot you like it.

to serve:

Slice the trout thinly and dress centre plate with 4-5 slices.
Drain off excess liquid from the cucumber and add to the plate.
Place three drops of the mayonnaise around the plate and drag a spoon through for effect.
Place sliced radish next to each mayonnaise swipe.
Drizzle herb oil (optional) and dress with cress or small salad leaf.

 RECOMMENDED WINE
Montagny 1er Cru Blanc –
Maison Albert Sounit – Côte Chalonnaise

FILLET OF OLD SPOT PORK ROLLED IN DRIED TROMPETTE MUSHROOM AND ASIAN SPICES, CRACKLING, WARM PORK BELLY, AND SAGE AND ONION BON BON

BY DAVID KELMAN

This is a play on pork, apple sauce, sage and onion and crackling using old spot pork but in a modern way.

Serves 4

Preparation time:
2-3 hours

Cooking time:
1-2 hours

Special equipment:
2 heavy flat trays
Clingfilm
Rubber rectangle baby food trays for the jelly
Small fat fryer
Fine sieve for the apple sauce
Meat slicer or very sharp knife

Planning ahead:
Cook the belly pork and shred when hot. Cook the pork crackling, roll and then freeze.

INGREDIENTS

pork fillet:

2 x 225g	pork fillet
10g	cep powder (or mushroom powder)
10g	tropette powder (or mushroom powder)
10g	khmeli suneli (from MSK) or chinese five spice

sage and onion bon bon:

200g	Maris Piper potatoes cooked then mashed
½	onion small diced and cooked in butter
5g	chopped sage cooked with the onion
	salt and pepper
1	egg
	splash of milk
30g	flour
100g	breadcrumbs

braised belly pork jelly:

125g	belly pork
575ml	of chicken stock
¼	stick of lemon grass
¼	chilli
1	sprig of tarragon
10g	fresh ginger
1	clove garlic
50ml	oyster sauce
50ml	honey
1	apple peeled and grated
5g	agar agar (MSK)

umbrian lentil and cabbage:

20g	of lentils
40g	of shredded Savoy cabbage

petit brunoise of ¼ carrot, ¼ leek, 1 shallot, and 100g of swede.

150ml	of chicken stock

apple sauce:

1	Granny Smith apples
100ml	cider

pork crackling:

½	large skin of pork.
	cep powder
	smoked paprika

to serve:

1	large baby carrot peeled and cooked

METHOD

pork fillet:

Trim all the fat and sinew off the fillet.
Roll it in the mushroom powder and the khmeli.
Roll tightly in clingfilm.
To cook, slow roast at 140°C for 12 minutes. Leave to rest for 10-15 minutes.

sage and onion bon bon:

Mix the onion, sage, mashed potato. Season and roll into 50g balls, Flour, egg wash and breadcrumb the balls then deep fry until golden brown.

braised belly pork jelly:

Put the lemon grass, chillies, garlic, tarragon, ginger, oyster sauce, and honey into a blender and mix well and pass.
Place the pork into a deep roasting tray, add the chicken stock and the above mixture and slowly braise for 4 hours.
When cooked strain off the liquid and keep it, pass trough muslin cloth.
Shred the pork, mix with the apple and season, add a little bit of the stock. Using 500ml of stock and the agar agar, bring to the boil.
Put the pork into the mould and top with the agar agar stock. Put into the fridge to set.

umbrian lentil and cabbage:

Wash the lentils and then cook in the chicken stock, when the lentils are just cooked. Add the cabbage and the brunoise of vegetable cook for a further 5 mins the take off the heat then season.

apple sauce:

Chop up the apples and put in with the cider.
Put into a pan and place a tight lid on top and cook until soft.
Pass through a sieve then put to one side.

pork crackling:

Cook the skin for 1 ½ hours.
Refresh.
Scrape off the fat and meat until clean, dust with salt, cep, and smoked paprika.
Roll up like a Swiss roll, roll in clingfilm tightly then freeze.
Slice very thinly on the meat slicer cook between 2 heavy trays and greaseproof for about 20 minutes. Season.

to serve:

Slice each pork fillet into five.
Place the warm pork jelly centrally on the plate.
On one side of the jelly spoon a little of the cabbage.
Sit the bon-bon on a little apple purée.
Cut root end of the carrot so it will sit high.
Place the sliced pork on top of the cabbage.
Dress with pork gravy and the rounds of crackling.

RECOMMENDED WINE
Rully & Rully 1er Cru Rouge –
Maison Albert Sounit – Côte Chalonnaise

PASSION FRUIT SOUFFLÉ, POMEGRANATE SORBET AND KIWI PASTEL BY DAVID KELMAN

I love the aromatic flavour in the passion fruit and pomegranate and this dessert blends the two fantastically.

Serves 4

Preparation time: 2-3 hours

Cooking time: 1-2 hours

Special equipment:
Small ramekins
Mixer with whisk
Small deep tray for the pastel
Ice cream machine

Planning ahead:
You can make the soufflé base, kiwi pastel and the pomegranate sorbet the day before.

INGREDIENTS

soufflé base:

250g	passion fruit juice
5	passion fruits (scoop out the fruit)
20g	cornflower (diluted with water)

passion fruit soufflé:

2	egg whites
160g	caster sugar
	lemon sherbet
	soft butter
1 tbsp	soufflé base

stock syrup:

750g	sugar
1150ml	water

pomegranate sorbet:

250ml	stock syrup
250ml	pomegranate juice
1	pomegranate (just the seeds)

kiwi pastel:

250ml	kiwi juice
8g	pectin powder
25g	caster sugar
250g	caster sugar
2g	citric acid (diluted with a little bit of water)
75g	glucose

kiwi and pineapple salad:

1	kiwi (peeled and diced)
100g	small diced pineapple
3g	sugar
2 drops	lemon juice

METHOD

soufflé base:

Boil the juice and fresh passion fruit. When boiling, add the cornflower and thicken to a paste. Cook out for ten minutes then strain through a fine sieve.

passion fruit soufflé:

Whisk the egg whites until white and fluffy, then slowly add the sugar until thick and glossy.
Put the soufflé base into a large bowl, add a little bit of egg and mix really well. Then fold the rest of the egg whites into the mix.
Butter the inside of 4 ramekins and then dust with lemon sherbet.
Place the soufflé mix into the ramekins until it is just over the top.
Smooth flat and then run your thumb around the inside of the ramekin to remove the soufflé mix away from the edge
Tap the ramekin on the table, place it in an oven of 200°C for 7 minutes.
Take out of the oven and dust with icing sugar, serve immediately.

stock syrup:

Put the ingredients into a pan and bring to the boil. When boiled, take off the heat and leave to cool.

pomegranate sorbet:

Put all the ingredients into a blender until they are mixed well, then pass through a fine sieve
Place into an ice cream machine until frozen and then place into a freezer.

kiwi pastel:

First mix 25g sugar and pectin powder together.
Boil the kiwi juice, then add the sugar and pectin powder.
Simmer, then slowly add the glucose and then the 250g of sugar.
When all the sugar has melted, boil until it reaches 106°C and then add the citric acid
Pour into a tray and place into the fridge to set.

kiwi and pineapple salad:

Mix all the ingredients together, place into a container and then into the fridge.

to serve:

Cut 2 small squares of the pastel per person and roll in sugar.
Place a small spoon of salad onto the plate, scoop a ball of sorbet onto the salad and place the 2 pastels next to the sorbet.
Take the soufflé out of the oven, dust with icing sugar and place on the plate.

RECOMMENDED WINE
Grains Nobles –
Rouvinez – Valais – Switzerland

LUCKNAM PARK

'An un-spoilt, country house living at its very best'

HYWEL JONES

Hywel Jones started his career as Chef de Partie in two three-star Michelin establishments; Chez Nico at 90 and Marco Pierre White. He then developed his skills as Junior Sous Chef at the Michelin-starred Le Soufflé. From there he went on to earn his own Michelin star working at Foliage restaurant at the Mandarin Oriental, Hyde Park where he was Head Chef for five years. He then became executive chef at Pharmacy restaurant in Notting Hill before moving to Lucknam Park in 2004. Since Hywel has been Head Chef at Lucknam he has achieved several accolades including Hotel Chef of the Year 2007, Best Restaurant outside London 2006 and one Michelin star.

Serves 4

Preparation time: 2 hours
Cooking time: 1 ½ hours

Special equipment:
Non-stick pan
Food processor
Fine sieve

Planning ahead:
The carrots, brandade mix and vinaigrette
may be prepared a day in advance.

INGREDIENTS

6	extra large scallops
16	marinated carrots
120g	cod brandade
60ml	tomato and cumin vinaigrette

marinated carrots:

16	peeled baby carrots
1	pinch saffron strands
2	finely chopped shallots
1	crushed clove of garlic
2 tbsp	olive oil
4 tbsp	orange juice
1 tbsp	chardonnay vinegar

brandade:

Makes a little more than required but will
keep well in the fridge for a few days.

100g	salted cod loin poached in garlic milk
100g	cooked, sieved, potato flesh
30ml	good olive oil
30g	grated aged parmesan
1 pinch	cayenne pepper

tomato and cumin vinaigrette:

8	very ripe cherry tomatoes roughly chopped
2	finely chopped shallots
1	clove of garlic, crushed
1 tsp	dry roasted cumin seeds, ground to a fine powder
1 tbsp	chardonnay vinegar
50ml	of light olive oil

ROAST SCALLOPS, BRANDADE FRITTERS, TOMATO AND CUMIN VINAIGRETTE, MARINATED BABY CARROTS

BY HYWEL JONES

Scallops are a favourite of mine as they can be prepared
and cooked so easily at home and my children love
playing with the shells.

METHOD

marinated carrots:

Cook the shallots, garlic and saffron in the oil until tender. Add the
vinegar and reduce to a syrup. Add the orange juice and reduce by two
thirds. Remove from the heat.
Cook the carrots in salted water until tender, drain and add to the
vinaigrette. Allot to cool. For best results prepare 1 day in advance.

brandade:

Mix drained cod and potato to a smooth purée.
Beat in the parmesan and olive oil.
Soften with a little of the cooking milk and season with the cayenne
and a little more salt if necessary.
Divide in 10g balls (3 each), coat in breadcrumbs and set aside.

tomato and cumin vinaigrette:

Cook shallots and garlic in a little olive oil.
Add cumin seeds and cook for 1 minute .
Add tomatoes and cook until dry.
Add vinegar and reduce to a syrup.
Blend until smooth and pass through a fine sieve. Whisk in the light
olive oil.

assembly:

Cut scallops in half and lightly season. Gently cook in olive oil until
golden (roughly 1 minute each side) .
Place three halves per plate and spoon vinaigrette in between.
Deep fry the fritters and place 3 per plate. Arrange carrots on top and
finish with either baby leaf salad leaves or picked herbs.

 RECOMMENDED WINE
Chevaliers Petite Arvine White
Vins des Chevaliers – Valais – Switzerland

TRIO OF ANDREW MORGAN'S BRECON LAMB, ORGANIC WATERCRESS, GREEN OLIVE PURÉE

BY HYWEL JONES

Being Welsh, lamb always plays a major role in my menus. A good friend of mine, Andrew Morgan, rears the best quality lamb that I have ever come across on his farm in Bwlch in the heart of the Brecon Beacons.

Serves 4

Preparation time:	3-4 hours
Cooking time:	3 hours

Special equipment:
Hand blender
Fine sieve

Planning ahead:
The shoulder, sweetbreads and purée may be prepared a day before.

INGREDIENTS

2 x 6oz	lamb loin fillets
150g	diced fatty lamb shoulder
2	large slices Parma ham
a few shredded basil leaves	
100ml	white wine
60g	watercress
4	plump lamb sweetbreads (optional)
2 ltr	chicken stock
100g	roughly chopped root vegetables
thyme and rosemary	
4	new potatoes
2 tbsp	double cream
a few assorted wild mushrooms	

green olive purée:

100g	pitted fresh green olives
1	finely chopped shallot
25g	butter
seeds from 3 cardamom pods	
2	celery sticks peeled and finely diced
1	sprig of thyme
50ml	white wine
100ml	chicken stock
50ml	orange juice

METHOD

braised lamb shoulder:

Gently colour the seasoned diced shoulder in a little olive oil. Remove from pan and colour two thirds of the root vegetables. Dust in a small teaspoon of flour and cook for one minute. Add wine and reduce to a syrup. Add lamb back to the pan and add enough chicken stock to cover. Bring to the boil. Add rosemary and thyme and cover. Cook in a low oven at 130°C for 2 hours until tender. Allow to cool in the braising liquor. Remove meat and gently flake discarding any sinews or fat. Season, mix in basil and moisten with a little of the cooking liquor.
Form into a cylinder shape using clingfilm and refrigerate to firm it up. Remove film and wrap in the Parma ham.

sweetbreads:

Soak overnight in salted water to remove any blood.
Rinse and gently poach in the remaining chicken stock along with the remaining root vegetables for 30 minutes. Cool.
Remove from liquor, pat dry and peel off any membrane.
Pass liquor through a fine sieve and reduce by two thirds .

new potatoes:

Peel and trim to a neat shape.
Colour gently in a pan and roast in oven until soft.

green olive purée:

Mix all ingredients together and cook until dry. Blend to a smooth purée.

assembly:

Season and seal the lamb fillets in olive oil. Cook at 160°C for 10-12 minutes. Sit it on some ruffled aluminium foil to prevent direct contact with the pan.
Allow to rest for 20 minutes.
Cut shoulder into 4 neat cylinders and pan fry until golden along with the sweetbreads that have been lightly dusted in seasoned flour.
Place a slash of the olive purée down the centre of plate. Arrange some wilted watercress to one side and the potato to the other. Place the sweetbreads on top of the potato, the shoulder at the base of the slash and carve the lamb and sit on the watercress.
Spoon a little of the reduced braising liquor around and scatter a few of the wild mushrooms around also.
Finally whisk the cream into the sweetbread stock and blend with a handblender. Spoon a little foam on top of the sweetbreads.

RECOMMENDED WINE
Il Pino Cinghiale Rosso –
Tenuta di Biserno – Tuscany – Italy

Serves 4

Preparation time: 3 hours (including time
for the parfait to
freeze)

Cooking time: 1 hour

Special equipment:
Heavy bottomed mixing bowl
Baloon or electric whisk
50mm cutter

Planning ahead:
Allow enough time to freeze the parfait.

INGREDIENTS

croustillant:

1   large peeled pineapple
4   sheets of spring rolls pastry
50g   butter
4 x 30g   discs of rum and raisin parfait
4 tbsp   coconut sorbet
icing sugar to dust

parfait:

2   egg yolks
20g   sugar
180ml   double cream
30g   raisins soaked in a good quality
dark rum

sorbet:

100ml   coconut milk (unsweetened)
35ml   water
60g   sugar
juice of lemon

CROUSTILLANT OF PINEAPPLE, RUM AND RAISIN PARFAIT, COCONUT SORBET

BY HYWEL JONES

This dessert is probably the most popular on our menu at present.

METHOD

croustillant:

Cut pineapple into four lengthways. Remove core and trim edges to create neat cylinders.
Dust with icing sugar.
Melt half the butter in a non stick pan and fry the pineapple until well caramelised. Retain the juices from the pan. Chill the pineapple pieces in the fridge.
Roll the pineapple in the spring roll pastry ensuring at least 2 layers all around. Brush with melted butter and dust with icing sugar. Cook in a hot oven (210°C) until golden and crispy (around 8 minutes).

parfait:

Whisk yolks and sugar in a bowl over steaming water until pale and fluffy. Allow to cool.
Whisk cream to ribbon stage and fold into egg mix.
Mix in raisins. Spoon onto a lined 1cm thick tray and freeze.
Cut into 50mm discs.

sorbet:

Mix ingredients and freeze in an ice cream maker.

assembly:

Cut ends off croustillant and cut in half diagonally. Stand on the plate.
Place parfait opposite and a spoon of the sorbet on top.
Drizzle the pineapple juices around with a few more of the soaked raisins.
Garnish with vanilla pod sticks and mint.

RECOMMENDED WINE
Cadillac – Château de L'Orangerie – Bordeaux

WHATLEY MANOR

'Classical French with a modern interpretation'

MARTIN BURGE

Martin Burge was awarded his second Michelin star in January 2009 for the acclaimed cuisine served in The Dining Room at Whatley Manor. Martin's cuisine is classical French with a modern interpretation. His passion for good food is inspired by working with some of the UK's most talented chefs in restaurants including Pied à Terre, L'Ortolan, Le Manoir aux Quat' Saisons and The Landmark. Other accolades include AA four Rosettes and *Which? Good Food Guide* recognising The Dining Room in the Top 30 Restaurants in the UK.

ROASTED LANGOUSTINE TAILS WITH CARAMELISED BACON AND SOY REDUCTION BY MARTIN BURGE

I like combining shellfish with eastern spices and this dish is representative of how we do this in The Dining Room.

Serves 4

Preparation time:	2 hours
Cooking time:	2 minutes (for the langoustines)

Special equipment:
A thick based pot with lid
Thermometer
Hand blender
Food processor
Liquidiser

Planning ahead:
To prepare this dish the bacon must be prepared two days in advance.

INGREDIENTS

langoustines:

12	langoustines, large
50ml	olive oil

soy glaze and reduction:

250ml	Ketchup Manis
6g	lemon grass
6g	peeled ginger
1.5g	garlic
1	red chilli

cauliflower purée:

250g	cauliflower finely chopped
65g	whipping cream
25g	butter
1.5g	white pepper
1.25g	salt

langoustine thai foam:

1.25 ltr	langoustine stock
15g	lemon grass
10g	ginger
2g	chilli
125g	milk
7g	stock syrup
	lemon to taste
	salt and pepper

garnish for the dish:

6	baby onions
30g	butter
100g	cauliflower
5g	olive oil
	salt and pepper
10g	sesame seeds

🍷 RECOMMENDED WINE
*Les Terrasses du Château Gris Blanc
Nuits-St-Georges – Burgundy*

METHOD

langoustines:

Set up a deep pan of boiling water and a bowl of iced water ready to cook your langoustines.

Prepare the langoustines by tearing the tails from the heads and removing the entrails by twisting the bottom part of the tail.

Plunge the tails into boiling water for 30 seconds and then into ice water to cool down quickly.

Peel the shells carefully away from the tails but leave the end part for presentation. Set aside in the fridge on kitchen paper ready to cook later.

soy glaze and reduction:

Chop the lemon grass, peeled ginger, red chilli and garlic into fine pieces. Mix the Ketchup Manis and all the finely chopped ingredients together and place into a small pan. Place the pan on a low heat and warm it to around 50°C and then set aside to infuse for one hour.

Pass through a fine sieve and store in the fridge in a plastic squeezey bottle ready to use. This can be made well in advance and stored in the fridge until needed.

cauliflower purée:

Place the finely chopped cauliflower into a steamer and cook on a high heat until soft in texture. Depending on how fine you cut the cauliflower this should be a quick process to retain flavour and nutritional value.

Place the cooked cauliflower into the liquidiser with the cream, butter and seasoning and blend until very smooth.

Pass through a fine sieve and cool it down quickly over a bowl of ice before storing in the fridge until needed.

langoustine thai foam:

Set up the food processor and blend the lemon grass, ginger and chilli to form a Thai paste and then divide this into two equal parts.

Place the langoustine stock into a pan with half the Thai paste and reduce over a moderate heat by 50 percent. Strain the reduced stock through a fine sieve into a smaller pan and add the second part of the paste and reduce by a further 50 percent. You should now have around 300ml of stock remaining. Strain through a fine sieve once again then add the milk, stock syrup, seasoning and lemon to taste and set aside to cool and then store in the fridge ready to use later.

garnish:

Peel and cut the baby onions into halves and cook gently in foaming butter with salt and pepper until golden brown and soft in texture.

Slice the cauliflower very thinly with a mandolin or a very sharp knife and season with a little salt, pepper and olive oil.

Toast the sesame seeds under the grill until light golden brown in colour.

to serve:

Caramelise the bacon under the grill until golden brown. Brush with the soy glaze until the bacon becomes sticky and a glaze is formed.

Take a frying pan and preheat on the stove in preparation to cook the langoustines.

Heat up the cauliflower purée in a small pan and keep warm.

Heat up the langoustine Thai foam in a small pan at around 60°C.

Season the langoustines with salt and pepper. Take the preheated hot frying pan and fry the langoustines in the olive oil until golden brown on one side and then flip the tails over to the other side. Pull the pan off the heat and allow the residual heat from the pan to cook the tails through. Note this whole cooking process should be done quickly to prevent the langoustines over cooking.

Assemble the dish in the following sequence:

Soy reduction	Onions	Cauliflower slices
Cauliflower purée	Bacon	Langoustine Thai foam
Sesame seed	Langoustine tails	

Chef's notes:

When you serve the langoustine Thai foam, make sure the temperature does not go above 60 degrees. This will then enable the structure to form properly and to create a light, airy foam.

ROASTED SQUAB PIGEON WITH CARAMELISED FOIE GRAS AND COFFEE SHERRY GEL

BY MARTIN BURGE

In this dish the bitterness of the coffee and the sweetness of the foie gras lend themselves particularly well to the earthy flavours of the squab pigeon.

Serves 4

Preparation time: 4 hours
Cooking time: 5-8 minutes (to cook the pigeon)

Special equipment:
Liquidiser

Planning ahead:
A reputable butcher will supply you with squab pigeons however make sure you give them plenty of notice to source them as they are only available from France.

INGREDIENTS

squab pigeons:

4	squab pigeons
50ml	olive oil

squab pigeon sauce:

250g	pigeon or duck bones
50g	olive oil
1.5ltr	chicken stock
50g	veal glace (optional)
50g	shallots
25g	sherry vinegar
300ml	medium sweet sherry
1g	garlic
1	sprig of thyme
½	bay leaf

cauliflower purée:

250g	cauliflower, finely chopped
65g	whipping cream
25g	butter
.5g	white pepper
1.25g	salt

sherry gel:

100ml	Pedro Ximenez sherry
25g	water
.75g	salt
4.25g	lemon juice
6g	veggie gel
25g	Pedro Ximenez sherry

coffee gel:

100ml	filtered espresso coffee
25g	water
20g	caster sugar
4.25g	lemon juice
7g	veggie gel
1.5g	salt
25g	Kahlua liqueur

foie gras:

200g	foie gras

garnish:

6 x	baby carrots
12 x	baby turnips
200g	baby spinach
20g	olive oil

RECOMMENDED WINE

Château Gris 1er Cru Rouge –
Nuits-St-Georges – Burgundy

METHOD

squab pigeons:

Remove the wishbone from the pigeon with a small sharp knife by following the bone structure and cutting it away. This is an important process to follow as it will make it easier to take the breasts off the carcase once the pigeon has cooked. You may also have a few feathers on the pigeon and these can be removed by gently burning the feathers with a blowtorch, then taking a small knife and scraping them away.

squab pigeon sauce:

Chop the bones into small pieces and roast in the oven with 20g of olive oil until light golden brown. In a medium size pan over a moderate heat add the remaining olive oil, sliced shallots, garlic, thyme and bay leaf and gently cook until the shallots are fairly soft and colourless.
Turn the heat up to a high temperature and then add the sherry vinegar and reduce until evaporated.
Add the sherry and reduce by half its volume and then add the chicken stock, optional veal glace and simmer for 2 hours skimming off any impurities.
Pass the stock through a fine sieve and return to a clean pan. Reduce the mixture to a sauce consistency. Cool down over ice water and store in the fridge until needed.

cauliflower purée:

Place the finely chopped cauliflower into a steamer and cook on a high heat until soft in texture. Make this a quick process to retain flavour and nutritional value.
Place the cooked cauliflower into the liquidiser with the cream, butter and seasoning and blend until very smooth.
Pass through a fine sieve and cool down quickly over a bowl of ice before storing in the fridge until needed.

sherry gel:

Add all the ingredients together leaving out the 25g of Pedro Ximenez into a small pan and simmer for two minutes. This method is important to follow to activate the veggie gel.
Now add the 25g of Pedro Ximenez to refresh the gel mixture and then set into a small lined container and refrigerate.
Once the gel has set and is firm to touch you can remove it from the container and cut into 1cm cubes.

coffee gel:

Add all the ingredients together except the 25g of Kahlua liqueur into a small pan and simmer for two minutes. This is important to follow to activate the veggie gel. Add the 25g of Kahlua liqueur to refresh the gel and then set into a small lined container and refrigerate. Once the gel has set and is firm to touch remove from the container and cut into 1cm cubes.

foie gras:

Cut the foie gras into four pieces and set aside in the fridge ready to cook later.

garnish:

Peel the carrots leaving the green top on and then cut into halves.
Remove the outside layer of the turnips with a small knife but keep the green tops on for presentation. Remove any large stems from the spinach and wash the leaves in a deep sink of cold water and repeat this process three times.

to serve:

Season the pigeon with salt and pepper. Place the pigeon into a moderately hot pan with a little olive oil. Colour the skin all over and then cook in a hot oven gas mark 5 for 8 minutes. Once the pigeon is roasted allow 15 minutes resting time after it's cooked to maximise the meat's tenderising process. Remove the legs and breast from the pigeon and keep warm ready to serve. Season the foie gras with salt and pepper and place directly into a hot pan caramelising both sides until golden brown.
Set up the steamer and cook the garnish starting with the turnips first, carrots second.
Fry the spinach in a large pan with a very small amount of olive oil.
Heat up the cauliflower purée and pigeon sauce in separate small pans and hold.

Assemble the dish in the following sequence:

Cauliflower purée
Spinach
Pigeon
Carrots
Foie gras
Turnips
Sherry and coffee gel
Pigeon sauce

Chef's notes:

Veggie gel can be replaced with normal leaf gelatine. If you decide to use leaf gelatine remember to soak it in cold water first and then dissolve into the warm mixture. Unlike veggie gel you must not boil leaf gelatine or the structure will break down and not set. Ratio to use would be 3g for 100ml of liquid to achieve a soft, textured result.

MANGO CANNELLONI WITH MINT ICE CREAM AND PINK GRAPEFRUIT BY MARTIN BURGE

This dish demonstrates how we use fresh mango in a variety of ways.

Serves 4

Preparation time:
3 hours (see planning ahead to save time)

Cooking time:
6 hours (after 3 hours, trim the frayed edges of the cannelloni crisps and cook for a further 3 hours)

Special equipment:

Hand blender
Ice cream machine
Silicone mat
Rectangle plastic stencil 5cm x 8cm
(this can be homemade from a Tupperware lid)
Cyclical object of 3cm diameter
3cm round plain cutter

Planning ahead:

Prepare the lime curd and mint ice cream a few days in advance to ease your workload.

INGREDIENTS

mango mousse:

200g	mango purée
60g	caster sugar
4g	leaf gelatine
100g	whipping cream
20g	lime juice

lime curd:

125g	lime juice
125g	caster sugar
50g	butter
2	limes, zest only
150g	Whole eggs

grapefruit jelly:

115g	pink grapefruit juice
115g	stock syrup 50/50
5.5g	leaf gelatine

coconut gel:

20g	desiccated coconut
100g	water
90g	coconut milk
75g	coconut purée
12.5g	caster sugar
.5g	salt
8g	Malibu
10g	veggie gel

mango cannelloni crisps:

200g	mango purée
22g	anti-humidity sugar*
1.5g	neutral acid

coconut foam:

100g	milk
100g	coconut purée
25g	desiccated coconut

mint ice cream:

100g	fresh mint
300g	milk
300g	cream
175g	caster sugar
7	egg yolks
5	drops Mint essential oil (optional)

coconut crisps:

20	strips of coconut
250g	stock syrup

to garnish:

1	pink grapefruit
1	mango
20	leaves of salad mache

🍷 RECOMMENDED WINE
Quintessence du Clos –
Domaine Le Clos des Cazaux

METHOD

mango mousse:

Dissolve the leaf gelatine in plenty of cold water until soft. Gently heat up the mango purée and caster sugar together in a pan. Dissolve the gelatine into this mixture. Pass through a fine sieve and allow to cool down. Whip up the cream to form a soft peak and then fold together with the mango purée and set in the fridge.

lime curd:

Heat up the lime juice caster sugar, butter and zest of lime together in a pan and set aside. In a separate bowl whisk your eggs until smooth and pour the hot lime mixture over the eggs and whisk until smooth. Place the combined mixture and cook over a bain marie until a thick curd is formed. Pass through a fine sieve into a bowl over iced water allowing the mixture to cool down quickly. Store in the fridge.

grapefruit jelly:

Soak the leaf gelatine in cold water until soft. In a pan heat up the grapefruit juice and stock syrup. Add the soaked gelatine to the pan and once dissolved strain through a fine sieve. Set into a plastic container lined with clingfilm, set in the fridge until firm to touch.

coconut gel:

Lightly toast the desiccated coconut under a grill. Mix together the toasted desiccated coconut and water in a pan and bring to the boil. Take off heat and set aside to infuse. Strain through a fine sieve. Add the remaining ingredients and simmer for three minutes to activate the veggie gel. Set into a plastic container lined with clingfilm. Set in the fridge until firm to touch.

mango cannelloni crisps:

Place the ingredients into a bowl and blend the mixture with a hand blender until smooth.

Using the stencil spread the mixture evenly onto a silicone mat and bake in a preheated oven at 105°C for 6 hours. After 3 hours, trim the frayed edges of the cannelloni crisps and cook for another 3 hours until the cannelloni crisps are completely dried out. Whilst hot wrap around a cyclical object of 3cm in diameter. Store the mango cannelloni crisps in a tightly sealed container containing silicone crystals.

coconut foam:

Lightly toast the desiccated coconut under a grill. Place the toasted desiccated coconut into a pan with the milk and coconut purée and gently heat until simmering. Set aside to infuse for 10 minutes. Strain the mixture through a fine sieve and once cool place in the fridge.

mint ice cream:

Place the mint and milk together in a pan and simmer. Whisk the sugar and yolks together in a bowl until smooth. Add the hot mint infused milk to the egg yolks and whisk until smooth. Return the mixture to the pan on a low heat and continue to stir until the mixture thickens. Do not allow the mixture to reach boiling point or it will curdle. Pass the mixture through a fine sieve into a bowl. Add the cream and mint essential oil. Cool down quickly over a bowl of iced water. Churn the mixture in an ice cream machine.

coconut crisps:

Place the coconut strips and stock syrup into a pan. Simmer until the coconut strips become translucent and slightly soft. Drain through a sieve and lay onto to a silicone mat. Cook in a moderately hot oven 175°C for approximately 10 to 15 minutes until golden brown and crisp in texture.

garnish:

Remove the outside layers of the grapefruit until only the flesh is remaining and then segment.

Remove the outside layer of the mango. Cut the fruit avoiding the stone. Thinly slice and divide the mango as required.

Wash the salad leaves in a deep bowl of iced water. Remove the salad leaves from the water. Drain and place in the fridge until required.

to serve:

Cut the coconut gel with a 3cm cutter. Sprinkle the tops with caster sugar and caramelise with a blowtorch.

Place the mango mousse into a piping bag and fill the mango cannelloni crisps with the mango mousse.

Assemble the dish in the following sequence:

Mango cannelloni
Coconut gel
Pink grapefruit jelly
Pink grapefruit segments
Mango slices
Lime curd
Quenelle of mint ice cream
Salad mache
Coconut crisps
Coconut foam

Chef's notes:

Many types of biscuit and tuilles go soft due to the humidity in the air. To prevent the mango cannelloni crisps going soft use silicone crystals and a tightly sealed container.

* Anti-humidity sugar is a SOSA product and can be purchased within the UK.

THE ROYAL CRESCENT

'Food that is innovative without being gimmicky'

GORDON JONES

Gordon trained at Birmingham College of Food and gained the first Gordon Ramsay scholarship before going on to work with Martin Wishart and Martin Blunos. Five years ago he joined the Royal Crescent Hotel as Demi-Chef progressing to Sous Chef and then to Head Chef. Gordon is always striving for excellence both in producing inspiring dishes for the menu and by using only the best produce and suppliers available, using local businesses wherever possible.

Serves 4

Preparation time:	30 minutes
Cooking time:	15-20 minutes

Planning ahead:
Make the langoustine stock a day ahead.

SHORT POACHED MONKFISH CHEEK, JERUSALEM ARTICHOKES, CAULIFLOWER "COUS COUS" LANGOUSTINE CLARIFICATION

BY GORDON JONES

I chose this dish for the cookbook because it's a wonderful light summery dish which incorporates different textures, flavours, techniques and also for its good looks!

INGREDIENTS

4	medium sized monkfish cheeks
1 ltr	langoustine stock for clarification

"cous cous":

1	banana shallot
1	clove of garlic
1	romanesco cauliflower, small
10g	Pommery mustard
3	drops white truffle oil
1 tsp	crème fraîche
salt and pepper	
squeeze of lemon juice	
verjus	
100g	baby spinach
50g	wild garlic

artichokes:

250g	Jerusalem artichokes
2	sprigs thyme
a knob butter	

garnish:

chives, finely chopped

METHOD

For the clarification make the langoustine stock and freeze in 2 inch thick blocks. Once frozen solid place the stock in muslin cloth and allow defrosting overnight into a tray. The stock in the tray should be crystal clear this is your clarification.

"cous cous":

For the "cous cous" finely chop the shallot, garlic and romanesco cauliflower, with all the stalks removed. The cauliflower should look like cous cous grains. Bind with a teaspoon of crème fraîche, mustard and season with salt, pepper, truffle oil and a little verjus.

monkfish:

Poach the monkfish cheeks in a little fish stock for 3-4 minutes remove from the stock and leave to rest for another 2 minutes.

artichokes:

Peel the artichokes cut them into discs and pan fry in a little thyme and butter until tender and golden brown.

to assemble:

Place the artichokes in a ring in the centre of the bowl and press. Next add the cauliflower cous cous then the wilted spinach and wild garlic so you end up with a little gateau of artichoke, cauliflower and spinach. Next place the poached monkfish cheek on top and sprinkle with finely chopped chives. Serve the consommé warm (not boiled) in a jug on the side and pour into the bowl at the table.

RECOMMENDED WINE

La Rosée du Château de Pressac –
Château de Pressac – Bordeaux

ROAST LOIN OF FALLOW DEER, CEP RISOTTO, ICE WINE VINEGAR JELLY, PARSLEY PURÉE

BY GORDON JONES

The venison is a really robust dish which combines sweet, sour, savoury, hot and cold and all of these flavours come together to form one of my favourite venison dishes.

Serves 4

Preparation time:	20 minutes
Cooking time:	20 minutes

INGREDIENTS

1	loin of fallow deer

risotto:

250g	Arborio rice
1 ltr	venison stock
2	banana shallots
1	clove of garlic
100ml	Madeira
50g	cep powder
50g	parmesan
25g	butter
Trimmings from ceps	

jelly:

250ml	ice wine vinegar
15g	powdered vegetable gelatine
bunch of flat leaf parsley	
salt and pepper to taste	

garnish:

mustard frills
parsley purée

250g	whole ceps
100g	crosne

METHOD

venison:

Portion the venison and season in chopped tarragon, salt and pepper and a little ground coffee beans, wrap in clingfilm and poach at 55.5°C for 25 minutes. Once cooked remove from the clingfilm and seal in a very hot pan and leave to rest.

risotto:

For the risotto finely chop one shallot and half a clove of garlic and sweat off with the diced stalks of the ceps and cep powder made from all the trimmings, add rice and cook for two minutes then deglaze with Madeira and carry on cooking slowly adding the venison stock a bit at a time until the rice is tender. Finish the risotto with parmesan and butter to give a creamy finish.

jelly:

For the jelly heat the ice wine vinegar up 65°C then add the vegetable gelatine, and cook out for a further 3 minutes then cool on a flat tray.

to assemble:

Pan fry the ceps. Place the risotto in a neat line on the plate and finely slice the venison and place on the risotto, then arrange the pan fried ceps and sweet pickled crosne on the venison. Cut the ice wine vinegar jelly into a long strip and pipe five dots of parsley purée. Garnish with the mustard cress and then sauce.

RECOMMENDED WINE

Château de Pressac –
Saint-Émilion Grand Cru – Bordeaux

CIGAR POACHED PLUMS, OAT CAKES AND BALVENIE ICE CREAM

BY GORDON JONES

This is a good autumnal dish that reminds me of Scotland so I had to include it to be true to my roots.

Serves 4

Preparation time: 40 minutes
Cooking time: 1-1 ½ hours

INGREDIENTS

plums:

4	mirabelle plums.
5g	mixed spice
fresh grated nutmeg	
1	vanilla pod
1	lemon, juiced
¼	of a Griffin cigar
250ml	stock syrup

oat cakes:

375g	oats
375g	plain white flour
9oz	butter
5g	salt
10g	bicarbonate of soda
75g	soft brown sugar
Balvenie whiskey, matured in port wood	

ice cream:

200ml	milk
250ml	double cream
50g	chestnuts
a splash of Balvenie whiskey	
100g	caster sugar
125g	egg yolk
50g	glucose syrup

METHOD

poached plums:

First infuse ¼ of the cigar in a little hot water, after 10 minutes remove the cigar from the water and squeeze out any excess liquid. Blanch the plums in water for 20 seconds then plunge into cold water to stop the cooking process; you should then be able to peel the plums. Place the peeled plums into a vacuum pack bag and add mixed spice, vanilla, nutmeg, stock syrup, the cigar water and a splash of lemon juice. Seal the bag and poach at 55.5°C for 35 minutes.

oat cakes:

For the oat cakes cream sugar and butter and then add all the dry ingredients and bind with a splash of whiskey. Chill the mix in the fridge for 20 minutes then roll out to the desired thickness and bake for 40 minutes at 140°C. As soon as the oat cakes are cooked remove them from the oven and cut into diamonds and cool on a cooling wire.

ice cream:

To make the ice cream heat milk and cream together with the glucose syrup, then mix the sugar and egg yolks and slowly pour the hot liquid over. Cook the custard until it coats the back of a spoon. Pass the mix through a fine sieve and chill over night. Add the whiskey to taste just before churning. Once the ice cream is churned add some of the chestnuts to the ice cream and mix being careful not to break the chestnuts up too much.

to serve:

Warm the poached plums in some of the poaching liquid, then arrange between the oat cakes and a little of the whiskey ice cream and some fresh blackberries. Blitz all the trimmings from the oat cakes with a little soft brown sugar until it resembles breadcrumbs, sprinkle a little of the crumbs on the plate and place a scoop of the ice-cream onto the crumbs. To garnish use a few blackberries, blackberry purée and quince purée.

RECOMMENDED WINE
Rasteau Rancio – Rhône

BUCKLAND MANOR

'Fresh local produce from the neighbouring Vale of Evesham.' 'One of the very finest restaurants in Gloucestershire'

MATTHEW HODGKINS

Matt's passion for cooking started at an early age when he first baked cakes with his two grandmothers. He enjoyed cooking at school and then went on to study at Worcester College. Following this he began his first position in the kitchen, as Commis, and worked his way up to Sous Chef and then finally as Head Chef at Buckland Manor. He has focused on refining his skills at Buckland and the team strive to produce outstanding dishes using the local produce of the area.

Serves 4

Preparation time: 15 minutes

Cooking time: 1 hour (setting time)

Special equipment:
Darimoulds

Planning ahead:
This can be made the day before serving.

INGREDIENTS

panna cotta:

375ml   double cream
175ml   whole milk
20g   stilton
3 ½   leaves of gelatine

salad:

6   figs
24   walnuts
butter and brown sugar
mixed leaves of rocket

CROPWELL BISHOP STILTON PANNA COTTA WITH ROASTED BLACK FIGS AND WALNUT SALAD

BY MATTHEW HODGKINS

On a lovely summer's day this simple dish has really outstanding flavours.

METHOD

panna cotta:

Soak gelatine in cold water.
Warm double cream and milk, add crumbled stilton.
Add gelatine and whisk until dissolved.
Leave to cool, pour into moulds before it sets.

salad:

Cut figs into quarters and sauté with walnuts in a little butter and sugar.

to serve:

Use a small knife to loosen panna cotta, place in centre of plate.
Spoon figs and walnuts around panna cotta and finish with leaves.

Chef's tip:

While mix is cooling, whisk every 10 minutes to prevent stilton settling on the bottom.

RECOMMENDED WINE
Calamin Grand Cru Blanc –
Louis Bovard – Vaud Switzerland

FILLET OF NEW SEASON LAMB WITH BLACK TRUFFLE CRUST, PARMESAN POTATOES AND LAMB REDUCTION

BY MATTHEW HODGKINS

In the Cotswolds you cannot beat new season lamb.

Serves 4

Preparation time: 30 minutes

Cooking time: 15-20 minutes

Special equipment:
Good quality non-stick pan

Planning ahead:
You can make the stock in advance.

INGREDIENTS

approx 16oz fillet new season lamb
1   black truffle finely diced
1   savoy cabbage
butter

lamb reduction:

lamb bones
1   carrot
1   leek
1   red onion

parmesan potatoes:

6   baking potatoes
2   cloves garlic
bunch fresh thyme
finely grated parmesan

METHOD

preparation:

Slice the cabbage and blanch in boiling water and refresh.
Prep the lamb and place in fridge.

reduction:

Roast the bones, carrot, onion and leek.
Place in a stock pot, add garlic and thyme and simmer for 1-2 hours until reduced.
Pass and chill.

potatoes:

Top and tail potatoes and cut into quarters, shape into barrels, keeping one side flat, then cut into the potato at an angle all the way along.
Roast.
When cooked, add chopped garlic, thyme and parmesan. Glaze under a hot grill.

lamb:

Seal the lamb well, add truffle and knob of butter, finish in hot oven.
When cooked pink, rest.

to serve:

Place stock in pan and reduce to a glaze. Heat cabbage in butter and place on plate. Serve the sliced lamb on top, with potatoes on the side. Finish with the reduction.

Chef's tip:

When preparing the lamb, make sure you remove all fat and sinew.

RECOMMENDED WINE
*Primus Classicus Cornalin Rouge –
Caves Orsat – Valais*

RICH DARK CHOCOLATE CAKE WITH BLOOD ORANGE ICE CREAM

BY MATTHEW HODGKINS

This is a lovely rich cake complemented well by the blood orange ice cream.
A fantastic way to finish off a meal.

Serves 4

Preparation time:	30 minutes
Cooking time:	50-60 minutes

Special equipment:
Ice cream machine

INGREDIENTS

cake:

100g	dark chocolate
100g	butter
½ tsp	instant coffee dissolved in 2oz boiling water
100g	muscovado sugar
100g	caster sugar
45g	self raising flour
40g	plain flour
15g	cocoa powder
Pinch	bicarbonate soda
2	eggs
40ml	buttermilk

ganache:

300g	dark chocolate, melted
150g	double cream
blood	orange ice cream
500ml	double cream
500ml	whole milk
12	egg yolks
200g	caster sugar
300g	blood orange purée

METHOD

cake:

Melt chocolate over a bain-marie, together with butter and coffee, leave to cool.

Mix together sugar, flour, cocoa and bicarbonate soda.

In a separate bowl, whisk together eggs and buttermilk then blend egg mixture into chocolate, until smooth.

Add dry ingredients, blend together.

Pour into lined 7 inch tin and bake for 1 hour at gas mark 3. Leave to cool.

ganache:

Bring cream to boil, pour over chocolate until smooth.

Pour over cake, leave to set.

ice cream:

Bring milk and cream to boil. Cream together yolks and sugar and pour cream mixture into eggs.

Return to pan, cook on low heat until mixture thickens, pass through sieve.

Leave to cool, add purée and churn in ice-cream machine.

to serve:

Place a slice of cake onto a plate, accompanied by a spoonful of ice cream.

Chef's tip:

Natural yoghurt can be used in place of buttermilk. As cake has good keeping qualities, you can keep and reheat in a microwave.

RECOMMENDED WINE
*Cristallo Vin de Fraise –
Thurgau – Switzerland*

MALLORY COURT

'Luxury country house hotel surroundings, fine food and wines are always at the forefront of your Mallory dining experience'

SIMON HAIGH

Simon joined Mallory Court Hotel as Head Chef in December 2001, was made Executive Head Chef in 2006 and was recently appointed Executive Head Chef of the Eden Hotel Collection. Prior to his move to Mallory, Simon spent seven years at Inverlochy Castle in Scotland, where he gained a Michelin star, followed by Seaham Hall in Northumberland. In January 2003 Simon and his team successfully regained a Michelin star which has been retained for the last seven years.

Serves 4

Preparation time: 24 hours

Cooking time: 40 minutes

Special equipment:
Mousse frame
Parisienne scoop

Planning ahead:
The foie gras needs to be marinated the day before cooking and the Brazan cheese needs to be sourced from a specialist cheese supplier.

TERRINE OF FOIE GRAS, SMOKED APPLE AND BRAZAN CHEESE WITH SALAD OF SMOKED DUCK, APPLE, BALSAMIC RAISINS

BY SIMON HAIGH

This may seem an unusual combination – cheese and foie gras – but the cheese has a great, light, smoky flavour to it, and also has a very similar texture to the foie gras. All in all it is a dish that just works.

INGREDIENTS

terrine:

1	lobe of foie gras
4	Granny Smith apples
100g	sliced Brazan cheese
100ml	ruby port
100ml	Madeira
20g	four spice
25g	salt
10g	white pepper

sherry vinegar to deglaze
a few drops of smoking essence

salad:

smoked duck:

salt	
100g	brown sugar
4g	dried orange peel
½	cinnamon stick
1	star anise
1	duck breast

poached apples:

1	Granny Smith apples
50ml	apple juice
30ml	calvados
15g	sugar

balsamic raisins:

30g	raisins
50ml	Madeira
20ml	balsamic vinegar
10ml	sherry vinegar

jelly:

125ml	white wine
375ml	sweet wine
100g	sugar
4	leaves of gelatine

to serve:

3	pain d'épice crêpes
3-5	sprigs of chervil

pain d'épice powder

METHOD

terrine:

Cut the foie gras into 2.5cm slices then marinate four 24 hours with the Madeira, ruby port, four spice, salt and pepper.
Peel, quarter and remove the core from the apples, place in a freezer bag with the smoking essence. Cook at 86°C in a water bath for 40 minutes until soft. (Alternatively, they can be cooked in sugar in a pan on the stove top).
Sear the foie gras in a hot pan on both sides, deglaze with the Sherry vinegar and place on a cooling wire. Reserve the fat from cooking the foie gras.
Line the terrine frame tightly with clingfilm. Put in a layer of foie gras, followed by a layer of smoked apples, a layer of cheese and another layer of foie gras, seasoning each layer. Pour over the fat from cooking the foie gras to seal any gaps. Place in the fridge over night.

salad:

smoked duck:

Trim and score the duck breast, rub with salt and leave for 2 hours. Rinse away the salt and place on a cooling wire.
Blend the sugar, star anise, cinnamon and orange peel at high speed until very fine. Line a pan with tin foil, sprinkle an even layer of the powder on the foil and place over a medium heat until it starts to smoke. Place the breast over the smoke, cover, and after 8 minutes remove from the heat and chill until ready for use.

poached apples:

Peel the apples then make into small balls using a parisienne scoop. Lightly poach in the apple juice, calvados and sugar.

balsamic raisins:

Bring the Madeira, balsamic vinegar, sherry vinegar up to the boil. Add the raisins, cover and take off the heat.

jelly:

Soak the gelatine in cold water. Mix all the other ingredients together in a pan and bring to the boil. Add the gelatine then pass through a chinoise and allow to cool. When firm, pass through a drum sieve before placing in a piping bag.

to serve:

Arrange a line of pain d'épice powder across the plate. Generously slice the foie gras terrine and lay across the powder. Thinly slice the duck breast into three slices and arrange with the apple and raisins (as in the picture). Season, pipe on the jelly, add the crêpes and the chervil.

RECOMMENDED WINE
Clos Louie Rouge –
Côtes de Castillon – Bordeaux

Serves 4

Preparation time: 1 hour (approximately)

Cooking time: 20 minutes

Special equipment:
Deep fat fryer

Planning ahead:
The duck legs need to be marinated and cooked up to three days in advance of starting the dish.

INGREDIENTS

2   whole mallards, plucked
         and drawn
50g   sea salt
30g   crushed black pepper
head of garlic
duck fat
2   additional Gressingham duck legs
         (already confit – see method
         opposite)
four spice
2   feuille de brik sheets
honey
vegetables to garnish

BREAST OF MALLARD, CONFIT LEG, CRISPY CONFIT

BY SIMON HAIGH

This is a great combination of wild and farmed duck, alongside the crispiness of the confit to give texture. Mallard do not really need to hang very long with the rich flavour coming naturally.

METHOD

duck confit:

Remove the legs from the mallards. Cover with the sea salt and black pepper, a sprig of thyme and the garlic, then cover and leave in the fridge over night.

The next day, wash off the salt mixture, pat dry with a clean cloth and place in a pan. Cover with duck fat and cook over a low heat until tender (2-3 hours approximately).

Remove from the heat and leave to cool. Trim as required then use straight away or leave in the duck fat until required.

breast of mallard:

Place the breasts in a dry pan skin side down and cook in a preheated oven at 160-170°C for approximately 12 minutes (a little longer if required well done). Keep in a warm place until required.

crispy duck roll:

Remove the meat from the two extra confit of Gressingham duck legs. Mix in a bowl, seasoning with a little four spice.

Roll the mixture in the feuille de brik sheets, sealing the edges with egg wash. Place on a tray in the freezer until required.

When required, remove from the freezer and place in a medium heat, preheated deep fryer until crispy. Remove, drain, season and cut as required.

N.B. If cut smaller, the rolls can be used as canapès or alternatively leave whole and use as a starter.

sauce suggestion:

Roast off any excess bones until brown. Add a little carrot, onion, leek, thyme, garlic and dried orange zest. Return to the oven until evenly browned. De-glaze with red wine, cover with chicken stock and reduce to the consistency required.

to serve:

Warm through the duck confit legs in a pan. When warm add a little honey to give a nice glaze and add a little sweetness. Remove the breast from the bone and carve as required. Arrange a confit leg on a plate with the duck breast and lay the crispy duck roll on top. Serve with vegetables of your choice. In the photograph we used beetroot, salsify, turnip, red cabbage and crosnes. These earthy flavours stand up well to the gamey mallard, but do not overpower it. Serve with the sauce of your choice.

 RECOMMENDED WINE
*Meursault 1er Cru Charmes –
Domaine du Pavillon – Burgundy*

Serves 4

Preparation and cooking time:
4 hours in total

Special equipment:
Blow torch or brulée iron
Kappa (specialist ingredient)

Planning ahead:
Everything on this dish needs to be done a
day in advance.

INGREDIENTS

baked crème brulée:

1 ltr	double cream
225g	caster sugar
12	egg yolks
2	vanilla pods

poached rhubarb:

	rhubarb
1 ltr	water
3	vanilla pods
800g	sugar
	grenadine syrup

ginger and advocaat ice cream:

300ml	cream
200ml	milk
6	egg yolks
200g	caster sugar
	stem ginger to taste
	advocaat

rhubarb bubble:

1 ltr	stock syrup
2	lemon grass sticks
6	slices of fresh ginger
	kappa
	poached rhubarb from previous recipe
	xantana

BAKED CRÈME BRULÉE, POACHED RHUBARB, GINGER AND ADVOCAAT ICE CREAM

BY SIMON HAIGH

This is one of my favourite combinations and reminds me of home, Yorkshire, where the best rhubarb comes from. This dish has had many incarnations – this is the present one.

METHOD

crème brulée:

Place the cream in a large saucepan along with the seeds and pods of the vanilla. Bring the cream up to the boil. Cream together the egg yolks and sugar – it is important that you do not whisk these together rapidly as then you will form a foam on top of the brulèe. When the cream boils, pour on to egg yolks and whisk gently making sure all the egg is incorporated into the cream. Strain into an oven dish and bake at 110°C, for 30 minutes, keep checking every 5 minutes after 20 minutes as all ovens vary. When set leave to cool.

rhubarb:

Cut the rhubarb width ways 1½ cm long and set to one side. In a large deep pan, bring the water, vanilla, sugar and grenadine up to the boil. You need enough grenadine to turn the water a dark pink colour. The grenadine is used to keep the pinkness of the rhubarb. When the liquor is at a rapid boil, carefully put all the rhubarb in, take off the heat and clingfilm the pan. Leave the pan covered until cool. You can then store the rhubarb in this liquor so the colour infuses.

ice cream:

Place the cream and milk into a saucepan and bring up to the boil. Whisk together the egg yolks and sugar. Pour the boiled milk and cream on to the egg yolks and sugar and whisk together. Return back to the pan and cook the mix until it reaches 80°C. When the mix reaches this temperature it means that the raw egg yolks are now cooked out. Take off the heat and strain. Now you have a plain ice cream base you can flavour with anything you want. Chop the stem ginger into small dice and add to the ice cream base, then add the advocaat to taste. Churn and freeze.

rhubarb bubble:

Blitz some of the poached rhubarb, pass and thicken with xantana until your mix is just holding together. Freeze this into semi-circle moulds.
Infuse the stock syrup with the lemon grass and ginger and leave to cool. Add the kappa – 2g for every 100g of liquor – and bring back up to simmer. Here you have an instant set jelly.
When your rhubarb has set in the freezer, bring it out and place a cocktail stick in each. While your jelly is still hot dip rhubarb in twice, this will give you a good coating. When each bubble is done, place in the fridge. This will then let the rhubarb defrost and give you an explosion when the jelly is broken.

rhubarb crisp:

All you need to make a rhubarb crisp is rhubarb and icing sugar. Cut the rhubarb into pieces 5cm in length, then slice thinly on a mandolin. Dust a silpat mat with icing sugar and lay out your thin rhubarb. Dust the top of the rhubarb. This draws out the natural moisture in the rhubarb. Place in a warm place until they are crisp.

to serve:

Cut out the brulee using a 6cm cutter, sprinkle the top with caster sugar and glaze with a blow torch until light brown. Arrange the rhubarb in the cutter standing on its ends, You will have to pack it fairly tightly to ensure the rhubarb remains standing when you remove the cutter.
Carefully arrange the rhubarb on a plate, place the brulee mix on top and place the bubble next to the brulée – remembering to remove the cocktail stick.
Place a ball of ice cream on the other side of the brulee, forming a neat line, add the rhubarb crisp and serve immediately.

 RECOMMENDED WINE
Cadillac – Château de L'Orangerie – Bordeaux

HAMBLETON HALL

AARON PATTERSON

Aaron Patterson is a youthful genius who started at Hambleton in 1984 and gained useful experience with Raymond Blanc, Anton Mosiman and others before returning to Hambleton as head chef in 1992. He may be lured from time to time to caper about in the television studio for such shows as Here's One I Made Earlier or Masterchef but his heart remains in the kitchen with his team of over 15 like-minded enthusiasts. Aaron is also an advocate of seasonal and locally sourced produce where possible — herbs, salads and berries from the kitchen garden and top-quality seafood and game dishes of all kinds (in season) are specialities.

'Strong seasonal
bias producing
quite brilliant,
assured cooking'

Serves 4

Preparation time: 30 minutes

Cooking time: 10 minutes

Special equipment:
Deep fat fryer

Planning ahead:
All parts of this recipe can be made the day before, except the scallops.

INGREDIENTS

8   large dived scallops
8   baby onions
3   onions finely chopped

onion bhaji:

3   white onions
3 tbsp   mild curry powder
100ml   passion fruit juice
chopped coriander leaves
2 tbsp   oil
2 tbsp   cornflour
20 x   white raisins
juice of 1 lime

tempura batter:

100g   plain flour
100g   cornflour
15g   salt
15g   baking powder
250ml   water

onion purée:

4   large white onions
100g   butter
sherry vinegar
lemon juice to taste

onions cooked in red wine and port:

8   baby onions
150ml   red wine
150ml   port
50g   butter
salt and pepper

the sauce:

8 x   ripe plum tomatoes
1 x   lemon grass stick
1 tbsp   lecithian
salt and pepper

RECOMMENDED WINE
Chevaliers Chardonnay –
Vins des Chevaliers – Valais – Switzerland

SEARED SCALLOPS WITH VARIATIONS OF ONION
BY AARON PATTERSON

Scallops are such a beautiful ingredient that it is very important not to interfere with the clarity of their flavour.

METHOD

onion bhaji:

Cook the finely chopped onion in a thick bottomed pan with the oil. Cook until soft and lightly coloured. Add the curry powder, raisins, passion fruit juice and cornflour. Continue to cook for 3 minutes until the corn flour starts to thicken the mixture. Season with salt, pepper, lime juice and chopped coriander. Leave to cool in the fridge. Place mixture in a piping bag and pipe straight lines about 2cm thick onto, greaseproof paper. Then freeze. When frozen cut into 2cm chunks. Mix together all ingredients for the batter.
Dip the bhaji chunks into the batter and deep fry in oil at 190°C until golden brown.

onion purée:

Cook onions in butter until very soft. Liquidise and pass through a fine sieve. Season with salt, pepper and lemon juice.

onions cooked in red wine and port:

Place onions in a small deep sided pan and cover with red wine and port and put in the butter. Top up with a little water if the onions are not quite covered in liquid. Boil until the onions are soft and the liquid has reduced to a syrupy consistency glazing the onions.

scallops:

Sear the scallops in a non stick pan with a little olive oil until golden brown. Approximately 2 minutes. Then turn over on to the other side and cook for a further 1 minute then allow them to rest. The scallop should not be hot in the middle. It should be just warm. Season with salt, pepper and lemon juice.

the sauce:

Blend the tomatoes and lemon grass in a food processor and drain in a muslin cloth overnight until all the clear liquid drops out of the tomatoes then add the lecithian, warm gently and season blend until a foam is formed.

to serve:

Put onion purée on the plate in three neat pools. Then the crispy onion bhajis, the red wine onions, the scallops and fnish with some lemon grass sauce.

Serves 4

Preparation time: 35 minutes

Cooking time: 10 minutes

Planning ahead:
Roll the puff pastry out 2mm thick and make the farce the day before.

INGREDIENTS

puff pastry
1	chicken breast
4	hare loins
2	whole eggs
2 tbsp	Armagnac
50ml	olive oil
30	raisins soaked in balsamic vinegar
40	pistachio nuts
4	thin pancakes

🍷 **RECOMMENDED WINE**
Riflessi d'Epoca Rosso –
Guido Brivio – Ticino – Switzerland

HARE WELLINGTON
BY AARON PATTERSON

This, surprisingly, is one of our best selling dishes at Hambleton Hall. The most important thing when making this dish is to have fresh hare otherwise the taste is too strong and vulgar.

METHOD

Roll out the puff pastry 2mm thick, 18cm long and 15cm in width and rest in the fridge. Make 4 thin pancakes and place in the fridge.

Dice up the chicken breast, put in a food processor along with the eggs and any lean hare trimmings. Add the Armagnac and blend until smooth. Slowly add olive oil, turn out into a stainless steel bowl and mix in the drained balsamic raisins and pistachios.

Season with salt and pepper.

Roll out clingfilm on a work surface and put a thin pancake on top. Using a palate knife spread out some of the blended stuffing evenly, on top of the pancake, approximately 2mm thick.

Put the hare loin on top and wrap up the package in clingfilm until a neat sausage shape has been achieved. Trim excess pancake from the ends and overlaps. Remove the clingfilm and now wrap the "sausage" in pastry so as to minimise any overlap. Seal the sides and ends of the pastry with egg white.

Put the Hare Wellington on to a roasting tin with a little vegetable oil and cook in the oven at 200°C. The parcel should have 4 sides when the first side is brown repeat the process until all sides of the Hare Wellington are of even colour, this should take about 10 minutes. Note: do not overcook as hare, like many other types of game is unpleasant if well done.

to serve:

Slice excess pastry off both ends and slice into 3 medallions. Position on suitable plate and serve with root vegetables and game sauce flavoured with prunes.

Chef's notes:

The pancake and the farce are not unnecessary complications. They are there to soak up the juices released during the cooking, and to ensure that the pastry does not become soggy.

CHOCOLATE OLIVE OIL TRUFFLE WITH BAKED BANANA AND PASSION FRUIT SORBET

BY AARON PATTERSON

This is my favourite and latest addition to our dessert menu, full of exciting flavours and textures.

Serves 4

Preparation time:	1 hour
Cooking time:	N/A

Special equipment:
Ice cream machine
Ice cream scoop

Planning ahead:
The sorbet, chocolate olive oil truffle and the chocolate crisps can all be made the day before.

INGREDIENTS

chocolate olive oil truffle:

200g	dark chocolate (50%)
20g	unsalted butter
20ml	warm water
1 ½	egg yolks
5g	cocoa powder
100ml	egg whites
135ml	olive oil

passion fruit and banana sorbet:

200ml	passion fruit juice
4	bananas
75g	sugar
50ml	lemon juice

pistachio praline:

4	baby bananas
4	chocolate crisps
4	banana crisps
2 tsp	Maldon rock salt
salt caramel	

caramelised pistachios and pistachio praline:

150g	sugar
50ml	water
handful of unsalted pistachios	
2	sheets of greaseproof paper

chocolate crisps:

100g	sugar
100g	glucose
45g	dark chocolate (70%)
1	Sheet of greaseproof paper

banana crisps:

lemon and sugar liquor (half lemon juice to half sugar)	
2	medium sized bananas

salted caramel:

125g	caster sugar
15ml	water
75ml	double cream
75g	unsalted butter
50ml	hot water
salt, to taste	

METHOD

chocolate olive oil truffle:

Firstly melt the chocolate and butter in a bowl over a Bain Marie then put to one side. In another bowl mix the egg yolks, cocoa powder and water then rapidly whisk in the olive oil making sure to pour the oil slowly so not to split the mix. This will make a chocolate mayonnaise. Take your egg whites and beat them into the chocolate until it becomes smooth and glossy then fold in the chocolate mayonnaise, put into a suitable container and refrigerate until the mix is set, approximately 4 hours.

passion fruit and banana sorbet:

Blend Passion Fruit Juice and Bananas in a food processor, add lemon juice and sugar. Pass through a fine sieve and churn in a sorbet machine.

caramelised pistachios and pistachio praline:

In a thick bottomed pan boil the sugar and water to caramel and add the pistachios. Stir until all the pistachios are separated from each other. With a fork remove half of the pistachios, a few at a time, and roll on greaseproof paper to remove any excess caramel, leave to set and place into an air tight container. Pour the remainder of the pistachios and caramel onto another sheet of greaseproof paper. Leave to set, break up and coarsely blend in a food processor to make the pistachio praline. Store in an air tight container.

chocolate crisps:

In a thick bottomed pan combine the sugar and glucose with enough water to dissolve both and heat to 158°C. Allow to cool slightly then beat in the chocolate and pour onto the greaseproof paper to set, then blend to a powder in a food processor. Lightly dust onto a tray lined with greaseproof paper using a fine sieve and heat in the oven at 200°C until the powder melts and is lacy in appearance. Cut into rectangles and allow to cool. Store in dry air tight containers

banana crisps:

Thinly slice bananas on a meat slicer as thinly as possible, lengthways with the skin on. Dip in the sugar solution and lay on a clingfilmed tray. Then dry under heat lamps or in an oven on 50°C until bananas are dry and crisp. Store in a dry airtight container.

salted caramel:

In a thick bottomed saucepan combine the sugar and 15ml water then heat to a dark caramel. Whisk in the cream and then the butter. Remove from the gas and add hot water and then add salt to taste. Allow to cool then pour into a squeezy bottle.

assembly:

To assemble the dish firstly you will need a large plate preferably square and a small scoop. Next score around the top of the four baby bananas and cook in the oven at 200°C until soft and the top layer of skin can be removed. Sprinkle caster sugar on the exposed flesh of the bananas and caramelise

Next scoop on to each plate at the top point two small perfect balls of chocolate olive mousse then, using a squeezy bottle, make large and small pools of caramel randomly around the plate. Place one banana on each plate in the left hand corner nearest to you. Place five pistachios randomly around the plate, leaving a space in the right hand corner nearest to you for a small pile of pistachio praline Next place a chocolate crisp into each of the chocolate balls and then scoop the passion fruit and banana sorbet onto the pistachio praline. Finally sprinkle Maldon sea salt around the plate and place your banana crisps into the sorbet with a sprig of mint and serve.

YNYSHIR HALL

'Succulent seafood with lobsters, crabs and shrimp landed at Aberystwyth and Borth'

SHANE HUGHES

Life really began for Shane in the kitchens he trained in. He saw that they provided a true sense of freedom, discipline and confidence all rolled into one, similar, he imagined to enlisting in the army, except he insisted on the Marines and chose to train in an elite cookery environment. Having been born abroad in South Africa and brought up in Manchester and Buckinghamshire he grew up directionless and unsure, but was sure of one thing, he loved to eat. After a fruitless education he went in search of some training and arrived at Hartwell House Hotel. A few years and some good advice later he found himself cooking in the kitchens of the Connaught Hotel in London and there began the classical benchmark of standards that he bases all his cuisine on today. If you skip forward to the present day you will see that Shane is devoted to his cooking and find that he considers himself truly lucky to have trained in such fantastic restaurants and hotels.

Serves 4

Preparation time: 3 hours (to create the jelly and the fish salad)

Cooking time: Seconds; just for the shellfish to lightly cure

Special equipment:
Metal rings
Clingfilm

Planning ahead:
Just find a good fish supplier and go for it!

INGREDIENTS

tomato jelly:

1.5kg	squeezed tomatoes
½ tsp	tabasco
1 tsp	celery salt
1 tbsp	worcestershire sauce
1 tbsp	sugar
12.5ml	white wine vinegar
200ml	chicken stock
2	sprigs of tarragon
1	clove of garlic
4	leaves of basil
2.5 tbsp	tomato ketchup
7	gelatine leaves
4	metal rings or moulds

fish:

8	langoustines
4	large scallops
1	lime
50ml	of good olive oil to marinate the fish

dressing:

simple vinaigrette

20ml	white wine vinegar
150ml	olive oil
2 tbsp	tarragon
pinch of salt and black pepper	
1	clove of garlic
1	bay leaf

to finish:

chopped tomato, chives and shallot
micro leaves
caviar (we use sustainable empirical baire but even keta or lumpfish roe will suffice as a garnish)

RECOMMENDED WINE
*Calamin Grand Cru Blanc –
Louis Bovard – Vaud – Switzerland*

SCALLOP AND LANGOUSTINE CARPACCIO WITH TOMATO JELLY AND CAVIAR

BY SHANE HUGHES

A light and fresh way of serving shellfish with a delicious hint of tomato and spice finished off perfectly with caviar.

METHOD

tomato jelly

Make a gastric with the white wine vinegar and sugar.
Set up the liquidiser and add all ingredients together. Blend until smooth.
Hang the purée of tomatoes in a muslin cloth, suspended over a bowl in the fridge.
When all of the liquid has dripped through the muslin, discard the remaining pulp.
Correct the seasoning of the liquid with salt, sugar and cayenne pepper.
Soak gelatine in ice water for 10 minutes.
Warm up the juice then add gelatine and stir until dissolved. Pour approximately 40g of the jelly into each mould – chill until set.

dressing

Combine the ingredients in a lidded jar, shake well and leave to infuse.

to serve

Complete the dish by cutting the fish into thick dice and dressing with lime juice, olive oil, salt and pepper – leave for 1 minute to marinate. Serve with jelly, salad and caviar.

Chef's tip:

This dish only works with the freshest fish available and served very quickly.
Micro leaves are nice but any lettuce would serve the same purpose.

Serves 6

Preparation time: 3 days (brine for at
least 24 hours for
maximum flavour)

Cooking time: 3 hours

Special equipment:
Butcher's string
Foil
A good braising pan

Planning ahead:
It's a good idea to pre-order the
ingredients from your butcher as they are
not mainstream cuts of pork.

INGREDIENTS

6	pigs' cheeks
2	pigs' tongues
1	pork belly
4	bottles of any strong ale
500g	salt
250g	each of chopped onion, carrot, celery and leek
5	gloves garlic
10g	coriander seeds
10	cloves
5	star anis
4	bayleaves
6	sprigs of thyme
400ml	white wine
400ml	red wine
250ml	sherry vinegar
200ml	clear honey
3 ltr	chicken stock
NOTE:	The pork is best served with a selection of root vegetables and creamy mash

BRINED AND BRAISED PORK

BY SHANE HUGHES

A delicious pork dish with deep rustic flavours, well worth the effort.

METHOD

stage 1:

Skin pork belly and remove any bones.
Roll pork cheeks and tongue in pork belly and tie firmly with string.
Boil salt and ale together – allow to cool – marinade pork in salt/ale brine for 24 hours.

stage 2:

Preheat heavy bottom saucepan and sauté vegetables and garlic until golden brown
– pour in sherry vinegar, honey, thyme, bay leaf, star anis, coriander seeds and cloves and
reduce by two thirds.
Add white and red wine – reduce by ½ – add chicken stock.
Remove pork from brine, wash lightly and dry thoroughly.
Sauté pork belly in olive oil until deep golden brown, add to stock and bring to simmer.
Foil the pan then put a lid on. Cook in the oven gas mark 3 / 150°C for 3 hours.
Remove from the oven and allow to cool entirely in the stock.
Remove from stock and pass juice through sieve and reduce while skimming until required
consistency.
Cut string off pork and serve with sauce and vegetables.

Chef's tip:

For perfect results take the string off the pork and roll in clingfilm then chill overnight and
the pork will slice perfectly before you reheat it with the sauce.

RECOMMENDED WINE
Riflessi d'Epoca Rosso –
Guido Brivio – Ticino – Switzerland

Serves 6

Preparation time: 2 hours

Cooking time: 40 minutes

Special equipment:
6 metal rings
1 sheet of silicone paper

Planning ahead:
Make sure all of your ingredients are
correct and the pastry is rested.

INGREDIENTS

100g	cooled, beurre noisettes (nut brown butter)
60g	eggs
40ml	double cream
5g	salt
455g	golden syrup (warmed)
60g	breadcrumbs
	zest of 1 lemon
25ml	lemon juice

sweet pastry:

500g	strong flour
125g	butter (unsalted)
85g	caster sugar
1	whole egg
2	egg yolks
1 tsp	lemon zest

TREACLE TART
BY SHANE HUGHES

METHOD

pastry:

Cream the butter and sugar with the lemon zest until it lightens in colour, then add flour and
all of the eggs.
Mix until a smooth paste. Roll and blind bake flat, on a tray, then cut out with metal rings
lined with silicone paper, leaving a layer of pastry in each ring.

tart:

Mix the butter with warmed syrup. Add to the eggs, cream and salt and mix together
Mix the breadcrumbs, lemon zest and juice into the syrup mixture.
Pour approx 100g of treacle mix into each lined ring, on top of cut out pastry already in them
and cook at 150℃ for approximately 40 minutes or until firm in the centre.

to serve:

Remove from ring and top with clotted cream.

Chef's notes:

Warm up the pastry discs before adding them to the rings to avoid cracking.

 RECOMMENDED WINE
Grains Nobles – Rouvinez Vins – Valais – Switzerland

MARLFIELD
HOUSE

'Fresh herbs, vegetables and fruit grown abundantly and gathered daily'

Serves 4

Preparation time:	20 minutes
Cooking time:	20 minutes

STEAMED MUSSELS WITH WILD GARLIC, SPRING ONIONS, FENNEL AND CURRY

MARLFIELD HOUSE RECIPE

INGREDIENTS

2kg	fresh mussels, scrubbed and de-bearded
	unsalted butter
1	bay leaf
1	sprig fresh thyme
100ml	dry white wine
1	onion, finely diced
1	leek, finely diced
1	celery stick, finely diced
1	head fennel, finely sliced
200g	broad beans
100g	baby spinach
100g	wild garlic, shredded
2	spring onions, finely sliced
1 tsp	curry powder
300ml	double cream
	sea salt and freshly ground pepper

garnish:

250g	pasta (preferably fresh)
4	sprigs dill
4	sprigs tarragon
4	sprigs chervil, snipped

METHOD

In a large saucepan, melt a knob of butter, add the onion and sweat until softened, add the bay leaf, thyme and a little ground pepper. Then add the mussels and white wine, cover and cook for 3-4 minutes, shaking the pan once or twice. Uncover the pan and strain reserving the juices. Discard any mussels that have not opened. Remove the mussels from their shell.

In a separate saucepan, melt a knob of butter and sauté the leek, celery and fennel until softened, add the teaspoon of curry powder and continue to cook for another minute. Add the reserved cooking juices from the mussels and reduce by half, then add the double cream and simmer for 5 minutes.

Finally add the wild garlic, broad beans, baby spinach, spring onions, mussels and pasta, season to taste.

to serve:

Divide the mussels between 4 warmed plates, garnish with fresh herbs.

RECOMMENDED WINE
Rully Blanc 1er Cru – Maison Albert Sounit – Côte Chalonnaise – Burgundy

Serves 4

Preparation time: 30 minutes

Cooking time: 40 minutes (for the partridge), 1-1½ hours (for the terrine)

ROAST PARTRIDGE WITH SMOKED GARLIC AND ROSEMARY POTATO AND PANCETTA TERRINE, BUTTERED SAVOY CABBAGE WITH CHESTNUTS

MARLFIELD HOUSE RECIPE

INGREDIENTS

partridge:

4	partridges (or other game bird or poultry)
olive oil	
1	bulb smoked garlic, separated into cloves, skin on
200ml	white wine
2	sprigs rosemary
250ml	chicken stock
salt and pepper	

for potato and pancetta terrine:

1 kg	potatoes
1	garlic clove
200g	butter, melted
12	long slices of pancetta
salt and pepper	

for buttered savoy cabbage and chestnuts:

1	small Savoy cabbage, finely shredded
1	large carrot, peeled and thinly sliced
butter	
1	onion, sliced
2	spring onions
8	whole chestnuts, sliced

METHOD

partridge:

Preheat the oven to 160°C (325°F). Season the partridges with salt and pepper. Heat 2 tablespoons of olive oil in a large frying pan, add the garlic and then brown the partridges on all sides. Roast for approximately 20-25 minutes.

Remove the partridges and garlic cloves from the pan, deglaze the pan with the white wine and add the rosemary, reduce the liquid by one half, add the chicken stock, simmer for 10 minutes and season to taste. When the sauce is smooth and thickened, strain and keep warm.

for potato and pancetta terrine:

Preheat the oven to 160°C.

Peel the garlic clove and use to rub the inside of a terrine mould (alternatively use a 9 inch round baking pan) and butter the bottom and sides.

Peel the potatoes and slice into thin rounds. Season and pour over the melted butter, mix thoroughly. Carefully layer the potatoes to the top of the terrine mould (baking pan), placing the pancetta strips in 3 alternative layers, evenly distributed through the potatoes.

Cover with kitchen foil, set in a bain-marie and bake for about 1-1½ hours, until the potatoes are tender. Turn out of the mould, slice and serve.

for buttered savoy cabbage and chestnuts:

Blanch the cabbage in salted, boiling water for 1 minute until tender. Drain.

Melt a knob of butter in a large saucepan and add the sliced onion and carrot, sauté until softened, add the savoy cabbage, sauté for a further minute then add the spring onions and chestnuts and serve.

to serve:

Place a slice of terrine on each plate. Remove the legs and breast meat from the partridges and arrange on plates, add cabbage and sauce.

RECOMMENDED WINE

Morey St Denis – Domaine Leymarie – Burgundy

Serves 4

Preparation time:	20 minutes
Cooking time:	45 minutes

QUEEN OF PUDDINGS WITH VANILLA AND CITRUS POACHED RHUBARB

MARLFIELD HOUSE RECIPE

INGREDIENTS

pudding:

100g	fresh white breadcrumbs
5 tbsp	caster sugar
450ml	milk
2 tbsp	butter
3	eggs, separated
1	vanilla pod seeds (alternatively few drops of vanilla essence)
1	lemon, zest only
3 tbsp	raspberry jam (or other sharp flavoured jam)

poached rhubarb:

4	stalks of rhubarb, peeled and chopped
1	vanilla pod
250g	caster sugar
300ml	water
2	oranges, juiced
2	lemons, juiced

METHOD

Preheat oven to 190°C, 375°F, gas mark 5

pudding:

In a bowl mix the breadcrumbs with 2 tablespoons of caster sugar.
Combine the milk and butter in a saucepan and bring to the boil, stirring until the butter has melted and pour over the breadcrumbs. Beat in the egg yolks, vanilla and lemon zest.
Grease 4 small (or alternatively one 1 litre) pie dishes lightly with butter and divide the breadcrumb mix, levelling them off, and bake for approximately 30 minutes, until the pudding is set and golden on top. Remove the pudding and leave to cool slightly.
Reduce the oven temperature to 170°C, 325°F, gas mark 3.
In a clean bowl whisk the egg whites until they form soft peaks, gradually add the remaining 3 tablespoons of caster sugar, continually whisking until they become stiff and glossy.
Take the raspberry jam and spread evenly over the puddings, then top with the meringue drawing it up in peaks.
Place the pudding in the oven and bake for 8-12 minutes until the meringue is set and golden in colour.

rhubarb:

To poach the rhubarb, slowly dissolve the caster sugar in the water, juice of lemons and oranges and vanilla pod. Place the rhubarb in the syrup and gently poach for 3-5 minutes being careful not to overcook. (should be softened but still hold a bite).

to serve:

Serve the pudding immediately with the poached rhubarb and syrup.

 RECOMMENDED WINE
Quintessence du Clos – Domaine Le Clos des Cazaux – Rhône

SHEEN FALLS LODGE

PHILIP BRAZIL

Dubliner Philip Brazil trained at the Dublin Institute of Technology 1989-1991 before honing his craft at Tinakilly House, Clarence House, Knockranny House, The Clarion and Sheen Falls Lodge. He describes his cooking style as 'Modern Irish with a European infusion'. While working with chefs from all over Europe he brings in some ideas from their countries. Phil also enjoys tailor making menus for the guests staying at Sheen Falls, not letting them miss what they've always liked. When not working in the kitchen, Phil can be found with his wife, Fidelma, cooking at home for family and friends, while sipping a glass of wine or cycling around Kerry.

'Magical woodlands
and cascading
waterfalls. Explore
the abundance
of Irish pubs and
Kenmare restaurants
brimming with old
fashioned Irish
hospitality'

Serves 4

Preparation time:	30 minutes
Cooking time:	20 minutes

Special equipment:
Food processor
Stick blender

Planning ahead:
The tapenade and the tomato dressing can be made a day in advance.

INGREDIENTS

soup:

600g	cherry tomatoes, quartered
440g	canned plum tomatoes, chopped
100ml	double cream

a good pinch and salt and freshly ground pepper

tapenade:

60g	stoned black olives
1	small garlic clove, crushed
3	tinned anchovy fillet, patted dry
2 tsp	capers, drained
2 tsp	olive oil

a squeeze of fresh lemon juice

tomato dressing:

2	plum tomatoes, halved
1	slice of garlic

a little olive oil

garnish:

4	round slices of mozzarella
4	round slices of toast
12	chopped cherry tomatoes

fresh basil leaves and rocket
parmesan shavings

WHITE TOMATO SOUP WITH MOZZARELLA AND TAPENADE

BY PHILIP BRAZIL

This soup is different to the traditional tomato soup with a chef's twist using the clear juice but also achieving the rich tomato flavour.

METHOD

soup:

Roughly chop the fresh tomatoes and blitz in a food processor with canned tomatoes and salt to taste until smooth. Lay a clean muslin cloth into a large sieve over a bowl and pour the puréed tomato into the sieve and allow to drain overnight.

The next morning, gently draw up and squeeze the muslin to get all the remaining juice. You should have a lovely translucent liquid. Discard the pulp. Just before serving, gently heat the liquid with the cream. Use a stick blender to bring the liquids together and season to taste. Set aside.

tapenade:

Crush the olives, anchovies and the capers in a pestle and mortar, mixing in the olive oil and the lemon juice at the end. Season with pepper only.

tomato dressing:

Pan-fry the tomatoes in olive oil until well coloured and softened. Then rub it though the sieve with the back of a ladle, adding a little olive oil to loosen it up. Drizzle it from a teaspoon.

to serve:

Spread some of the tapenade on the toast and top with mozzarella. Grill lightly until melted and scatter with some chopped cherry tomato. Place on a serving plate. Garnish with basil and rocket leaves. Gently reheat the soup and pour into preheated soup bowls. Drizzle with tomato dressing and serve with toast.

RECOMMENDED WINE
La Contrada Merlot Bianco –
Guido Brivio – Ticino – Switzerland

Serves 4

Preparation time: 1 ½ hours
Cooking time: 1 hour

Special equipment:
Non-stick frying pan

Planning ahead:
Pre-order the halibut and clams from your fishmonger or deli.

FILLET OF HALIBUT WITH GREEN AND WHITE ASPARAGUS, STEAMED CLAMS AND JAMESON WHISKEY BUTTER, SQUID INK PASTA AND TOMATO SALAD

BY PHILIP BRAZIL

Halibut is a fish that I particularly like to work with. Asparagus, when in season, has a good taste, is colourful and easy to prepare. The Jameson butter gives the dish the real lift though.

INGREDIENTS

halibut:

4	fillets of halibut each 140g prepared weight (skinned and prepared by fishmonger)
25g	Jameson whiskey

salad:

100ml	olive oil
16	cherry tomatoes (quartered)
2	shallots (finely sliced)
½	flat parsley bunch (chopped)

sea salt and freshly ground pepper for seasoning

asparagus:

15ml	olive oil
500g	asparagus (white)
5	thyme sprigs (picked and chopped)
1	lemon (juiced)

clams:

500g	clams in their shells
1	bay leaf
1	garlic clove (crushed)
25g	white wine
125g	chicken stock
tabasco sauce	
15g	cream
225g	unsalted butter

pasta:

squid ink pasta from good deli or supermarket, allow 65g per person, 260g total

METHOD

tomato salad :

Simply mix the cherry tomatoes with 25ml of the olive oil, ¼ of the sliced shallot ¼ chopped parsley. Season with sea salt and freshly ground pepper. Cover and set aside for 1 ½ hours at room temperature.

asparagus:

Wash the asparagus tips and slice from bottom to top with a speed peeler to give you nice long strips. Preheat a frying pan with 15ml olive oil and ¼ of the thyme. Add asparagus and toss quickly for 1 to 2 minutes. Set aside.

clams:

Preheat a small pot and add the clams, white wine, the rest of the shallots, bay leaf, garlic, chicken stock and cover with a lid. Cook for 2 to 3 minutes until shells have opened fully. Then pour ¾ of the cooking liquid into a separate pot for the sauce. Cover the clams with clingfilm and keep warm. Reduce the cooking liquid with cream until a tablespoon remains. Lower the heat and slowly whisk in the cold diced butter. Season with lemon juice and a splash of tabasco. Set aside and keep warm.

pasta:

Boil 2 litres of water seasoned with salt only. Add the pasta and cook for 8 to 10 minutes until al dente.

halibut:

Preheat a non-stick frying pan with 25ml of olive oil. Place the seasoned fillets presentation side down for 2 minutes until it reaches a golden colour. Now turn carefully and cook for another 2 to 3 minutes. At this point, add the whiskey. Spoon it over the fillets as they cook.

to serve:

Have four preheated plates ready. Drain and season the cooked pasta and twist into neat bundles. Place the warm asparagus beside the pasta. Take the fish and place alongside not hiding the asparagus. Take the warm clams and garnish evenly. Sprinkle the tomato salad around the plate and spoon butter sauce generously around. Serve immediately (use the photo as a guide).

 RECOMMENDED WINE
Vacqueyras Vieilles Vignes Blanc –
Domaine Le Clos des Cazaux – Rhône

Serves 4

Preparation time: 30 minutes

Cooking time: 8-10 minutes

Special equipment:
Non-stick dariole moulds
Piping bag

Planning ahead:
Prepare the balsamic forest fruits in
advance.

INGREDIENTS

fondant:

120g	caster sugar
150g	eggs
95g	chocolate drops (70%)
90g	unsalted butter
40g	flour (plain)

balsamic forest fruits:

125g	frozen forest fruits
25g	caster sugar
½	cinnamon stick
½	vanilla pod
10g	honey
2 tbsp	balsamic vinegar
100g	red wine
20g	cornflour

to serve:

good quality vanilla ice cream

mint sprigs

WARM CHOCOLATE FONDANT WITH BALSAMIC FRUITS AND VANILLA ICE CREAM

BY PHILIP BRAZIL

Chocolate is everybody's favourite and the fondant is simple to prepare
and serve. The berries and ice cream marry it all together.

METHOD

fondant:

Preheat the oven to 180°C and butter 4 moulds.
Melt the chocolate and butter in a bowl over warm water stirring all the time and set aside.
Now beat the eggs and sugar in a bowl over warm water, until you get a good stiff foam.
Remove from heat and allow to cool by whisking.
Add the warm chocolate mix to the egg mix and fold in the sieved flour.
Fill a piping bag with the mixture and fill the moulds ¾ way full. Bake for 8-10 minutes – this
should give you a soft liquid centre.

balsamic forest fruits:

Simply place all ingredients except the fruit, red wine and cornflour into a pot and bring to
the boil. Mix the red wine and cornflour together, remove liquid from heat and stir in the
wine mixture. Return to the heat, stirring to achieve a syrup. Now add the berries and warm
through.

to serve:

Spoon the berry mix onto a plate and turn out the fondant. Using a hot spoon, scoop a nice
ball of ice cream onto the plate. Dust with icing sugar and add a sprig of mint to garnish.

RECOMMENDED WINE
Cristallo Vin de Fraise –
Thurgau – Switzerland

FARLAM
HALL

BARRY QUINION

After college Barry started in the kitchen at The Bell at Aston Clinton, one of the founder members of Relais & Châteaux in the UK. From there he moved to a Relais in Switzerland and then back to the UK to The Waterside Inn at Bray under Pierre Koffmann. This was followed by a change to front of house, as by then the family's plan was to have their own hotel. He has been happily in charge of his own kitchen since the move to Farlam Hall in 1975 and now runs the hotel with his wife Lynne and sister Helen.

'A meal to delight the tastes and also satisfy the inner man – or woman'

Serves 4

Preparation time:	10 minutes
Cooking time:	3-4 minutes

KING PRAWNS WITH CHILLI AND GARLIC

BY BARRY QUINION

An easy, straightforward recipe.

INGREDIENTS

16	king prawns (peeled and veined)
2	pak choi heads, blanched and core removed
¼	green chilli finely chopped
¼	red chilli finely chopped
½	garlic cloves, crushed

sweet chilli sauce

virgin olive oil

salt and pepper to taste

METHOD

Fry the prawns gently on one side in a little virgin olive oil until they change colour, add chopped chilli and garlic and turn the prawns over to colour.

Cook very briefly, remove from the pan, keep warm.

in the same pan, stir fry the blanched pak choi until it is warmed through, season to taste.

Arrange the pak choi in the centre of a white plate in a tight mound.

Arrange the prawns on top.

Spoon some sweet chilli sauce around the edge of the plate.

Chef's tip:

Buy the chilli sauce, it is easy to make but very time consuming.

RECOMMENDED WINE
ZD Chardonnay –
ZD Winery – California

Serves 4

Preparation time: 30 minutes

Cooking time: 25 minutes

Planning ahead:
The quail can be prepared the day before serving.

LANCASHIRE QUAIL, FILLED WITH A CHICKEN AND HERB MOUSSE WITH A RED WINE SAUCE AND WILD MUSHROOMS

BY BARRY QUINION

Something a little different but easier to do than you may think.

INGREDIENTS

4	boned quail
1	chicken leg, medium
	chopped herbs (such as parsley, chives, coriander)
150ml	cream
500ml	chicken stock
1	glass red wine
2	knobs butter
250g	wild mushrooms (the best you can get)
2	medium shallots finely chopped

METHOD

quail

Remove the skin, bone and sinew from the chicken leg, roughly chop the meat, put in a food processor and whiz until smooth, slowly add the cream and herbs (do not over mix), then season.

Open up the quail, remove any sinew or bone, season, add the mousse, re-shape. Roll in clingfilm like a sausage, tie up the ends, refrigerate until needed. Put the wrapped quail into a pan of cold water, bring to the boil and simmer for 10 minutes. Remove the quail from the water and drain in a colander. Remove the clingfilm. Melt one of the knobs of butter in a frying pan and colour the quail gently, remove from the pan and put in a low oven to keep warm. In the same pan cook the wild mushrooms and one shallot. Remove and drain on kitchen paper.

red wine sauce

Put the remaining chopped shallot in a thick bottomed saucepan with the glass of wine and reduce to almost nothing, add the chicken stock, reduce by half or until you are happy with the consistency. Remove from the heat and whisk in the remaining knob of butter. Season and strain.

to serve:

You may like to make a little mashed potato to put the carved quail on to. This makes the presentation easier and means you do not have to provide a potato dish separately. Add sauce.

Chef's tip:

Prepare the quail the day before. You can make the sauce in advance but do not add the butter until you finish the dish.

RECOMMENDED WINE
ZD Pinot Noir –
ZD Winery – California

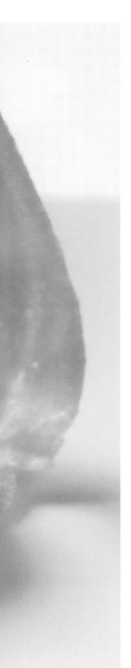

SPICED APPLE CAKE SERVED WITH CALVADOS ICE CREAM AND CARAMELISED APPLES

BY BARRY QUINION

A really refreshing autumn pudding but can be enjoyed all year round.

Serves 4

Preparation time: 30 minutes (shortbread),
15 minutes (ice cream)

Cooking time: 20 minutes (shortbread),
2-3 hours (cooling and churning ice cream)

Special equipment:
4 x 7cm rings

Planning ahead:
The shortbread can be made well in advance.

INGREDIENTS

shortbread:

25g   caster sugar
50g   butter
100g   plain flour

spiced apple cake:

2   large cooking apples peeled, cored and cut into medium sized pieces
½   lemon, juice and zest
25g   butter
50g   wholemeal breadcrumbs
25g   demerara sugar
1 tsp   mixed spice

calvados ice cream:

3   egg yolks
75g   caster sugar
150ml   milk
150ml   cream
75ml   calvados

METHOD

shortbread:

Sieve the flour. Mix in the fat and sugar with the flour. Combine all the ingredients to a smooth paste. Roll carefully on to a floured surface ½ cm thick. Place on a lightly greased baking sheet, bake in a moderate oven for approximately 15-20 minutes. Before it becomes too cool, cut out four rings.

spiced apple:

Put the lemon juice and zest in a stainless steel pan along with the apple pieces and cook gently with a lid on until the apple is soft. Allow to cool.
Fry the breadcrumbs in the butter, not too fast, remove from the heat, add the spices and sugar, allow to cool on a plate. Make sure it is all mixed well.
Place a shortbread in the bottom of each ring. Put an eighth of the apple sauce on top of each and then an eighth of the crumb mix on each, repeat again so you finish with a level crumb topping. Allow to set and then turn out of the ring and serve with calvados ice cream.

ice cream:

Whisk the egg yolks and sugar until pale.
Boil the milk, add to the egg mixture, return to the pan and cook until it coats the back of a spoon.
Remove from the heat and pour into a bowl, add the cream and calvados straight away to stop it cooking on. If you over cook the eggs and milk and it curdles, liquidise the mix and it will come back.
Allow to cool, refrigerate for an hour at least before putting in the ice cream maker to churn.

to serve:

When the cakes have set, turn out of the rings, onto individual plates, and serve with a scoop of the ice cream.

Chef's tip:

Make the day before, it sets better. You can buy some vanilla ice cream to serve with this but if you have an ice cream machine, calvados ice cream is easy to make.

RECOMMENDED WINE
*Liqueur au Calvados –
Lecompte*

GILPIN LODGE
COUNTRY HOUSE

'Warm smiles, fresh flowers, real fires and friendly, unpretentious service. Classically based yet thoroughly modern'

RUSSELL PLOWMAN

Russell trained for three years at the Relais & Châteaux, three Michelin-starred Waterside Inn at Bray and two years at the Michelin-starred L'Ortolan before joining Gilpin in January 2009. With very seasonal menus and a particular interest in butchery, he makes the most of fantastic local suppliers, 'Cumbria and the Lake District are at the forefront of supplying some of the top restaurants and we're so lucky to have these on our doorstep — and of course we get the pick of the bunch before it go elsewhere.'

Serves 4

Preparation time: 1 hour

Cooking time: 2 hours

Special equipment:
Tweezers
Bain-marie

BALLOTINE OF ORGANIC SALMON WITH HORSERADISH AND POTATO MOUSSE AND A BEETROOT SALAD

BY RUSSELL PLOWMAN

A piece of top quality salmon with the classic marriage of pickled beetroot and horseradish is a wonderful way to kick-start the meal, and the colours are superb.

INGREDIENTS

salmon ballotine:

1	fillet organic salmon (best quality available); approx 1.5 kg off the bone

beetroot liquor:

12	large beetroots
415g	sugar
750ml	red wine
400ml	red wine vinegar
400ml	water
5	bay leaf
5	sprig thyme
35g	salt
10	black peppercorns

horseradish and potato mousse:

450g	ratte potatoes peeled and washed
4	leaves of gelatine
100ml	milk
450ml	whipping cream
250g	crème fraîche
75g	horseradish relish
salt and pepper	
cayenne pepper	
lemon juice	

beetroot purée:

500g	cooked beetroot, diced
1 ltr	beetroot cooking liquor
salt and sugar to taste	

METHOD

salmon:

Fillet and pin bone the salmon.
Cut down the centre of each fillet lengthways to achieve four fillets without the dark flesh.
Top and tail each fillet and lightly season with sea salt and cayenne pepper.
Roll tightly in clingfilm into sausage shape, tie ends.
Poach in a bain marie at 45°C for 1 hour.
Chill in ice bath and refrigerate.

beetroot liquor:

Bring all ingredients to the boil before cooking the beets.
Gently simmer beets with lid on until cooked through.
Leave beets and liquor to cool; remove beets to slice.

horseradish and potato mousse:

Cook potatoes in seasoned water till soft.
Soften gelatine in cold water.
Bring the milk and 150ml of whipping cream to boil and whisk in the gelatine; purée in food processor.
Mix potatoes with crème fraîche, horseradish relish and gelatine until smooth and pass through fine sieve.
Put in fridge, wait until it's semi set and fold in the remaining cream which has been lightly whipped.
Season to taste.

beetroot purée:

Simmer the beetroot, dice in the liquor for 30 minutes until very soft.
Strain the beets and purée until silky smooth adding some of the liquor to achieve the correct consistency.
Pass with fine sieve and season to taste.

to serve:

To achieve a smooth finish, use a sharp serrated knife to cut. Use a piping bag for the purée, and a squeezy bottle for the mousse.

Chef's tip:

Everything except the mousse can be made the day before.

 RECOMMENDED WINE
ZD Chardonnay
ZD Wineries – California

Serves 4

Preparation time: 2 hours

Cooking time: 4 hours

ROASTED BEST END AND BRAISED SHOULDER OF HERDWICK LAMB WITH GARLIC AND POTATO PURÉE, AND MOREL MUSHROOMS

BY RUSSELL PLOWMAN

One of the first Lake District suppliers I visited was Hazel and her Herdwick lamb at Yew Tree Farm in Borrowdale. It really did live up to the hype, and I let the produce speak for itself in this dish.

INGREDIENTS

lamb:

600g	boned and rolled lamb shoulder
2 ltr	lamb stock
150g	butter
2	shallots
1	carrot
2	heads of garlic
400g	French trimmed piece of best end Herdwick lamb (ask your butcher)
50ml	olive oil
160g	lamb sweetbread, blanched and peeled

garlic and potato purée:

3kg	Desirée potatoes
100g	coarse rock salt
250ml	whipping cream
4	cloves garlic
200g	unsalted butter

vegetables:

100g	wild garlic
100g	morel mushrooms
200g	green beans
200g	peas

METHOD

shoulder:

Start the preparation for the lamb shoulders a day in advance.
In a heavy based frying pan caramelise the boned and rolled lamb shoulder to a deep golden brown in a little vegetable oil.
Once browned remove from the pan and roast the carrot, shallot and garlic before adding to the lamb shoulder.
Then cover with lamb stock, bring to a boil and skim.
Put in an oven set at 150°C and cook slowly for two to three hours or until the meat is tender.
Allow to cool, but while the shoulder is still warm, roll in clingfilm to form a large cylinder.
When cold, cut into disks, pass the stock through a chinoise and reduce until a sauce consistency.

best end:

To cook the best end, caramelise the fat in olive oil, skin side down, cook the fat until rendered and finish with a little butter, salt and pepper.
Finish in the oven for 6 minutes, leaving to rest the meat for a further 6 minutes.

sweetbread:

Whilst the rack is resting baste the shoulder disks in the stock and pan roast the sweetbread until golden brown. Heat the garnishes and sauce, carve the rack and serve.

garlic and potato purée:

Prick the potatoes, bake on a bed of rock salt at 150°C for 1½-2 hours.
Scoop out the potatoes, pass through fine sieve.
Bring cream to the boil with the butter and garlic, strain onto the dry potatoes and mix together to achieve a smooth purée. Season with salt and pepper.

vegetables:

Wilt wild garlic in a butter/water emulsion.
Lightly clean morels in warm water, dry; softly fry (low heat) in butter and season.
Trim beans, cook in boiling salted water until soft. Drain and split lengthways for presentation.
Cook peas in boiling salted water.

to serve:

Always dress the plate with the vegetables first, and carve the meat at the last possible minute before serving.

Chef's tip:

When braising the lamb shoulder, make sure the meat is fully relaxed before rolling in clingfilm, so it absorbs as much of the stock as possible. This can be done the day before.

 RECOMMENDED WINE
ZD Cabernet Sauvignon –
ZD Wineries – California

RHUBARB MARSHMALLOW WITH GINGER JELLY AND SWEET WINE GRANITÉ

BY RUSSELL PLOWMAN

A childhood favourite ingredient that lends itself to some really interesting flavours, the granité and jelly are a very refreshing contrast to the sweet, soft marshmallow.

Serves 4

Preparation time:	2 hours
Cooking time:	1 hour

Special equipment:
Jam thermometer
Domes or non-stick tian mould
Parisienne scoop (melon baller)
Blowtorch
Ice cream machine

INGREDIENTS

rhubarb poaching liquor:

1kg	pink rhubarb, peeled and cut into 4cm batons
800g	water
300g	caster sugar
4g	vanilla pods (1)

genoise blanche:

6	whole eggs
300g	caster sugar
300g	strong white bread flour
75g	ground almonds
125g	butter, melted

white wine granité:

250g	water
50g	caster sugar
150g	Coteaux de Lyon sweet wine

ginger jelly:

50g	water
140g	rhubarb poaching liquor
25g	caster sugar
25g	chopped ginger
2	soaked gelatine leaves

marshmallow:

40g	fresh egg whites
25g	water
90g	caster sugar
¾	soaked gelatine leaf
1	small lime, juiced
ice cream or sorbet as desired	

METHOD

rhubarb poaching liquor:

Place all the ingredients into a large flat bottomed pan, and bring to a light boil.
Reduce heat to minimum.
Add the baton rhubarb and poach very slowly at 150°C in the oven, covered by foil, until al dente.
Remove from the heat, and cool in a large shallow container.
Reserve in the fridge until required.

rhubarb purée:

Take 100g poached rhubarb and blend with a touch of poaching liquid to make a smooth purée.

genoise blanche:

Whisk the eggs and sugar together.
Sieve the flour and almonds, and mix well.
Machine whisk until maximum volume is achieved .
Fold carefully into the mix, keeping maximum volume.
Add a little mix in to the melted butter and mix well, fold gently back into the mix.
Fill loaf tin ¾ full and cook in fan oven at 170°C for 20-35 minutes.
Check with a wooden stick, when stick remains clean remove from oven and cool on wire racks.
De-mould and clingfilm when cold.
Once cooled, remove crusts and portion sponge to 1x3cm slices.

white wine granité:

Boil 50g of the water with the sugar.
Remove from the heat, and add the remaining water.
Mix with the wine and pass through a fine sieve.
Strain into a large metal container.
Freeze at -21°C until frozen.
Scrape as required.

ginger jelly:

Infuse the water, poaching liquor, sugar and the ginger for 10 minutes.
Add the gelatine, mix well and strain through a fine sieve.
Place into a small plastic container.
Clingfilm, set in the fridge.

marshmallow:

Whisk egg whites into soft peaks (start to do this when the sugar and water mix reaches 116°C)
Cook the water and sugar, when the mix reaches 121°C, add the soaked gelatine to the syrup.
Pour the mixture onto the egg whites and whisk until cool, then add the lime juice.
Fill domes as required, scoop out the centres, fill with desired flavour ice cream/sorbet and freeze.

to serve:

Make sure that the marshmallow with ice cream is placed on the (cold) plate at the very last minute before serving. Garnish with coriander cress.

Chef's tips:

Everything except the jelly can be made the day before, allowing the sweetness of the rhubarb to develop. Quick cheat: buy Madeira sponge instead of making the genoise blanche; if making yourself, be careful folding in the flour and almond to achieve maximum volume.

RECOMMENDED WINE
Inniskillin Ice Wine – Canada

SHARROW BAY COUNTRY HOUSE

'An experience
to be shared and
cherished with
magnificent views
of the lake and fells'

COLIN AKRIGG

Colin Akrigg, began his career when he joined Sharrow Bay in 1968 as a 15 year old kitchen porter from a nearby farm. Even as a 13 year old Colin was hugely ambitious: 'I knew exactly what I wanted, I wanted to be the head chef at Sharrow Bay'. His talents were quickly recognised and under the guidance of the late Francis Coulson, Colin became head chef in 1997 and achieved a Michelin star the following year, a feat that has remarkably been achieved for the last 11 consecutive years. Over the years Colin has trained some of the industries' top chefs such as Paul Heathcote and continues, alongside his highly-talented young team, to develop the world famous cuisine at Sharrow Bay.

MARK TEASDALE

Mark Teasdale was born and raised on a farm in Mungrisedale, close to Sharrow Bay. Mark joined the Sharrow Bay kitchen as Chef de Partie in 1996, working under the award-winning team of Colin Akrigg and Juan Martin. Mark was made Assistant Head Chef in 2006 and introduced the first in a series of culinary podcasts, which was at the time a pioneering concept for the industry. Mark was recently involved in the Von Essen culinary tour which visited Lower Slaughter and the Royal Crescent hotel in Bath and according to Mark was a 'fantastic experience to work alongside such upcoming enthusiastic chefs.'

Serves 4

Preparation time: 45 minutes
Cooking time: 5 minutes

Special equipment:
4 inch non-stick frying pan
18 inch frying pan
Parchment paper

Planning ahead:
Ensure you use a good chicken stock.
The velouté and pancetta can be
prepared in advance.

INGREDIENTS

8	scallops
250g	baby spinach
4	pieces of pancetta
4	quails' eggs

shrimp risotto:

150g	arborio rice
25g	butter
100ml	white wine
400ml	vegetable or fish stock
zest of ½ lemon	
200g	potted shrimps (to add at last minute)

velouté sauce:

12g	butter
2	shallots
½	leek
450ml	double cream
150ml	Noilly Prat
1	stick lemon grass
1	clove of garlic
2	sprigs of rosemary
a dash of lemon juice	
roes off the scallop	
pinch of cayenne pepper	

CARAMELISED SCALLOPS WITH BUTTERED SPINACH, SHRIMP RISOTTO, CRISPY PANCETTA, FRIED QUAIL'S EGG AND A SCALLOP VELOUTÉ

BY COLIN AKRIGG AND MARK TEASDALE

METHOD

shrimp risotto:

Sweat off 1 medium onion, 1 small clove of garlic, zest of lemon and seasoning to taste in the butter until onion is translucent. Add the arborio rice and stir until coated with the onions. Add the white wine stirring continuously until evaporated. Add the fish or vegetable stock a ladle at a time until evaporated. Keep adding the stock until the rice is cooked. Finish with Morecambe shrimps in butter, fresh soft herbs and a little cream. Serve immediately.

pancetta:

Place the pancetta flat between 2 sheets of parchment paper and two heavy flat baking trays – cook at 200°C until golden – approximately 7 minutes – leave to cool, it will crisp.

spinach:

Pick off stalks from baby spinach. Cook in a hot, large saucepan with a knob of butter and seasoning. Pat dry excess liquid with a kitchen towel.

scallops:

Halve the scallops and fry in a hot pan, 30 seconds on each side until caramelised and warmed through, taking care not to overcook.

velouté sauce:

Sweat off the leeks, shallot, onion and lemon grass in a little butter. Add the Noilly Prat, reduce by ¾. Add the scallop roes and cream. Bring to simmer and cook for 2 minutes.
Take off the heat and add the garlic, rosemary and season to taste. Add the lemon juice to taste and pinch of cayenne pepper.
Strain the liquid.

fried quail's egg:

Fry the quail eggs and add on top of the risotto at the last minute.

to serve:

Place a bed of spinach onto the centre of the plate in a rectangular shape.
Place risotto on top of the spinach.
Place 4 scallop halves on top of the risotto.
Pour velouté around the edge of the spinach.
Place a strip of the pancetta on top of the scallops and then finally a fried quail egg on top of the pancetta.

 RECOMMENDED WINE
Mercurey Blanc –
Maison Albert Sounit – Côte Chalonnaise

BEST END AND BRAISED SHOULDER OF HERDWICK LAMB WITH CREAMED SAVOURY CABBAGE, SHALLOT AND THYME ROSTI, PEA PURÉE AND A TOMATO AND ROSEMARY SAUCE

BY COLIN AKRIGG AND MARK TEASDALE

Serves 4

Preparation time: 20 minutes
Cooking time: 6 hours

Special equipment:
Magimix/blender
Non-stick rosti pan
Fine sieve

Planning ahead:
Prepare the rosti in advance; it is easier
to cut when it is cold and it can then be
reheated. The sauce can also be made in
advance.

INGREDIENTS

best end of lamb (French trimmed):

125g	brioche, crumbled
	chopped chervil
	chopped thyme
	pinch lemon zest
	grain mustard

shoulder of lamb:

85g	butter
70g	plain flour
½	onion
1	carrot
1	stick of celery
1	clove of garlic
1	sprig of thyme
1	sprig of Rosemary
250ml	red wine
500ml	chicken stock

rosti:

2	large Maris Piper potatoes
2	large shallots
3	sprigs of thyme

savoury cabbage:

1	head cabbage
50g	carrots
50g	celeriac
4 tbsp	double cream

pea purée

250g	peas

tomato and rosemary

2	plum tomatoes
2	sprigs of rosemary
2	cloves of garlic
1 tsp	oregano
125ml	tomato juice
500ml	chicken stock
250ml	demi glaze
	seasoning to taste

🍷 RECOMMENDED WINE
Beaune Blanc –
Domaine des Clos – Beaune
Aloxe Corton 1er Cru
Clos des Marechaudes – Burgundy

METHOD

best end of lamb:

Seal meat on both sides in a hot frying pan with a little oil.
Place seasoned lamb best end on a cooking rack on a baking tray. Bake for 8 minutes at 200°C, then turn and cook the meat for a further 8 minutes.
On the service side spread a thin layer of grain mustard, then a layer of herb crust, made with brioche crumble, chopped chervil, a pinch of lemon zest and fresh chopped thyme. Blitz together to make a green crumb.

braised rolled shoulder of lamb:

Seal meat all round until golden in a frying pan with a little oil. Put meat in a casserole dish.
Brown the onion, carrot, celery, garlic, thyme, rosemary. Add flour and mix well, then add red wine and chicken stock. Bring all these to the boil then transfer to the oven.
Cook in the oven at 110°C for 6 hours or until cooked. Then roll tightly in cling film.
When cooled, put in fridge. When cutting the meat, leave in the clingfilm. Heat up in the cooking juice to serve.

rosti:

Place the potato in cold seasoned water and bring to the boil. Cook for 5 minutes then place in cold water. Take the skins off. Grate the potato and season.
Sweat the shallots and thyme in a little butter until softened, but not browned.
In a rosti pan place some oil, butter and add a ¼ of the grated potato. Add the shallot then add another ½ of the grated potatoes.
Colour on both sides until golden brown. Place in the oven. Cook for 30 minutes, leave to cool then cut into triangles and reheat before serving.

savoury cabbage:

Pull off tough outer green leave from the cabbage. Do not use these.
Blanch the leaves in boiling water for 3 minutes. Plunge into iced water, then drain and shred finely.
Finely dice the onion, carrots and celeriac. Cook in butter until cooked. When ready to serve add 4 tbsp of double cream to the cabbage, carrots and celeriac until the cream is absorbed and heated throughout.

pea purée:

Blanch peas until cooked (approximately 3 minutes). Place in iced water. Put in a blender and purée, place through a fine chinoise. Add 1 tsp of mint jelly and mix.

tomato and rosemary:

Roast the trimmings from the best end of lamb as well as 2 plum tomatoes and the garlic until golden brown. Place in a pan with all the other ingredients, simmer until right consistency. Pass through a fine chinoise.

to serve:

On a serving plate place the potato rosti.
Next to the rosti place the shoulder of lamb, and add the pea puree to the top of it.
Next to the lamb put a metal ring and press the cabbage into it, and then remove the metal ring.

Serves 4

Preparation time: 45 minutes

Cooking time: 20 minutes

Special equipment:
Stencil
4 inch jelly moulds
6 inch square tin

Planning ahead:
The jelly can be prepared the day before.

CRANBERRY JELLY, ORANGE POLENTA CAKE AND A COINTREAU MASCARPONE

BY COLIN AKRIGG AND MARK TEASDALE

INGREDIENTS

cranberry jelly:

300g	cranberries
125g	sugar
1	orange, juice and zest
75ml	white wine
250ml	water
½	cinnamon stick,
1	star anise,
3	leaves of gelatine/pint liquid

orange polenta cake:

1	egg
50g	soft butter
25g	self raising flour
25g	fine polenta
	zest and juice of ½ orange
25g	sugar

cointreau mascarpone:

125g	mascarpone
45g	caster sugar
25ml	orange juice
25ml	Cointreau
½	leaf gelatine
125ml	double cream

tuile:

40g	butter
50g	icing sugar
1	egg white
40g	plain flour

candied orange:

1	orange
226g	sugar
284ml	water

orange sauce:

4	oranges
56g	sugar

RECOMMENDED WINE
*Château La Truffière –
Monbazillac – France*

METHOD

jelly:

Place the cranberries, sugar and juice and zest of orange in a bowl and stand over boiling water for at least an hour in order to relinquish the cranberry juice.
Bring the white wine and water to the boil and pour onto the cranberries. Strain the mixture through cheese cloth and measure the liquor. Soften the gelatine in cold water for 5 minutes and add to the hot liquor. Pass and set in 4oz pudding basins.

cake:

Cream butter and sugar until pale, add the egg and beat vigorously. Finally fold in the flour, polenta and zest.
Bake at 180°C in a 6 inch square cake tin, greased and lined, for approximately 20 minutes until risen and golden.
Make a syrup with orange juice and 40g sugar and brush onto the cooked cake. Cool and cut into ½ inch squares.

cointreau mascarpone:

Beat mascarpone and sugar until smooth. Warm Cointreau and orange juice and add gelatine (which has been softened in cold water). Add liquid to mascarpone and mix. Softly whip the cream and fold into the mixture, chill in the refrigerator.

tuile:

Beat the egg whites and sugar until mixed together.
Add the melted butter to the mixture and fold in the flour. Leave to rest in a fridge overnight.
Spread the mixture thinly onto baking parchment, and cut out using a plastic stencil in the shape of a cross.
Place cross onto a baking tray and cook at 150°C until golden in colour.
Spread the cross shape over the base of a pudding basin.
Carefully peel away from the basin and keep.

candied orange:

Peel one orange with a potato peeler, and cut into thin juliennes.
Place in a pan of boiling water and strain.
Repeat this process 4 times to remove all bitterness from the orange julienne.
Place the sugar in a saucepan and add the water. Bring to the boil.
Add the orange julienne to the syrup and allow to boil for one minute.

orange sauce:

Strain the juice of 4 oranges and add the sugar.
Bring the mixture to the boil and allow to reduce and then place in the fridge to chill.

how to serve:

Peel one orange cut into thin rounds (3 slices per plate).
Drizzle orange sauce over plate.
Place 3 slices of orange onto the centre of each plate.
Put cranberry jelly on top of the oranges.
Place tuile biscuit on top of the cranberry jelly.
Quenelle one portion of the cointreau cream and place on the tuile biscuit.
Cut out five small squares of polenta cake and place around the edge of the plate, and add in between a piece of candied orange.
Add a small sprig of mint to the cointreau cream.

AIRDS HOTEL

'On the romantic coast of Argyll in the Scottish Highlands. Impeccable, yet informal and friendly service giving you plenty of time to talk to your friends, enjoy the food or simply admire the breathtaking view'

PAUL BURNS

Paul Burns, Head Chef at The Airds Hotel, Port Appin, Argyll, began his career in Scone, Perthshire, where he grew up. Working, aged 15, as a kitchen porter, his genuine talent was quickly spotted and he was promoted to Commis Chef and went on to work under the tutorage of some of Scotland's best chefs. At 23 he was awarded three rosettes by the AA for food and has worked consistently at this level ever since. Paul has been a Master Chef of Great Britain for many years and was honoured to be made a "fellow" in 2007 at the age of 36.

Serves 4

Preparation time:	30 minutes
Cooking time:	30 minutes

PUFF PASTRY CASKET WITH SQUAB PIGEON AND WILD MUSHROOMS

BY PAUL BURNS

The squab pigeon is one of my favourite meats and served with a rich sauce in the pastry with locally picked wild mushrooms makes this an ideal autumn/winter dish. The squab can easily be replaced with rabbit or lamb fillets with the wild mushrooms replaced with cultivated mushrooms.

INGREDIENTS

4	breasts of squab pigeon
4	pieces of puff pastry – (8cm x 8cm and 1cm thick)
1	egg
	salt and pepper

sauce:

200g	wild mushrooms finely chopped – pied de mouton, chanterelles and oyster mushrooms
½	an onion, finely chopped
1 tsp	tarragon, fresh, finely chopped
1	good splash of brandy
1	good splash of Madeira
300ml	chicken stock
150ml	double cream
25g	pickled walnuts, finely chopped
50g	unsalted butter

to serve:

4	sprigs of chervil

METHOD
Preheat the oven to 375-400°F

pastry case:

Brush the puff pastry squares with the beaten egg. Cut around the top of the puff pastry 5mm from the edge to form a smaller square (this will then form the lid of the pastry case). Bake on a tray for 8-10 minutes. Remove from the oven, place the "lid" on one side for later and throw away any unbaked pastry. Keep warm until ready to use.

sauce:

Lightly fry the onion in a little of the butter and add the mushrooms. Cook for 3-4 minutes. Add the Madeira and Brandy and reduce by boiling rapidly.
Remove the mushrooms and add the chicken stock. Reduce by half and then add the double cream and cook until a nice creamy consistency is reached.
Add the mushrooms back and bring to the boil. Add the tarragon and pickled walnuts. Add the remaining butter and allow to melt. Keep warm.

squab pigeon:

Season and gently fry the squab pigeon on both sides for 2 minutes. Keep warm in the oven until ready to use.
Carve the squab pigeon in preparation.

to serve:

Retrieve the cooked pastry case and "lid" and place the mushroom mixture and the sliced pigeon on top of the pastry. Place on a serving plate and drizzle a little of the remaining sauce onto the plate. Place the "lid" of the pastry case on top and garnish with sprigs of chervil.

 RECOMMENDED WINE
Clos Louie Rouge –
Côtes de Castillon – Bordeaux

Serves 4

Preparation time:	40 minutes
Cooking time:	20 minutes

BRAISED FILLET OF OBAN TURBOT WITH A LIGHT BROTH OF SHELLFISH

BY PAUL BURNS

On the west coast of Scotland we have a fabulous choice of locally caught fish and shellfish. To make this simple dish taste even better try sourcing your own local supplied fish to help keep the "Fresh is best" policy.

INGREDIENTS

400g	prime turbot fillet
4	king scallops
4	large langoustine tails, peeled
500g	large, fresh mussels, thoroughly washed
4	shallots, finely chopped
1	medium carrot, cut into thin strips and blanched
12	small asparagus spears, blanched
1	white leek, cut into thin strips and blanched
2	tomatoes, skinned, de-seeded and diced
300ml	fish stock
200ml	vegetable stock
350ml	dry white wine
300ml	double cream
2 tsp	dill, chopped
25g	unsalted butter (cut into cubes and placed in the fridge)

salt and pepper to season

METHOD

Cut the turbot into 4 equal portions and place in the fridge
Place 8 large mussels in the fridge then steam the remaining mussels in the vegetable stock together with a splash of wine until they are open (this should take about 2 minutes). Carefully remove the mussels from their shells and place to one side until required.
Melt one cube of butter in a frying pan and add the finely chopped shallots. Cook until soft.
Add the wine and reduce by two thirds. Add the fish stock and again reduce by two thirds.
Add the double cream and simmer for two minutes.
Remove the 4 pieces of turbot from the fridge and season lightly with salt and pepper. Place all 4 pieces in the pan and cook for two minutes, turning once.
Season the scallops and langoustines and add to the pan. Turn over after one minute.
Take the remaining mussels from the fridge and together with the carrot, leek and asparagus and add to the pan. Simmer gently.
When the mussels start to open, add the mussels already cooked and the chopped dill. Place a lid over the pan and continue to simmer until all the ingredients are hot through.
Remove the pan from the heat. Add the diced tomatoes and stir in the butter carefully.
Once the butter has melted, stir and serve immediately in four equal portions.

Chef's tip:

Be careful when cooking mussels – never force open a mussel. Any mussels which do not open during cooking MUST be discarded and thrown away.
The secret of this dish is good preparation. Ensure the ingredients are prepared and at hand, before starting to cook.
If you are a lover of shellfish you may add or take away any of the shellfish ingredients.

RECOMMENDED WINE
Dezaley Medinette Blanc –
Louis Bovard – Vaud – Switzerland

Serves 4

Preparation time:	4 hours (minimum, for the mousse to set)
Cooking time:	N/A

"AIRDS" VANILLA BEAN MOUSSE WITH CASSIS, POACHED GARDEN BERRIES AND COULIS

BY PAUL BURNS

"Airds" vanilla mousse is a light creamy dessert with the added pleasure of our own home grown berries. In late summer/early autumn the hedgerows also give an added luxury of brambles with a truly individual flavour.

INGREDIENTS

to prepare the vanilla mousse:

2	vanilla pods
½ ltr	double cream
70g	caster sugar
1 ½	leaves of gelatine (soaked in cold water)

poached berries:

200g	caster sugar (you can use less sugar if you prefer)
200ml	water

juice of ½ a lemon
a selection of fresh berries (washed with stalks removed)
cassis

raspberry coulis:

250g	fresh raspberries
100g	icing sugar

juice of ½ a lemon or lime
5   mint leaves to garnish

METHOD

vanilla mousse:

Scrape the vanilla pods into 150ml of the cream and add the sugar.
Simmer and leave to infuse for 2 minutes.
Add the gelatine and pass through a fine sieve.
Lightly whip 350,l of cream and then fold into the vanilla cream.
Combine the two completely.
Pour into moulds.
Allow to set in the fridge for a minimum of 4 hours.

poached berries:

Add together the water, lemon juice, a good splash of cassis and sugar and allow to simmer for 5 minutes. This makes up the stock syrup
Wash the berries and place in a bowl.
Remove the hot syrup from the pan and pour over the berries. Leave to cool.

raspberry coulis:

Place the fresh raspberries and the juice of the lemon in a blender or food processor and blend for 10 minutes, slowly adding the icing sugar. The amount of icing sugar can vary depending on how sweet you want the coulis to be. Pass through a fine sieve.

to serve:

Remove the mousse from the moulds by placing half the mould in boiling water for about 2 seconds and then turn out onto serving plate. Drain the berries from the syrup and arrange round the mousse. Finally drizzle the coulis over the berries and place mint leaves around the berries before serving.

RECOMMENDED WINE
Saumur Rouge Sparkling –
Domaine de la Paleine – Saumur

GLENAPP
CASTLE

'A fairytale castle on the rugged and beautiful Ayshire coast. Imagine exquisite rooms, outstanding cuisine, fine wines and exceptional service – a world apart'

ADAM STOKES

Adam grew up in Lincolnshire where he completed catering school, before joining the kitchen brigade at fellow Relais & Châteaux Hambleton Hall, where he spent several years before joining Glenapp Castle. Following culinary experiences in London and Paris he has created an individual style which incorporates a sophisticated blend of traditional combinations and inventive twists. The best British and finest local ingredients such as Ballantrae crab and Ayrshire lamb are seen on his daily changing six course menu. He was recently awarded Gourmet Menu of the Year at the Scottish Chef Awards 2009.

Serves 4

Preparation time: 1 ½ hours
Cooking time: 10 minutes

Special equipment:
Non-stick pan
Japanese mandolin

Planning ahead:
You can make the purée and the oil two
days before.

ROASTED SEA BASS WITH COCKLES, A FENNEL AND VANILLA SALAD AND A FENNEL AND DILL PURÉE

BY ADAM STOKES

I love this beautifully simple dish. It showcases Scotland's fantastic fish and seafood. To capture the true magic of this dish you will need the freshest line caught wild sea bass and beautifully fresh plump cockles.

INGREDIENTS

sea bass and cockles:

1kg	wild line caught sea bass (scaled and filleted into 4 portions) – can be substituted for sea bream
15	cockles
50g	Sauternes – sweet wine
olive oil	
butter	

fennel and vanilla salad:

½	bulb of fennel
1	vanilla pod
25ml	grapeseed oil

fennel and dill purée:

½	bulb of fennel – finely sliced
150g	water
8g	Pernod
25ml	double cream
chopped dill	

to season
lemon juice
vanilla oil
salt

METHOD

fennel and vanilla salad:

Vanilla Oil – marinade the vanilla pods in grapeseed oil and leave in a warm place for 24 hours. 30 minutes before serving, slice the fennel on a mandolin and season with salt, lemon and the vanilla oil. Leave to soften in a warm place for 20 minutes. Save some vanilla oil to glaze the fish just before serving the dish.

fennel and dill purée:

Slice the fennel finely with a mandolin, place in a pan with the water and Pernod, boil until soft (approximately 15 minutes) and strain – keep this cooking liquid. Put the softened fennel and double cream into a food blender and blend whilst gradually adding the cooking liquid until a smooth purée is produced. Finally, add the dill.

sea bass and surf clams:

Heat the olive oil in a non-stick pan, sear the fillets of sea bass and season with salt and a squeeze of lemon. Finish with a knob of butter and glaze with vanilla oil. Place the surf clams and Sauternes in a hot pan and cook until the clams open (approximately 1 minute) at which point season with salt and lemon.

to serve:

Place the fennel and vanilla salad in a small heap slightly off centre on the plate. Add the sea bass on top (skin side up). For the tear drop of fennel and dill purée, put a spoonful of purée onto the plate and drag the back of a spoon through the spoonful. Dress the dish with the surf clams, glaze the top of the sea bass with vanilla oil and drizzle a little vanilla oil over the plate.

 RECOMMENDED WINE
Buxus Villette Sauvignon Blanc –
Louis Bovard – Vaud – Switzerland

Serves 4

Preparation time: 2 hours

Cooking time: 15 minutes

Special equipment:
Japanese mandolin
Round cutters

Planning ahead:
You can make the hot-pot mix and celeriac the day before.

ROASTED LOIN OF AYRSHIRE ROE VENISON WITH CELERIAC, SZECHUAN AND HOT-POT

BY ADAM STOKES

This dish represents the use of two parts of the deer, the better known loin and the cheaper haunch. Each cut is dealt with very differently. The hot-pot adds a traditional British aspect as well as acting as a sauce for the dish.

INGREDIENTS

roasted loin of venison:

380g venison loin
salt
Szechuan pepper – or black pepper if preferred

celeriac purée:

½ celeriac (diced)
100ml chicken stock
50ml double cream
50g smoked bacon (chopped)

hot-pot mix:

50g venison haunch (diced)
50g mixture of carrot, shallot and ceps – other mushrooms (diced) can be used if preferred
25g morteaux sausage (diced)
50g bouillon
pinch of garlic and thyme (diced)
pinch of salt and Szechuan pepper
pinch of tarragon

hot-pot top:

1 large Maris Piper potato
knob of melted clarified butter

to season:
lemon
the hot-pot mix and purée
salt

METHOD

celeriac purée:

Add cream, chicken stock and smoked bacon to pan with celeriac and cook gently until soft. Place in food processor and blitz until smooth then season with salt and a squeeze of lemon.

hot-pot mix:

Place haunch, carrots, ceps, shallot, morteaux sausage, garlic and thyme into a red hot pan and cook with a little colour. When soft add bouillon, seasoning and tarragon. Cook until hot-pot liquor is at the right consistency and full of flavour.

hot-pot top:

Slice the peeled potatoes very thinly on a mandolin (alternatively with a knife) then cut out with a round cutter (2-3cm diameter). Place the thin rounds in a little clarified butter then place in a non-stick pan in a round formation and cook until golden brown. Season with salt and leave in a warm place.

roasted loin of venison:

Cut venison into four equal portions and sear in hot oil until coloured on each side. Set meat aside. When ready to serve the other components of the dish, place the venison portions in a pan with hot butter and cook for approximately 6-7 minutes turning constantly. Set aside to rest for 2 minutes.

to serve:

The celeriac purée and hot-pot mix should be served hot and the hot-pot top warm. Put the hot-pot mix in a small pan handle dish (alternatively use a ramekin dish) with the top on and place to one side of the plate. Place purée onto plate with the sliced pink venison on top.

 RECOMMENDED WINE
*Dezaley Grand Cru Rouge –
Louis Bovard – Vaud – Switzerland*

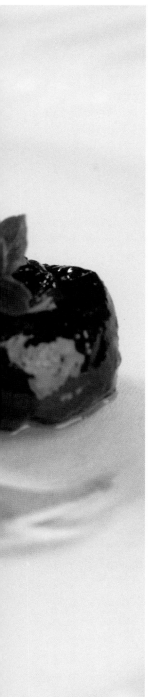

Serves 4

Preparation time: 1 ½ hours

Cooking time: N/A

Special equipment:
Silicone paper
Sugar thermometer

Planning ahead:
You can make the parfait up to a week in advance.

INGREDIENTS

caramelised pear and macadamia nuts:

4	waxed tipped pears
60g	macadamia nuts
100g	sugar
½	vanilla pod

juice of ½ lemon
mint
caramel sheet (cooling a thin sheet of caramelised sugar on a silicone/greaseproof sheet)

macadamia praline parfait:

75g	sugar
30g	water
1	egg
3	egg yolks
1	vanilla pod (seeds only)
300g	double cream

silicone/greaseproof sheets

earl grey and prune jelly:

1 tbsp	Earl Grey tea leaves
50ml	stock syrup
25ml	white wine
25ml	water
8	prunes (4 for garnish)
1	leaf of gelatine

CARAMELISED WAX TIPPED PEAR WITH MACADAMIA PRALINE PARFAIT AND AN EARL GREY AND PRUNE JELLY

BY ADAM STOKES

This unusual combination of ingredients makes a truly fabulous dessert.

METHOD

caramelised pear and macadamia nuts:

Place 50g of the sugar in a pan and heat to a caramel, add the nuts and when evenly coated, place them on a silicone/greaseproof sheet to cool. Heat the remaining 50g of sugar to a caramel, then add the peeled and quartered pears. When the pears have an even coating of caramel, add the half pod of vanilla and the lemon juice to glaze. Place on a baking tray to cool.

macadamia praline parfait:

To make a sugar mix: boil the sugar and water to 121°C. Whisk eggs in food processor until light and fluffy then pour onto the sugar mix making an egg mix. In another bowl, whisk the cream and the contents of the vanilla pod into a soft peak. Fold the cream mix and the egg mix together and add the cooled caramelised nuts. Place this mixture onto a long flat tray lined with silicone/greaseproof sheets and place flat in the freezer to set.

earl grey and prune jelly:

Bring the stock syrup, white wine, water and tea leaves to the boil in a pan. Add four prunes and the gelatine, cover and leave to infuse for 1 hour. Strain through a sieve, removing the prunes and tea leaves and then leave the jelly to set in the fridge.

to serve:

Place the cold pears on the plate followed by a neatly cut slice of parfait. Garnish plate with small cubes of jelly and the remaining prunes, mint and a thin caramel sheet.

Chef's tip:

Presentation is down to the cutting of the pears and parfait.

 RECOMMENDED WINE
*Liqueur au Calvados –
Lecompte*

INVERLOCHY CASTLE

'Scotland's finest luxury hotel located amongst the glens, lochs and mountains of the West Highlands of Scotland. The best personal service'

MATTHEW GRAY

Matthew Gray was appointed Head Chef at Inverlochy in 2000, having joined the hotel in 1995 and been promoted to Sous Chef in 1997. Matthew was born and raised in Elderslie, Renfrewshire, Scotland. He initially followed his father into the hospitality industry, completing a degree in hotel management at Napier Polytechnic, Edinburgh in 1990. However, he subsequently decided that hospitality wasn't for him, and trained instead as a chef.

Serves 4

Preparation time: 30 minutes (for the lobster)

Cooking time: 8 minutes (roughly, for an 800g lobster)

Special equipment:
Fryer

Planning ahead:
Hang the yoghurt and breadcrumb 24 hours before.

INGREDIENTS

lobster:

1   lobster cooked (800g, for two people)

cauliflower salad:

1   tomato concasse (peel, seeded and diced)
cooked cauliflower florettes
chopped chives

french vinaigrette:

1   egg yolk
100ml   balsamic
75ml   raspberry vinegar
60ml   sherry vinegar
        (step 1)
2½g   salt
5g   sugar
8g   Dijon mustard
300g   ground nut oil
        (step 2)
250g   cream (step 3)
1   clove of garlic
rosemary (step 4)
basil
3 tbsp French dressing
1 tbsp crème fraîche

yoghurt beignet:

250g   good quality natural yoghurt
tobasco, to taste
dried breadcrumbs
salt and pepper

SCOTTISH BLUE LOBSTER, CAULIFLOWER SALAD AND YOGHURT BEIGNETS

BY MATTHEW GRAY

This lobster dish is one of our most popular on the menu to date.

METHOD

Hang the yoghurt in a muslin overnight to remove excess moisture. Season with salt and pepper and tobasco. Roll into balls and breadcrumb. Remove shell from lobster and cut into desired size. Make the dressing by mixing the ingredients together in the above order i.e. 1, 2, 3 and 4. Add crème fraîche to dressing base before using.

how to serve:

Mix the cauliflower, concasse, chives and vinaigrette together. Season to taste. Deep fry beignets until golden. Season. Place salad on the plate and neatly arrange the lobster and beignets on top. Garnish with Chervil. Extra dressing can be put on plate if desired.

Chef's tip:

If lobster is too expensive it can be substituted with prawns. The yoghurt mix can be lightly frozen to make it easier to panne.

 RECOMMENDED WINE
Cuvée des Huitres Champagne – Grand Cru – Bruno Vesselle – Bouzy

HIBISCUS CRUSTED VENISON MEDALLIONS, YOUNG LEEKS AND A BLACK PEPPER DRESSING

BY MATTHEW GRAY

Simple but tasty!

Serves 4

Preparation time:	30 minutes (to infuse black pepper dressing)
Cooking time:	10 minutes (for the venison)

Planning ahead:
You can make the purée and black pepper dressing in advance.

INGREDIENTS

black pepper dressing:

100ml	good quality olive oil
1	lemon, juiced
20	turns, milled coarse black pepper

salt to taste

butternut squash purée:

1	small butternut squash diced
1	shallot sliced
2	sprigs of thyme
20g	butter
200ml	cream

salt and pepper

charred young leeks:

12	baby leeks (trimmed)

ground nut oil
sea salt to taste

venison medallions:

hibiscus powder

12	venison medallions

salt and pepper

METHOD

black pepper dressing:

Mix all the ingredients together.
Leave to infuse flavours.

butternut squash purée:

Sauté the shallots and thyme and diced butternut squash in butter. Season with salt and pepper, add chicken stock and cook until very soft. Add cream, bring to the boil. Blend until you have a nice smooth purée. Season to taste if needed. The purée can be made in advance if desired.

charred young leeks:

Wash baby leeks and dry. Lightly cover with oil. Chargrill on both sides, they should still be crunchy.
Season lightly with sea salt.

venison medallions:

Pan fry venison medallions in hot oil until coloured on both sides. Remove from pan and leave to rest. Sprinkle with hibiscus powder and keep warm.

assembly:

Place some squash on the plate.
Lay on the baby leeks and place the venison medallions as desired. Finish with the black pepper dressing.

Chef's tip:

The venison is best served pink. Being medallions these are easy to overcook – be careful.

RECOMMENDED WINE
*Vougeot Clos de Village Rouge –
Domaine Leymarie – Burgundy*

Serves 4

Preparation time: 1 ½ hours (for the
                    chocolate cream,
                    including freezing
                    time)

Cooking time: 15 minutes (for the
                    chocolate cream)

Special equipment:
Sugar thermometer
Martini glasses

Planning ahead:
You can make the granité in advance.

INGREDIENTS

chocolate cream:

500g	cream
90g	sugar
3	yolks
80g	milk chocolate
50g	praline paste

granité:

500g	raspberries
300g	water
100g	sugar
1	lemon, juiced

chocolate nougatine:

125g	sugar
75g	glucose
25g	butter
25g	dark chocolate

🍷 **RECOMMENDED WINE**
*Cristallo Vin de Fraise –
Thurgau – Switzerland*

CHOCOLATE AND PRALINE CREAM WITH RASPBERRY GRANITÉ

BY MATTHEW GRAY

I chose this dessert as it is so easy to put together yet looks and tastes sublime – especially when presented in a martini glass.

METHOD

Cook sugar to caramel. Add warm cream. Bring to the boil. Pour onto eggs.
Bring up to 85°C.
Add melted chocolate and praline paste.
Pass. Leave to cool.
Cook raspberries with water, sugar and lemon juice.
Liquidise, pass.
Freeze in container.
Cook sugar and glucose to light caramel, add butter and chocolate.
Pour onto tray. Once set blitz and sprinkle onto greaseproof.
Melt in oven.

to serve:

Put the cream into martini glasses. Top the cream with raspberry granité, garnish with fresh raspberries and chocolate nougatine.

Chef's tip:

The milk chocolate can be substituted with dark or white chocolate.
This dish works well with any berries.

KINLOCH HOUSE

'In the very heart
of Scotland
with a belief
in the value of
freshness and
quality'

ANDREW MAY

New Zealand born Andrew May began his cooking career at the age of 18. At a young age he moved to the UK, spending several years working throughout Britain in a number of fine dining establishments. He then travelled extensively in Europe, Zimbabwe and South Africa where he extended his repertoire while discovering new ingredients and techniques. On returning to the UK, Andrew moved to Perthshire where he decided to settle and started working at Kinloch House. He was promoted to Head Chef in 2006 where he was able to pay close attention to detail from the supplier to the table, giving a consistency of performance in the kitchen and a belief in the value of freshness and quality. He enjoys making full use of the excellent and readily available local produce from Perthshire.

Serves 4

Preparation time:	30 minutes
Cooking time:	15 minutes

Special equipment:
Ring moulds

Planning ahead:
The day before: cook the crab, allow to cool, remove meat and take your time to thoroughly pick through it to remove the shell.

INGREDIENTS

100g	white crab meat
4 tbsp	mayonnaise
1 tsp	grapefruit juice
1 tsp	chives – chopped
salt and pepper	
2	avocados – ripe
vinaigrette	
4	plum tomatoes – seeded and skinned, chopped in very small pieces

gazpacho:

675g	plum tomatoes – ripe
4g	tarragon
2	red peppers
1	slice of white bread/ no crust
25ml	white wine
125ml	olive oil
½	cucumber
½ tbsp	tomato purée
½	clove garlic
dash	tabasco sauce
1	shallot
1 dstsp	sugar
7g	basil
salt and pepper	

garnish:
Finely chopped, skinned tomatoes and cucumber.

TIAN OF SCOTTISH CRAB WITH GAZPACHO
BY ANDREW MAY

We find this dish exceptionally refreshing as well as visually impressive. Fresh, local crab is a spring/summertime delight.

METHOD

tian:

Place white meat in bowl, add mayonnaise, grapefruit juice and chives and combine together. Check for seasoning.
Peel, stone and roughly chop the avocados, mix with a squeeze of lemon juice and a drizzle of vinaigrette.
Place 4 round moulds on a tray and fill with layers of avocado, crab and finally tomato, pressing down each layer to give a good shape.

gazpacho:

Roughly chop the first eight ingredients, add the remaining ingredients, and refrigerate overnight.
Liquidise then pass through a sieve

to serve:

Place tian of crab in centre of plate and remove the ring. Surround with chilled gazpacho sauce and finely chopped, skinned tomatoes and cucumber.

RECOMMENDED WINE
Chablis Grand Cru Moutonne –
Domaine de la Moutonne – Burgundy

SLOW COOKED FEATHERBLADE STEAK WITH HORSERADISH POTATO PURÉE, ROAST VEGETABLES AND A RED WINE SAUCE

BY ANDREW MAY

Although this dish takes a little time to prepare and cook, the end result is so succulent and tasty it is worth the effort.

Serves 6

Preparation time:	45 minutes
Cooking time:	2 ½ hours

Special equipment:
Potato ricer/masher

Planning ahead:
The beef needs to be tied with string. It can be cooked the day before and refrigerated which allows the shape to form. The vegetables can be pre-blanched so they are ready to be reheated.

INGREDIENTS

1kg	featherblade of beef
3	medium onions, peeled
2	carrots, peeled
250ml	red wine
1	head garlic
500ml	beef stock
2 tbsp	tomato purée
1	bay leaf
1	sprig of thyme
olive oil	

horseradish potato purée:

680g	Maris Piper potatoes, peeled and chopped
115g	butter
240ml	hot milk
1 tbsp	creamed horseradish
salt and pepper	

vegetables:
spinach
baby carrots
parsnips (turned)
sauté parsnips
green beans
butter
honey
salt and pepper for seasoning

METHOD

Preheat oven to 180°C.
Brown the featherblade in a heavy large saucepan or oven casserole dish on a high temperature using the olive oil. Season meat during this process.
Roughly chop the onions and carrots, add them to the beef and continue to cook until the blade is sealed and brown.
Add the red wine, herbs, garlic and beef stock and bring the liquid to a low simmer and cover. Place casserole in the oven at 180°C for 2½-3 hours. You may need to top up the stock with water.
Once the blade is very tender, gently remove from the stock and allow to cool for 5-10 minutes.
Roll the blade in clingfilm in a swiss roll fashion, making a uniform sausage shape, tighten ends and tie.
Now add tomato purée to stock and reduce until sauce consistency.

horseradish potato purée:

Cook potatoes in boiling salted water until tender. Drain and pass through a ricer.
Place potatoes in a bowl with butter, half the milk and creamed horseradish. Whip together and pass through a fine sieve.
Place in a saucepan and whisk in remaining milk until the mixture has ribbon-like consistency. Season to taste.

vegetables:

Sauté spinach with butter, salt and pepper.
Peel carrots into shape and boil in salted water until tender.
Sauté parsnips in pan with oil until lightly coloured, add a little honey and seasoning and roast in oven for 4 minutes.
Boil green beans in salted water for 3 minutes and refresh.

to serve:

Cut featherblade into six equal size portions and gently reheat in the sauce.
Place spinach in the centre of a heated plate and place the steak on the spinach.
Put a line of potato next to the steak then arrange the vegetables together and drizzle red wine sauce around plate.

RECOMMENDED WINE
Morey Saint Denis Rouge – Domaine Leymarie – Burgundy

DUO OF CHOCOLATE MOUSSE WITH SOFT MILK CHOCOLATE CENTRE AND RASPBERRY COULIS

BY ANDREW MAY

This dessert is one of the most popular in the restaurant so it was an obvious choice, and everyone loves chocolate!

Serves 4

Preparation time: 30 minutes

Cooking time: 15 minutes, then 2 hours in the fridge

Special equipment:
Sugar/jam thermometer
Ring moulds
Blow torch (optional)

Planning ahead:
Make the chocolate triangles and tear drops in advance. The chocolate glaze can be made the day before.

INGREDIENTS

coulis:

112.5g	fresh or frozen raspberries
50g	caster sugar
7.5ml	lemon juice

milk chocolate ganache – (for centre):

100ml	cream
42.5ml	water
25ml	butter
60g	milk chocolate

chocolate Glaze – (for top of dessert):

90g	dark chocolate
20ml	water
41.5ml	milk
21g	sugar
31.5ml	cream
21g	glucose

dark chocolate mousse:

55g	dark chocolate
75ml	water
20g	butter
100ml	double cream
1½ (30g)	egg yolks
45g	egg whites
50g	caster sugar

white chocolate mousse:

150g	white chocolate
37.5ml	water
250ml	double cream
2	leaves gelatine
25g	caster sugar

METHOD

coulis:

Place raspberries in a liquidiser along with the sugar and lemon juice. Blitz until smooth then pass through a fine strainer. If sauce is too thick add a little water to thin it down, check sweetness and add more sugar to desired taste. Chill before serving.

milk chocolate ganache – (for centre):

Place chocolate and butter in a bowl and set over a pan of simmering water until melted, heat water and cream, add to chocolate mixture, mix thoroughly and pour into deep tray and freeze.

chocolate glaze – (for top of dessert):

Boil together milk, cream, water, sugar and glucose.
Add to chocolate, mix until melted, leave to cool.

dark chocolate mousse:

Melt chocolate and butter over bain-marie, and allow to cool slightly Whisk the yolks until light and fluffy, meanwhile, boil the sugar and water to 120°C.
Once the sugar has reached 120°C, pour slowly into whisking egg yolks and continue to beat until the mixture is cold.
Whip cream to soft peaks, whisk whites to soft peaks.
Fold chocolate into yolk mixture, fold cream through then finally fold the whites into the mix.

white chocolate mousse:

Melt chocolate over bain-marie. Soak gelatine in cold water and semi whip cream.
Heat water and sugar until warm enough to dissolve gelatine in.
Add gelatine leaves to warmed sugar/water and dissolve.
Add the mix to the chocolate and mix thoroughly, fold into semi whipped cream.

to assemble dessert:

Pipe chocolate mousse into a mould half way up.
Cut rounds from the frozen ganache and place into centre, working quickly as this will defrost quickly.
Pipe white chocolate mousse into the mould until full. Scrape off any excess to level the mould. Place in fridge to set.
Once set place chocolate glaze on top and level, place in fridge again for 15 minutes to set the glaze.

to serve:

Using a blow torch or the heat from your hands, un-mould the dessert on to a plate and decorate with chocolate garnishes and raspberries and pour raspberry coulis around the plate.

 RECOMMENDED WINE
Cristallo Vin de Fraise –
Thurgau – Switzerland

KINNAIRD

JEAN-BAPTISTE BADY

Jean-Baptiste joined Kinnaird as a Sous Chef in early 2004 and took over as Head Chef in 2007. He is driven in his belief that sourcing produce from local farmers and producers delivers the essential freshness and authenticity required to truly create "taste on a plate" and, where possible, he uses the best of Scottish produce. Jean-Baptiste has worked at many revered Relais & Châteaux properties including La Côte d'Or Bernard Loiseau with three Michelin starred chef Bernard Loiseau. From Bernard, Jean-Baptiste learnt to understand food and how to keep it simple yet tasty. He also learnt how you inspire a team in a calm and cheery working environment and he now runs his kitchen in the same style, encouraging learning in a relaxed and constructive environment.

'Each meal is
a celebration
sourced mainly
from Scotland's
natural larder'

LANGOUSTINE, CRISPY OYSTER, RATTES POTATO

BY JEAN-BAPTISTE BADY

This dish is all about beautiful Scottish seafood. Loch Fyne is only one hour away from Kinnaird so the freshness is guaranteed. This dish would be perfect for early autumn when the oysters are at their best.

Serves 4

Preparation time:	45 minutes
Cooking time:	25 minutes

Special equipment:
Deep fat fryer

INGREDIENTS

8	large langoustines
12	oysters
200g	peeled and cooked rattes potatoes
15g	finely chopped shallots
5cl	sherry vinegar
10g	shopped dill
5cl	olive oil
0.2 ltr	fish stock
salt	
0.1 ltr	cream
100g	coarse sea salt

tempura mix:

3 tbsp	flour
2 tbsp	cornflour
1 tbsp	baking powder
10cl	sparkling water

METHOD

Open the oyster and peel the langoustine, wash carefully the oyster shells and reserve. Make the tempura batter.
Reheat the fish stock add the cream reduce by a third, without boiling keep warm.
Reheat the potato and crush them. Add the olive oil, shallots, sherry vinegar, dill and seasoning.
Coat eight of the oysters in tempura and deep fry until crispy. Pan sear the langoustine and finish the velouté by blending the four remaining oysters into the warm sauce.

to serve:

Wet the sea salt and divide onto four plates. Place three of the reserved oyster shells per serving on top of the wet sea salt, fill with potato then top two shells with a langoustine and one with an oyster. Froth the velouté with a small whisk, and spoon over the langoustine.

RECOMMENDED WINE
Cuvée des Huitres Champagne – Grand Cru – Bruno Vesselle – Bouzy

LOIN OF WILD BOAR, BUTTERNUT SQUASH PURÉE, POTATO MILLE-FEUILLE, BLACK MUSTARD SEED JUS

BY JEAN-BAPTISTE BADY

I've chosen this dish because wild boar is not something usual on a menu, but is one of our best sellers. The meat is always tender and tasteful, for me the flavours are very important.

Serves 4

Preparation time:	1 hour
Cooking time:	1 ½ hours

Special equipment:
1 deep rectangular mould
(14cm x 6cm x 5cm)

INGREDIENTS

1	large butternut squash
250g	butter
0.1 ltr	cream
1kg	Maris Piper potato
1	loin of wild boar (about 1.2 kg)
10g	black mustard seed
0.2 ltr	veal jus
4	banana shallots
400g	baby navet
0.2 ltr	cider
1	Braeburn apple
salt and pepper	

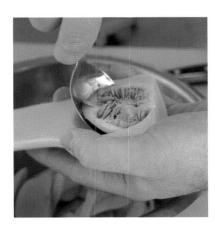

METHOD

Preheat the oven at 180°C for the potato, the squash, and the boar.

Peel and finely slice the potatoes and melt the butter in a pan. Coat the potatoes in the warm butter, then layer them into the mould, seasoning each layer. Bake for 30 minutes and allow to cool.

Peel and dice the butternut squash, wrap in kitchen foil and bake for 20 minutes.

Remove from the foil and purée in a blender with the cream, 20g of butter and seasoning.

Trim the loin of boar, reserving the trimmings for the sauce, portion off 4 cutlets and leave the rest whole.

For the sauce, roast the trimmings and apple together, deglaze with the cider, reduce by half, pass through a fine chinoise then add the veal jus and reduce to a sauce consistency.

Peel and blanch the baby navets, peel and slice the shallots into 1.5cm rings.

Roast the loin of wild boar for 8 to 10 minutes then allow to rest for at least 10 minutes, meanwhile, pan fry the cutlets and shallots together.

to serve:

Cut the potato into 4 slices, brush with butter and place in the oven. Reheat the purée, finish the sauce with the black mustard seed, glaze the navet in butter. Slice the loin and plate as illustrated.

Chef's tip:

In this dish the mustard seeds bring a hint of heat to balance the sweetness of the butternut squash. But the most important thing is to make sure that no flavour blinds another, this is very important for me.

 RECOMMENDED WINE
*Chambolle Musigny 1er Cru –
Domaine Leymarie – Burgundy*

Serves 4

Preparation time: 1 hour

Cooking time: 20 minutes and a
                      further 8 minutes
                      before serving

Special equipment:
4 ramekin moulds
(7cm diameter)

Planning ahead:
You can prepare the sorbet the day before.

INGREDIENTS

6	fresh basil leaves
30g	finely chopped confit lemon (can be replaced by bitter lemon marmalade)
100g	whole milk
4	eggs
20g	cornflour
10g	soft butter
100g	caster sugar
100g	water
1	leaf of gelatine
100g	lemon juice
	zest of 1 lemon (organic)
10g	icing sugar

HOT LEMON AND BASIL SOUFFLÉ

BY JEAN-BAPTISTE BADY

I've picked this dish for its originality. Basil and lemon work well together in savoury dishes, but are very rarely seen as a combination in a sweet dish. This dish is perfect on a sunny summer's day.

METHOD

Soak the gelatine leaf into cold water.

Boil the water with 50g of sugar and pour over 80g of lemon juice, then infuse with the fresh basil for 5 minutes. Add the gelatine, pass through a fine sieve and freeze (allow 12 hours in the freezer before using).

Bring the milk to boil. In the meantime, mix 2 egg yolks with 30g of sugar and the cornflour. Pour one third of the boiling milk over the mix, stir well and return this mix into the pan with the remaining milk. Cook as a light custard taking care not to bring to a boil, allow to cool down.

Prepare ramekin mould by coating inside with 10g of soft butter and spread with sugar.

Whisk 4 egg whites until firm peaks, add in 20g of sugar and 10g lemon juice, whisk until meringue is smooth and firm. In a separate bowl, mix together the confit lemon, 10g of lemon juice and chopped basil, then fold the meringue gently into this mix.

Preheat the oven to 170°C, put the mixture into the mould and bake for 8 minutes.

to serve:
Scrape the granité with a fork and place it in a cold glass.
Sprinkle icing sugar over the top of the soufflé, put on a plate next to the granité and serve immediately.

RECOMMENDED WINE
Château La Truffière –
Monbazillac – France

THE PERFECT CHEESEBOARD

Where did cheese come from as a savoury dessert? And where does it fit into a meal?

Cheese has been around since the time of the ancient Egyptians, and in many countries, especially in the Western world, has become a staple of menus and often a part of a nation's culture. General Charles De Gaulle famously asked 'How can you govern a country which has 246 varieties of cheese?' And in France cheese has become something of a national icon, from the creamy simplicity of Brie and Camembert to the subtle fruitiness of Comté and the magnificent richness of Vacherin-Mont d'Or and Époisses. In the UK, too, there are classic cheeses recognised around the world: Stilton is probably the most famous, but Cheddar became so popular that it has lost its regional connotation and is now made everywhere, and Cheshire and Wensleydale have long histories. In recent years, cheeses such as Lord of the Hundreds and Stinking Bishop have made their appearance — indeed, the UK now produces some 450 varieties of cheese whilst France has moved on to around 1,000. What Charles De Gaulle would have made of that we shall never know.

Cheese on the restaurant menu is a different matter: in the distant past it was the food of the poor, who couldn't afford to slaughter their livestock but could turn the milk into a protein-rich food. As with all artisanal products, its simple quality and easy availability insinuated it on to the menus of the gourmands, and Brillat-Savarin wrote extensively about the French cheeses of his day in Physiologie du Goût (published in 1825), at a time when French gastronomy was beginning to take over the western world.

In those days a meal was very much more substantial than those we know today, especially in the days of service à la française, in which all the dishes would be placed on the table at the same time, for the guests to pick and choose for themselves. One menu which has survived from this period is that of a wedding feast in 1571, which offered 14 starters, ranging from salads to roast mutton; 21 main courses, from venison broth to roast swan; and 17 desserts, only one of which was cheese. Service à la française was subsequently replaced by service à la russe, which we would recognise today as dishes served in sequence — usually soup, fish,

meat, cheese and a sweet dessert or fruit — and by the end of the 18th century cheese had found its niche on the tables of the rich.

Since then there has been a split in the French and British approaches to cheese at the table. In France cheese is consumed before the dessert, whilst in Britain, at least until recently, it was always consumed afterwards. The reason for this is probably to do with wine. In France the meat course would always be accompanied by a robust red wine, and the cheese allowed diners to finish it off before moving on to something sweet. In Britain, however, from the early 18th century, the gentry had an addiction to Port, which was seen as the only accompaniment to cheese. Given that, even in those days, Britain enjoyed a wider variety of wines from around the world than France and that main courses might very well have been accompanied by light wines such as Hock and Mosel and even Champagne, the sweet-dessert course would be a useful palate-cleanser before approaching the very robust flavours of the Port and the cheese.

A good modern cheeseboard will, of course, have been selected from the restaurateur's chosen affineur, and offer the full range of flavours to complement whatever dishes the chef has created for the menu: after a main course of delicate fish and seafood, for example, a softer, younger cheese such as Brie or Camembert or perhaps something Swiss such as Emmenthal or Raclette might be appropriate. For more savoury dishes, there are "spicy" cheeses — Pont l'Évêque and Reblochon, for example, have a classic, aromatic style which follows roast meats and game with similarly robust flavours. For the follow-up to a well-hung grouse or a haunch of venison, blue cheeses come into their own: Stilton, Roquefort, Dolcelatte and Fourme are several excellent examples.

To the purist, choosing a cheese is akin to choosing a wine — in a good restaurant, trust your sommelier and waiter (or affineur if they have one of their own) to suggest something appropriate to "crown" the meal, both in the glass and on the plate. You may be surprised.

THE PERFECT ACCOMPANIMENT

If you wish to purchase any of the wines that we have recommended to accompany the delicious dishes in this book, please visit:

www.harrisonvintners.co.uk

WORLD CLASS WINES

SPAIN   FRANCE   HUNGARY

ITALY

SWITZERLAND

USA   CHILE   ARGENTINA

SOUTH
AFRICA

AUSTRALIA   NEW ZEALAND

THE BEST OF HARRISON VINTNERS

This diverse collection of independent growers and small estates has one great thing in common; all share a passion for "terroir" which dictates both quality and quantity. They do not produce volume; they make distinctive wines with great character and finesse which are designed to give pleasure and satisfaction when married with appropriate cuisine.

www.harrisonvintners.co.uk

Albert Bichot – Burgundy

Founded in 1831 and currently headed by Albéric Bichot, the House owns several wonderful domains including Pavillon in Pommard; Clos Frantin in Vosne-Romanée; Long-Depaquit and the legendary Grand Cru Moutonne in Chablis. Excellent wines with real "goût de terroir".

Albert Sounit – Burgundy

Founded in the 1930's and located in the Ch. Jeaunet in Rully, the House produces outstanding Côte Chalonnaise wines from the Appellations of Rully, Mercurey and Montagny.

Bruno Vesselle – Grand Cru Champagne

In the Grand Cru village of Bouzy, where his family has lived for several generations, Bruno owns 42 acres of vineyards. His Champagne receives a minimum of 2½ years ageing in the bottle before release. His "Cuvée des Huitres" has zero dosage and was specially created to complement seafood.

Château Camplazens – Languedoc

Located in La Clape, on the site of a former "pleasure camp" for the Roman Legions, the estate is owned by Peter and Susan Close. They regularly receive medals for each of their wines and their Syrah 2006 was voted "Best Red Wine" in the Top 100 Vin de Pays 2007.

Château de L'Orangerie – Premières Côtes de Bordeaux

Owned by the Icard family since 1790 and currently run by Jean-Christophe who produces a delightful range of red, white and rosé wines, including a most impressive dessert wine from Cadillac.

Château de Pommard – Burgundy

A jewel of Burgundy! The Château dates from 1725 and is surrounded by a clos, a single walled vineyard, of some 50 acres. A continuous process of selection through the various stages of production results in only the finest finished wine gaining the Château label. Burgundy in the old style with potential for great age.

Château de Pressac – St. Émilion Grand Cru

Here in 1453, the treaty was signed after the Battle of Castillon, ending The 100 Years War and the 300 years of English rule of Bordeaux. Now owned by M. Quenin who makes beautifully rich, fruity and firm Clarets which, quite rightly, are frequent gold medal winners. His excellent rosé is juice run off from the Grand Cru vats.

Clos Louie – Côtes de Castillon

A unique vineyard of pre-phylloxera vines, the oldest in Bordeaux! Pascal Lucin tends his ancient vines with the utmost care and makes his wine in the traditional way: trodden by foot and bottled without filtration. Due to the great age of the vines, fewer than 5,000 bottles of this amazing Cru Artisan can be produced each vintage.

Cristallo Vin de Fraise – Switzerland

A unique wine! Made solely from fresh, ripe, fermented strawberries by Peter Knup and Jürg Beiner in Thurgau. Rich and intense strawberry flavours make this an excellent accompaniment to chocolate and most desserts. Also, having a clean fresh acidity, it makes a good partner for most cheeses.

Domaine Bressy-Masson – Rasteau, Rhône

Rasteau Rancio is a rarity these days as less than 5% of the entire vineyard area is dedicated to producing Vins Doux Naturel (VDN). Marie-France Masson's wine is 100% old-vine Grenache, deliberately oxidised in oak casks. Sweet on the palate with a dry finish, it has similarities with Port/Madeira/Sherry.
An experience!

Domaine de La Paleine – Saumur

At Puy Notre Dame on the local "tuffeau" which imparts something very special to the vines, M. Vincent produces the finest selection of Saumurs we have ever tasted. Most impressively, this encompasses the whole spectrum of Sparkling, White, Rosé, Red and Dessert!

Domaine des Clos – Beaune

Benigne Bichot and his son Gregoire have 10 acres of prime vineyards around Beaune producing wines in the classic style. They also produce a lovely, delicate Beaune Blanc which is a bit of a rarity today.

Domaine Le Clos des Cazaux – Vacqueyras Rhône

Owned by the families Vache and Archimbault who are among the oldest in Vacqueyras with cellars dating from the 12th Century. The irrepressible Jean-Michel Vache makes outstanding Vacqueras and Gigondas plus, when botrytis allows, a unique red and a unique white dessert wine.

Domaine Leymarie – Burgundy

Winemakers since 1933 and proud owners of Le Clos du Village, which was once the garden of the world famous Clos de Vougeot. Jean-Charles

also makes a delightful Chambolle-Musigny and a fine, firm Morey-St.-Denis from his other two vineyards.

Domaine Lupé Cholet – Burgundy

Formerly owned by Madame Innes La Comtesse de Mayol de Lupé and now safely in the hands of Bichot, this estate has two unique possessions: Ch. Gris, the only terraced vineyards in Burgundy and Clos de Lupé, the only vineyard within the town of Nuits-St-Georges.

Domaine Pardon et Fils – Beaujeau

For six generations, the Pardon family has been making some of the finest Crus of Beaujolais with true "goût de terroir". They also provide a most valuable export service for a number of other family domains which are too small to have such a commercial structure. The Crus of Beaujolais at their finest.

Eric Chevalier – Val de Loire Atlantique

The family vineyards of Domaine de L'Aujardière, near Grand Lieu, were taken over by Eric in 2006 and, with his first vintage, he took first prize for "Best White Wine" in the Top 100 Vins de Pays 2007. This was his Fié Gris (aka Sauvignon Gris) which he had persuaded his family not to re-plant with the ubiquitous Sauvignon Blanc!

Fabrice Feytout – Pécharmant

Ch. Beauportail is in the little known Appellation of Pécharmant, north-east of Bergerac. This very individual red wine is in the classic Bordeaux style but with some added spice from its 5% Malbec. In addition, Fabrice makes a most satisfying Monbazillac dessert wine at his parents' estate, Ch. La Truffière.

Guido Brivio – Ticino, Switzerland

Cellars carved into the rock of Mt. Generoso provide perfect conditions for ageing these wonderful red wines which, due to the similarity of soils, closely resemble fine Pomerol. Guido also produces a White Merlot, "La Contrada", by running off the juice before it takes any colour from the skins.

Inniskillin – Canada

Established in 1975 by Donald Ziraldo and Karl Kaiser, this is Canada's premier Estate winery. Rated in the "Top 100 Wines of the World", their Icewine comes solely from grapes frozen on the vines naturally; no bunches are artificially frozen. Handpicked at night when frozen, in temperatures of -10°C and pressed immediately.

Lecompte Calvados

Settled in the heart of Normandy, in the Pays d'Auge, Hervé Pellerin works with double distilled ciders coming solely from fruit grown in that area. His is "Production Artisanale", true Calvados, without any additives or topping up of casks. They have delightful aromas, are wonderfully smooth and, on the palate, seem to last forever! His 12 year old was voted "Best Spirit" at Vinexpo 2007.

Lodovico Antinori — Tuscany

Having sold Ornellaia in 2002, it is the Tenuta di Biserno estate which now takes centre stage. Working with his brother Piero and Umberto Mannoni, striking wines of the utmost quality are being produced here and, not yet at Ornellaia price levels, they offer superb value!

Louis Bovard — Vaud, Switzerland

For centuries, the Bovards have worked their domain at Cully on the shore of Lake Geneva but, in 1994, Louis Bovard created something amazing: he grafted onto old Chasselas rootstock, Sauvignon Blanc! The resulting wine, "Buxus", was voted by the Jury Découverte, Vinexpo 2005 as one of the world's Top 10 Most Interesting Wines.

Rouvinez Vins — Valais, Switzerland

Owners of some 80 acres of vineyards and creators of the excellent "Primus Classicus" selection of rare and unusual varieties, Rouvinez are at the forefront of innovation in Valais. Jean-Bernard's first ever vintage of Grains Nobles took Gold in 2000 at the Concours Mondial de Bruxelles with the record score of 98/100.

Vins des Chevaliers — Valais, Switzerland

Situated in Salquenen, a pretty town of vineyards near Sierre, Vins des Chevaliers are producers of wines in the classic Swiss style: very clean, with beautiful fruit and mineral notes and that great freshness so redolent of Swiss mountain air!

ZD Wines — Napa Valley

Under the great vision and drive of Norman deLeuze these past 40 years, ZD has become one of the most revered of producers. Their Chardonnay has won the IWS Decanter Award 3 times and their wines have graced the tables at The White House over 3 administrations. They are one of only two certified "Organic Handlers" and their winery runs completely on solar power!

Directory of Relais & Châteaux United Kingdom & Ireland Properties

● Relais & Châteaux Properties in the UK and Ireland   ● Grands Chefs Relais & Châteaux

Airds Hotel
Port Appin, Argyll PA38 4DF
– United Kingdom
Tel.: + 44 (0)1631 730236
Fax: + 44 (0)1631 730535
airds@relaischateaux.com
www.airds-hotel.com
Owners: Shaun and
Jenny McKivragan
Maître de Maison: Robert McKay

Amberley Castle
Amberley, BN18 9LT Arundel (West
Sussex) – United Kingdom
Tel.: + 44 (0)1798 831992
Fax: + 44 (0)1798 831998
amberley@relaischateaux.com
www.amberleycastle.co.uk
Owner: Andrew Davis
Maître de Maison: Oliver Smith

Buckland Manor
Buckland Manor, Buckland
near Broadway WR12 7LY
(Worcestershire) –
United Kingdom
Tel.: + 44 (0)1386 852626
Fax: + 44 (0)1386 853557
buckland@relaischateaux.com
www.bucklandmanor.co.uk
Maître de Maison: Nigel Power

Chewton Glen
Christchurch Road, New Milton
BH25 6QS (Hampshire) –
United Kingdom
Tel.: + 44 (0)1425 275341
Fax: + 44 (0)1425 272310
chewton@relaischateaux.com
www.chewtonglen.com
Maître de Maison:
Andrew Stembridge

Farlam Hall
Brampton CA8 2NG (Cumbria)
– United Kingdom
Tel.: + 44 (0)1697 746234
Fax: + 44 (0)1697 746683
farlam@relaischateaux.com
www.farlamhall.co.uk
Owners and Maîtres de Maison:
Quinion and Stevenson Families

The Fat Duck
High Street, Bray SL6 2AQ
(Berkshire) – United Kingdom
Tel.: + 44 (0)1628 580333
fatduck@relaischateaux.com
www.fatduck.co.uk
Maître de Maison and Grand
Chef Relais & Châteaux: Heston
Blumenthal

Gidleigh Park
Chagford TQ13 8HH (Devon)
– United Kingdom
Tel.: + 44 (0)1647 432367
Fax: + 44 (0)1647 432574
gidleigh@relaischateaux.com
www.gidleigh.com
Owners: Andrew and
Christina Brownsword
Maître de Maison: Sue Williams
Grand Chef Relais & Châteaux:
Michael Caines MBE

Gilpin Lodge
Country House & Spa
Crook Road, Near Windermere
LA23 3NE (Cumbria) – United
Kingdom
Tel.: + 44 (0)1539 488818
Fax: + 44 (0)1539 488058
gilpin@relaischateaux.com
www.gilpinlodge.co.uk
Owners and Maîtres de Maison:
Cunliffe Family

Glenapp Castle
Ballantrae KA26 ONZ (Ayrshire)
– United Kingdom
Tel.: + 44 (0)1465 831212
Fax: + 44 (0)1465 831000
glenapp@relaischateaux.com
www.glenappcastle.com
Owners: Graham and Fay Cowan
Maîtres de Maison: Graham and
Fay Cowan, John Orr

Gravetye Manor
Near East Grinstead RH19 4LJ
(West Sussex) – United Kingdom
Tel.: + 44 (0)1342 810567
Fax: + 44 (0)1342 810080
gravetye@relaischateaux.com
www.gravetyemanor.co.uk
Owners: Andrew N. Russell and
Mark T. Raffan
Maître de Maison: Andrew Russell

Hambleton Hall
Hambleton, Oakham – Rutland
LE15 8TH – United Kingdom
Tel.: + 44 (0)1572 756991
Fax: + 44 (0)1572 724721
hambleton@relaischateaux.com
www.hambletonhall.com
Owners: Tim and Stefa Hart
Maître de Maison: Chris Hurst

Inverlochy Castle
Torlundy-Fort William, Scotland
PH33 6SN – United Kingdom
Tel.: + 44 (0)1397 702177
Fax: + 44 (0)1397 702953
inverlochy@relaischateaux.com
www.inverlochycastlehotel.com
Maître de Maison: Calum Milne

Kinloch House
Blairgowrie PH10 6SG (Perthshire)
– United Kingdom
Tel.: + 44 (0)1250 884237
Fax: + 44 (0)1250 884333
kinloch@relaischateaux.com
www.kinlochhouse.com
Owners: Allen Family
Maître de Maison: Graeme Allen

Kinnaird
Kinnaird Estate, By Dunkeld PH8
0LB (Perthshire) – United Kingdom
Tel.: + 44 (0)1796 482440
Fax: + 44 (0)1796 482289
kinnaird@relaischateaux.com
www.kinnairdestate.com
Owner and Maître de Maison:
Constance Cluett Ward

Le Gavroche
43 Upper Brook Street, London
W1K 7QR – United Kingdom
Tel.: + 44 (0)20 7 499 1826
Fax: +44 (0)20 7 491 4387
gavroche@relaischateaux.com
www.le-gavroche.co.uk
Owners: Michel Roux Jr.
and Albert Roux
Maître de Maison:
Emmanuel Landré
Grand Chef Relais & Châteaux:
Michel Roux Jr.

Le Manoir Aux Quat' Saisons

Church Road, Great Milton, Oxford OX44 7PD (Oxfordshire) – United Kingdom
Tel.: + 44 (0)1844 278881
Fax: + 44 (0)1844 278847
4saisons@relaischateaux.com
www.manoir.com
Owner: Raymond Blanc
Maître de Maison: Tom Lewis
Grands Chefs Relais & Châteaux: Raymond Blanc and Gary Jones

Longueville Manor

Longueville Road, St Saviour JE2 7WF (Jersey) – United Kingdom
Tel.: + 44 (0)1534 725501
Fax: +44 (0)1534 731613
longueville@relaischateaux.com
www.longuevillemanor.com
Owner: Malcolm Lewis
Maître de Maison: Pedro Bento

Lower Slaughter Manor

Lower Slaughter GL54 2HP (Gloucestershire) – United Kingdom
Tel.: + 44 (0)1451 820456
Fax: + 44 (0)1451 822150
slaughter@relaischateaux.com
www.lowerslaughter.co.uk
Maître de Maison: Andrew Thomason

Lucknam Park

Colerne-near Bath SN14 8AZ (Wiltshire) – United Kingdom
Tel.: + 44 (0)1225 742777
Fax: + 44 (0)1225 743536
lucknam@relaischateaux.com
www.lucknampark.co.uk
Maître de Maison: Harry Murray MBE

Mallory Court

Harbury Lane, Bishops Tachbrook, Leamington Spa CV33 9QB (Warwickshire) – United Kingdom
Tel.: + 44 (0)1926 330214
Fax: + 44 (0)1926 451714
mallory@relaischateaux.com
www.mallory.co.uk
Owner: Sir Peter Rigby
Maître de Maison: Mark E. Chambers

Marlfield House

Courtown Road R742, Gorey Co. Wexford – Ireland
Tel.: + 353 (0)53 9421124
Fax: + 353 (0)53 9421572
marlfield@relaischateaux.com
www.marlfieldhouse.com
Owners: Ray and Mary Bowe
Maîtres de Maison: Margaret and Laura Bowe

The Royal Crescent Hotel

16 Royal Crescent, Bath BA1 2LS – United Kingdom
Tel.: + 44 (0)1225 823333
Fax: + 44 (0)1225 339401
crescent@relaischateaux.com
www.royalcrescent.co.uk
Maître de Maison: Sharon Love

Sharrow Bay Country House

Lake Ullswater, Howtown, Penrith CA10 2LZ (Lake District) – United Kingdom
Tel.: + 44 (0)1768 486301
Fax: + 44 (0)1768 486349
sharrow@relaischateaux.com
www.sharrowbay.co.uk
Maître de Maison: Andrew King

Sheen Falls Lodge

Kenmare Co. Kerry (Kerry) – Ireland
Tel.: + 353 (0)64 6641600
Fax: + 353 (0)64 6641386
sheenfalls@relaischateaux.com
www.sheenfallslodge.ie
Owner: Bent Hoyer
Maître de Maison: Alan Campbell

Summer Lodge Country House & Spa

9 Fore Street, Evershot DDT2 0JR (Dorset) – United Kingdom
Tel.: + 44 (0)1935 482000
Fax: + 44 (0)1935 482040
summer@relaischateaux.com
www.summerlodgehotel.co.uk
Owner: Beatrice Tollman
Maître de Maison: Charles Lotter

The Vineyard at Stockcross

Newbury RG20 8JU (Berkshire) – United Kingdom
Tel.: + 44 (0)1635 528770
Fax: + 44 (0)1635 528398
vineyard@relaischateaux.com
www.the-vineyard.co.uk
Owner: Sir Peter Michael
Maître de Maison: Andrew McKenzie
Grand Chef Relais & Châteaux: John Campbell

The Waterside Inn

Ferry Road, Bray SL6 2AT (Berkshire) – United Kingdom
Tel.: + 44 (0)1628 620691
Fax: + 44 (0)1628 784710
waterside@relaischateaux.com
www.waterside-inn.co.uk
Owners: Michel Roux and Alain Roux
Maître de Maison: Diego Masciaga
Grands Chefs Relais & Châteaux: Michel and Alain Roux

Whatley Manor

Easton Grey, Malmesbury SN16 0RB (Wiltshire) – United Kingdom
Tel.: + 44 (0)1666 822888
Fax: + 44 (0)1666 826120
whatley@relaischateaux.com
www.whatleymanor.com
Owners: Alix Landolt and Christian Landolt
Maître de Maison: Peter Egli

Ynyshir Hall

Eglwysfach, Machynlleth SY20 8TA (Powys – Mid-Wales) – United Kingdom
Tel.: + 44 (0)1654 781209
Fax: + 44 (0)1654 781366
ynyshir@relaischateaux.com
www.ynyshirhall.co.uk
Maître de Maison: Joan Reen

RECIPES: Alphabetical index of recipes ordered by property

Longueville Manor

Poached tail of Jersey lobster with Lumo cured ham chowder, garden vegetables and micro salad, 100
Roast fillet of Angus beef with oxtail ravioli, grilled foie gras and woodland mushrooms, 102
Hazelnut sablé with "Jivara" chocolate, sesame ice cream and a balsamic reduction, 104

Lower Slaughter Manor

Home cured Donnington trout, white radish, sesame marinated cucumber, wasabi mayonnaise and micro cress, 142
Fillet of old spot pork rolled in dried trompette mushroom and Asian spices, crackling, warm pork belly, and sage and onion bon bon, 144
Passion fruit soufflé, pomegranate sorbet and kiwi pastel, 146

Lucknam Park

Roast scallops, brandade fritters, tomato and cumin vinaigrette, marinated baby carrots, 152
Trio of Andrew Morgan's Brecon lamb, organic watercress, green olive puree, 154
Croustillant of pineapple, rum and raisin parfait, coconut sorbet, 156

Mallory Court

Terrine of foie gras, smoked apple and Brazan cheese with salad of smoked duck, apple, balsamic raisins, 186
Breast of mallard, confit leg, crispy confit, 188
Baked crème brûlée, poached rhubarb, ginger and advocaat ice cream, 190

Marlfield House

Steamed mussels with wild garlic, spring onions, fennel and curry, 214
Roast partridge with smoked garlic and rosemary, potato and pancetta terrine, buttered Savoy cabbage with chestnuts, 216
Queen of puddings with vanilla and citrus poached rhubarb, 218

The Royal Crescent Hotel

Short poached monkfish cheek, Jerusalem artichokes, cauliflower "cous cous", langoustine clarification, 168
Roast loin of fallow deer, cep risotto, ice wine vinegar jelly, parsley purée, 170
Cigar poached plums, oat cakes and Balviene ice cream, 172

Sharrow Bay Country House

Caramelised scallops with buttered spinach, shrimp risotto, crispy pancetta, fried quail's egg and a scallop velouté, 252
Best end and braised shoulder of Herdwick lamb with creamed savoury cabbage, shallot and thyme rosti, pea purée and a tomato and rosemary sauce, 254
Cranberry jelly, orange polenta cake and a Cointreau mascarpone, 256

Sheen Falls Lodge

White tomato soup with mozzarella and tapenade, 224
Fillet of halibut with green and white asparagus, steamed clams and Jameson whiskey butter, squid ink pasta and tomato salad, 226
Warm chocolate fondant with balsamic fruits and vanilla ice cream, 228

Summer Lodge Country House & Spa

Pan seared Lyme Bay scallops with sweet shallot purée, confit Maris Piper potatoes, parsley and caper dressing, 108
Roast loin of Dorset lamb and braised shoulder "shepherd's pie" with Savoy cabbage and rosemary jus, 110
Summer Lodge trio of lemon, lemon curd, lemon sherbet and lemon thyme jelly, 112

The Vineyard at Stockcross

Risotto wild mushrooms, cep espuma, balsamic, 54
Organic salmon "mi-cuit", spiced lentils, foie gras, 56
"Roast chicken" smoked gnocchi and sweetcorn, 60
Cucumber, lime, mango, yoghurt, 64
Black forest gateau, 66

The Waterside Inn

Rock fish soup lightly scented with saffron, garnished with flaked cod and a slice of seaweed flavoured bread, 16
Smooth risotto of Cornish hen crab, squid filled with "véneré" rice and clams, 18
Fillet of salmon cooked "en papillote" with pine needles, served with deep fried leaves of pak-choï and a star aniseed sauce, 20
Selection of "Suffolk Texel" lamb and pastilla with confit lemon, served with a medley of simmered pulses and jus enhanced with ras-el-hanout, 22
Warm golden plum soufflés, 24

Whatley Manor

Roasted langoustines with caramelised bacon and soy reduction, 160
Roasted squab pigeon with caramelised foie gras and coffee sherry gel, 162
Mango cannelloni with mint ice cream and pink grapefruit, 164

Ynyshir Hall

Scallop and langoustine Carpaccio with tomato jelly and caviar, 204
Brined and braised pork, 206
Treacle tart, 208

Index of Recipes

SOUP

Rock fish soup lightly scented with saffron, garnished with flaked cod and a slice of seaweed flavoured bread, 16

White tomato soup with mozzarella and tapenade, 224

SALAD

Cropwell Bishop Stilton panna cotta with roasted black figs and walnut salad, 178

Leek and truffles with mustard vinaigrette, 86

Lobster mango salad, 44

Roasted winter vegetables, 92

Terrine of foie gras, smoked apple and Brazan cheese with salad of smoked duck, apple, balsamic raisins, 186

RISOTTO

Caramelised scallops with buttered spinach, shrimp risotto, crispy pancetta, fried quail's egg and a scallop velouté, 252

Risotto wild mushrooms, cep espuma, balsamic, 54

Smooth risotto of Cornish hen crab, squid filled with flaked cod and a slice of seaweed flavoured bread, 16

SOUFFLE

Soufflé Suissesse, 42

FISH

Crab
Smooth risotto of Cornish hen crab, squid filled with "vénéré" rice and clams, 18

Tian of Scottish crab with gazpacho, 290

Halibut
Fillet of halibut with green and white asparagus, steamed clams and Jameson whiskey butter, squid ink pasta and tomato salad, 226

The Sound of the Sea, 28

Langoustine
Langoustine, crispy oyster, rattes potato, 300

Roasted langoustines with caramelised bacon and soy reduction, 160

Scallop and langoustine Carpaccio with tomato jelly and caviar, 204

Seared Hebredian scallops with a fricassee of cockles, mussels and langoustine, 132

Lobster
Lobster mango salad, 44

Poached tail of Jersey lobster with Lumo cured ham chowder, garden vegetables and micro salad, 100

Scottish blue lobster, cauliflower salad and yoghurt beignets, 280

Mackerel
The Sound of the Sea, 28

Monkfish
Short poached monkfish cheek, Jerusalem artichokes, cauliflower "cous cous", langoustine clarification, 168

Mussels
Seared Hebredian scallops with a fricassee of cockles, mussels and langoustine, 132

Steamed mussels with wild garlic, spring onions, fennel and curry, 214

Prawn
King prawns with chilli and garlic, 232

Red Mullet
West Country red mullet, sweet and sour carrots, tomato fondue and Scottish langoustines, 126

Salmon
Ballotine of organic salmon with horseradish and potato mousse and a beetroot salad, 242

Fillet of salmon cooked "en papillote" with pine needles, served with deep fried leaves of pak-choï and a star aniseed sauce, 20

Organic salmon "mi-cuit", spiced lentils, foie gras, 56

Organic salmon minestrone with macaroni, 124

Scallops
Caramelised scallops with buttered spinach, shrimp risotto, crispy pancetta, fried quail's egg and a scallop velouté, 252

Ceviche of tuna and sea scallop with shaved fennel salad, 88

Hand-dived scallops cauliflower and curry, parmesan and truffle, 116

Pan seared Lyme Bay scallops with sweet shallot purée, confit Maris Piper potatoes, parsley and caper dressing, 108

Roast scallops, brandade fritters, tomato and cumin vinaigrette, marinated baby carrots, 152

Scallop and langoustine Carpaccio with tomato jelly and caviar, 204

Scallops with celeriac puree and soy and truffle vinaigrette, 72

Seared scallops with variations of onion, 196

Seared Hebredian scallops with a fricassee of cockles, mussels and langoustine, 132

The Sound of the Sea, 28

Sea Bass
Roast fillet of sea bass, parsnip puree and caramelised garlic, 46

Roasted sea bass with cockles, a fennel and vanilla salad and a fennel and dill purée, 272

Trout
Home cured Donnington trout, white radish, sesame marinated cucumber, wasabi mayonnaise and micro cress, 142

Tuna
Ceviche of tuna and sea scallop with shaved fennel salad, 88

Turbot
Braised fillet of Oban turbot with a light broth of shellfish, 264

Braised fillet of turbot, oyster, cucumber and wasabi jus, 90

Yellowtail
The Sound of the Sea, 28

GAME AND POULTRY

Chicken
"Roast chicken" smoked gnocchi and sweetcorn, 60

Duck
Breast of mallard, confit leg, crispy confit, 188
Wild duck with girolle mushrooms, 48

Foie Gras
Pan-fried duck foie gras with braised chicory with orange and raisins, 76
Terrine of foie gras, smoked apple and Brazan cheese with salad of smoked duck, apple, balsamic raisins, 186

Hare
Hare wellington, 198

Partridge
Roast partridge with smoked garlic and rosemary, potato and pancetta terrine, buttered Savoy cabbage with chestnuts, 216

Pheasant
Roast pheasant with lentils, and pumpkin and cumin purée, 74

Pigeon
Puff pastry casket with squab pigeon and wild mushrooms, 262
Roasted squab pigeon with caramelised foie gras and coffee sherry gel, 162

Quail
Lancashire quail, filled with a chicken and herb mousse with a red wine sauce and wild mushrooms, 234
Roasted quail with herb purée and rosemary gnocchi, 78

Venison
Hibiscus crusted venison medallions, young leeks and a black pepper dressing, 282
Roast loin of fallow deer, cep risotto, ice wine vinegar jelly, parsley purée, 170
Roasted loin of Ayrshire roe venison with celeriac, Szechuan and hot-pot, 274
Saddle of venison, celeriac and sauce poivrade, civet of venison with pearl barley, venison and frankincense tea, 32

Wild Boar
Loin of wild boar, butternut squash purée, potato mille-feuille, black mustard seed jus, 302

MEAT

Beef
Roast fillet of Angus beef with oxtail ravioli, grilled foie gras and woodland mushrooms, 102
Slow cooked featherblade steak with horseradish potato purée, roast vegetables and a red wine sauce, 292

Lamb
Best end and braised shoulder of Herdwick lamb with creamed savoury cabbage, shallot and thyme rosti, pea purée and a tomato and rosemary sauce, 254
Cannon of spring lamb with gratin potatoes, asparagus and minted hollandaise, 134
Fillet of new season lamb with black truffle crust, parmesan potatoes and lamb reduction, 180
Rack of Laverstoke Park lamb pistachio crust, sweetbreads and black olive jus, 118
Roast loin of Dorset lamb and braised shoulder "shepherd's pie" with Savoy cabbage and rosemary jus, 110
Roasted best end and braised shoulder of Herdwick lamb with garlic and potato purée, and morel mushrooms, 244
Selection of "Suffolk Texel" lamb and pastilla with confit lemon, served with a medley of simmered pulses and jus enhanced with ras-el-hanout, 22
Trio of Andrew Morgan's Brecon lamb, organic watercress, green olive puree, 154

Pork
Brined and braised pork, 206
Fillet of old spot pork rolled in dried trompette mushroom and Asian spices, crackling, warm pork belly, and sage and onion bon bon, 144
Loin of wild boar, butternut squash purée, potato mille-feuille, black mustard seed jus, 302

DESSERTS

Apple
Spiced apple cake served with calvados ice cream and caramelised apples, 236

Banana
Chocolate olive oil truffle with baked banana and passion fruit sorbet, 200

Cakes and Gateaux
The BFG! (black forest gateau), 36
Black forest gateau, 66
Rich dark chocolate cake with blood orange ice cream, 182
Spiced apple cake served with calvados ice cream and caramelised apples, 236
Spiced fig cake, lemon jelly and toasted almond foam, 128

Chocolate
Chocolate and praline cream with raspberry granité, 284
Chocolate olive oil truffle with baked banana and passion fruit sorbet, 200
Duo of chocolate mousse with soft milk chocolate centre and raspberry coulis, 294
Rich dark chocolate cake with blood orange ice cream, 182
Trio of chocolate: dark chocolate mousse on a sable biscuit, milk chocolate parfait and white chocolate ice cream, 80
Warm chocolate fondant with balsamic fruits and vanilla ice cream, 228

Cherry
Spiced cherries in Kriek beer, 50

Cranberry
Cranberry jelly, orange polenta cake and a Cointreau mascarpone, 256

Index of Recipes